AF880223

Welcome to Microsoft® Office 2010

JILL MURPHY
Trainer and Consultant

LABYRINTH
LEARNING™

El Sobrante, CA

President:
Brian Favro

Acquisitions Editor:
Jason Favro

Managing Editor:
Laura Popelka

Production Manager:
Rad Proctor

eLearning Production Manager:
Arl S. Nadel

Editorial/Production Team:
Sandy Jones, Sheryl Trittin, Betsy Walker

Indexing:
Joanne Sprott

Cover Concept:
Huckdesign

LABYRINTH
LEARNING™

Welcome to Microsoft Office 2010
by Jill Murphy

Labyrinth Learning
P.O. Box 20818
El Sobrante, California 94820
800.522.9746
On the web at lablearning.com

ITEM: 1-59136-380-2
ISBN-13: 978-1-59136-380-4

Manufactured in the United States of America.

0 9 8 7 6 5 4 3 2 1

Welcome to Microsoft Office 2010

Table of Contents

Quick Reference Table Summary vii
Preface viii

LESSON 1

Word – Working with Word Basics 1

Discovering Just How Suite It Is 3
Defining Word 3
  Starting Word 2010 4
  Exploring the Word Window 7
Introducing the Ribbon 8
  ToolTips 9
  Contextual Tabs 9
  Varying Button Arrangements 10
Introducing the Toolbars 10
  The Quick Access Toolbar 10
  The Mini Toolbar 11
Opening Documents 12
  Downloading and Storing Exercise Files 12
  Opening Documents Created in Earlier Versions of Word 12
Navigating in a Word Document 14
  Navigating with the Scroll Bar 14
  Recognizing Different Mouse Pointer Shapes 15
  Navigating with the Keyboard 17
Closing Documents 19
Starting a New Blank Document 19
Getting Help in Word 2010 21
Exiting from Word 22
Concepts Review 23
Skill Builders 25

LESSON 2

Word – Writing a Letter and a Resume 29

Typing a Cover Letter 31
  Line and Paragraph Spacing 31
  Nonprinting Characters 32
  AutoComplete 33
  The Enter Key and Word Wrap 36
  Using the Bullets Feature 37
Saving a Document 39
  Save Compared to Save As 39
  Saving a Modified Document 41
Printing a Document 43
Using a Word Table to Organize a Resume 45
  Merging Cells and Centering Data in a Cell 45
  Navigating in Tables and Adding Rows 48
  Resizing Column Widths and Row Heights 48
  Removing Borders from a Table 52
Creating an Envelope 54
  The Envelopes and Labels Dialog Box 54
Concepts Review 56
Skill Builders 58

LESSON 3

Word – Editing the Business Etiquette Column 63

Selecting Text 65
  The Selection Bar 65
  The Typing Area 65
  Selection Techniques 66
Editing Techniques 69
  Add, Delete, and Replace Text 69
  AutoCorrect 69
  Spelling & Grammar Checker 72
  Undo and Redo 72
Moving and Copying Text 74
  Move and Copy Text 74

Finding and Replacing Text 77
Find with the Navigation Pane 77
The Find and Replace Dialog Box 78
Concepts Review 82
Skill Builders 84

LESSON 4

Word – Encouraging Recycling with Flyers 89

Formatting with the Ribbon 91
Fonts. 91
The Font Group 92
Font Size. 92
Formatting with the Mini Toolbar 92
Using Live Preview with Galleries 93
Saving a Document to a New Folder 97
Creating a New Folder 97
Setting Paragraph Alignment 99
The Alignment Buttons 99
Creating WordArt 100
Formatting WordArt 101
Contextual Tabs on the Ribbon 102
Selecting, Sizing, and Rotating WordArt . . . 102
Using Clip Art 105
Searching for Clip Art 105
Rotating Clip Art 108
Resizing Clip Art 108
Wrapping Text 111
Positioning an Image 111
Cropping Clip Art Images 112
Concepts Review 115
Skill Builders 117

LESSON 5

Excel – Tracking Firefighter Training 125

Understanding Excel 127
Starting Excel 2010 127
Exploring the Excel Window 128
Understanding Workbook Organization . . . 128
Mouse Shapes in Excel 129
Navigating in a Spreadsheet 130
Using the Scroll Bars to Navigate 130
Using the Keyboard to Navigate 132
Freezing Panes 133
Entering Data in a Spreadsheet 136
Completing and Canceling Cell Entries . . . 136
Editing in Excel 139
Aligning Cell Contents 140
Working with Ranges of Cells 141
Moving and Copying Data 144
Copying Data. 145
Sorting Data. 147
Kinds of Sorts. 147
Structuring an Effective List 147
Working with Columns and Rows 149
Resizing Columns and Rows 149
Inserting and Deleting Columns and Rows 150
Concepts Review 154
Skill Builders 156

LESSON 6

Excel – Budgeting with Calculations and Charts . . 161

Defining Formulas 163
Excel's Mathematical Operators 163
How to Type a Formula 164
Using Built-in Functions 167
How Functions Are Constructed 167
The AutoSum Button 167
Calculating with AVERAGE, MAX, and MIN 171
Copying Formulas and Functions 172
Using Charts to Visualize Data 174
How Do I Know Which Cells to Select? . . . 174
Embedded Charts Compared to Chart Sheets 176
Using Design Tools 182
Concepts Review 189
Skill Builders 191

LESSON 7

PowerPoint – Creating Powerful Presentations . . 199

Presenting PowerPoint 201
Starting PowerPoint 201
Introducing the PowerPoint Window 202
Navigating in a Presentation 203
Using PowerPoint Views 206
Creating a Presentation 209
Using PowerPoint Themes 209
Typing Text in a Slide 210
Working with Slide Layouts 211
Presentation Design Tips 213
Adding Clip Art to a Presentation 214
Delivering the Slide Show 217
Delivery Tips 217
Navigating in Slide Show View 218
Adding Animations and Transitions to the Show 220
Animating Your Slide Show 220
Adding Transitions to Your Slide Show 221
Concepts Review 223
Skill Builders 225

LESSON 8

Access – Accessing Raritan Clinic East 231

Defining Access Databases 233
What Is a Database? 233
Exploring the Access Environment 233
Starting Access 233
Identifying Elements of the Access Window 234
Using Database Templates 234
Creating a Blank Database 234
Designing a Database 235
Identifying Features of the Database Window 236
Using the Navigation Pane 236
Creating Tables in Datasheet View 237
Working with Tables 237
Identifying Table Guidelines 238
Identifying Field Data Types 239
Navigating Tables and Entering Data 242
Working with Tabs and Closing Database Objects 242
Previewing and Printing Data 244
Setting Up Data to Print 244
Checking Data Accuracy 244
Examining the Preview Window 244
Closing a Database and Exiting Access 248
Concepts Review 250
Skill Builders 251

Glossary *253*
Index *256*

Quick Reference Table Summary

Access Tasks

Identifying Access Data Types 240

Excel Tasks

Completing and Canceling Cell Entries 137

Copying Data with Copy and Paste 145

Deleting, Replacing, and Editing Data 139

Freezing Columns and Rows 134

Inserting and Deleting Columns and Rows 150

Moving Data with Cut and Paste 144

Navigating with the Keyboard in Excel 133

Outlining Common Excel Functions 167

Reviewing Excel's Mathematical Operators 163

Selecting Cell Ranges 142

PowerPoint Tasks

Navigating in a Slide Show 218

Navigating in PowerPoint 203

Windows Tasks

Naming Folders 98

Navigating with the Keyboard 17

Opening, Closing, and Starting a New Document 19

Saving Documents 42

Word Tasks

Editing Text 69

Finding and Replacing Text 78

Moving and Copying Text 74

Selecting Text 66

Preface

Welcome to Microsoft® Office 2010 provides a survey of Office 2010 applications. Students get an introduction to Word, Excel, PowerPoint, and Access. The book begins with four Word lessons, which cover such topics as the Ribbon, navigation techniques, AutoComplete, tables, editing text, AutoCorrect, character formatting, special text effects, and more. In the two Excel lessons, students enter and edit data, construct simple formulas, and depict data using column and pie charts. PowerPoint topics include creating a new presentation, working with layouts and design themes, creating animations and transitions, and more. And finally, in the Access lesson students will explore the Access application window, create a new database, and print datasheets.

For almost two decades, Labyrinth Learning has been publishing easy-to-use textbooks that empower educators to teach complex subjects quickly and effectively, while enabling students to gain confidence, develop practical skills, and compete in a demanding job market. We add comprehensive support materials, assessment and learning management tools, and eLearning components to create true learning solutions for a wide variety of instructor-led, self-paced, and online courses.

Our textbooks follow the *Labyrinth Instructional Design,* our unique and proven approach that makes learning easy and effective for every learner. Our books begin with fundamental concepts and build through a systematic progression of exercises. Quick Reference Tables, precise callouts on screen captures, carefully selected illustrations, and minimal distractions combine to create a learning solution that is highly efficient and effective for both students and instructors.

This course is supported with *comprehensive instructor support* materials that include printable solution guides for side-by-side comparisons, test banks, customizable assessments, customizable PowerPoint presentations, detailed lesson plans, preformatted files for integration to leading learning management systems, and more. Our unique WebSims allow students to perform realistic exercises for tasks that cannot be performed in the computer lab.

Our *eLab assessment and learning management tool* is available to supplement this course. eLab is an intuitive, affordable, web-based learning system that helps educators spend less time on course management and more time teaching. eLab seamlessly integrates with your Labyrinth textbook.

Visual Conventions

`Type this text`	Anything you should type at the keyboard is printed in this typeface.
TIP!	Tips, Notes, and Warnings are used throughout the text to draw attention to certain topics.
Command→ Command→ Command, etc.	This convention indicates how to give a command from the Ribbon. The commands are written: Ribbon Tab→Command Group→ Command→Subcommand.
QUICK REFERENCE	Quick Reference tables provide generic instructions for key tasks. Only perform these tasks if you are instructed to in an exercise.
	Hands-On exercises are introduced immediately after concept discussions. They provide detailed, step-by-step tutorials so you can master the skills presented.
	The Concepts Review section includes both true/false and multiple choice questions designed to gauge your understanding of the concepts introduced in the lesson.
	Skill Builder exercises provide additional hands-on practice with moderate assistance.

LESSON 1

Word – Working with Word Basics

In this lesson, you will learn the basics of Microsoft Office Word 2010. You will start Word, work with the Ribbon interface, open a document, learn navigation techniques for moving around the document, and start a new document. Finally, you will get familiar with Word's Help feature.

LESSON OBJECTIVES

After studying this lesson, you will be able to:

- Identify key parts of the Word 2010 interface
- Open and close existing documents
- Start new documents
- Navigate in a document using scroll bars and the keyboard
- Use Word's Help feature
- Exit from Word

Student resources ***labyrinthelab.com/wtmo10***

Case Study: Exploring Word

Jasmine Morales will attend Central Community College in the fall, and she wants to learn Word 2010 to help with her school assignments. She just got a new laptop with Word 2010, and she's ready to explore the Word window.

Jasmine says that Word's Ribbon interface is intuitive and easy to use.

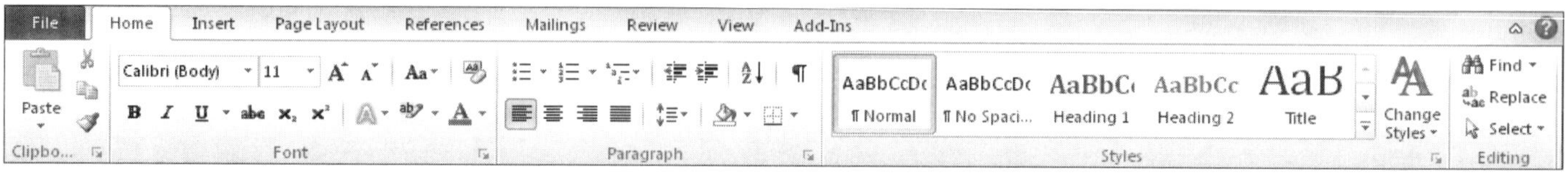

Jasmine received a product brochure written in Word 2003 as an email attachment from the local gardening store. The Compatibility Mode indicator in the title bar lets Jasmine know the document was created in an earlier version of Word. She has the option of leaving the brochure in the Word 2003 format or converting it to the Word 2010 format.

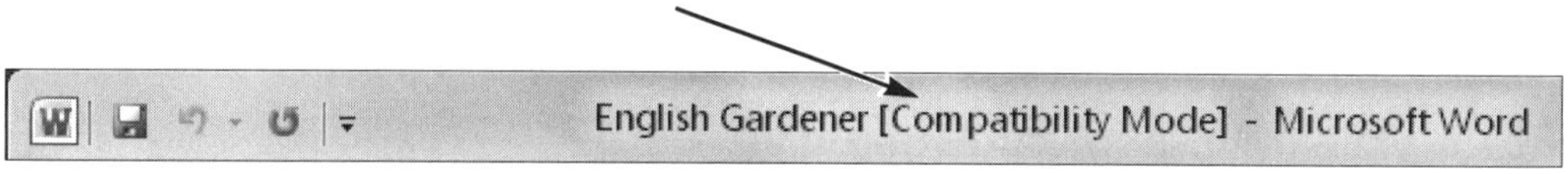

If Jasmine wants to share the document with her gardening friend who uses Word 2003, she won't convert the document. If she wants to be able to use a document created in Word 2003 and also use all of Word 2010's new features, she will convert the document.

Discovering Just How Suite It Is

Microsoft Office 2010 is a suite of software programs. A suite is several programs usually sold together as one package, which is less expensive than buying them individually. In this course, you will learn to work with Word, Excel, PowerPoint, and Access—four of the most popular software programs in the Office 2010 suite.

- **Word 2010:** This word-processing program allows you to create documents, such as a letter or an envelope, and then make changes without having to retype the information. Other Word documents include memos, reports, and fancy flyers.
- **Excel 2010:** A spreadsheet program makes organizing numbers and financial information and performing calculations a breeze. A budget is a good example of something you might create in a spreadsheet program. Other ideas include sales reports, billing statements, and graphs.
- **PowerPoint 2010:** Whether you are giving a presentation to your community center or your work colleagues, PowerPoint lets you produce elegant electronic slide shows with little effort. The tools built into this program will make any presentation a hit!
- **Access 2010:** Organizing very large amounts of data is how a database program shines. If you have a collection of hundreds of CDs or a parts inventory, you can keep track of them in a database.

One of the great things about a software suite is that all programs share common features and a similar design. This means that when you have learned one program, you can quite easily learn another. And, moving information between various programs in the suite is a snap.

Defining Word

Word 2010 is the name of the word-processing program that is part of the Microsoft Office 2010 suite of programs.

As in all word-processing programs, you use Word 2010 to electronically create and edit text. After creating a document, you can make editing changes. You can make big changes too, like adding or deleting a couple of paragraphs in the middle of a page. When you do, the existing text moves out of the way to make room for the new text, or it collapses to close the gap when you delete text. Other editing changes like moving or copying text within a page or from one page to another are also easy to do.

Word is great for formatting text, too, and it also provides special features like Spelling & Grammar. There's even an AutoCorrect feature that fixes many mistakes for you. Imagine that!

Starting Word 2010

You start Word from the Start button, which appears on the taskbar in the bottom-left corner of your Windows Desktop. The appearance of the Start button varies depending on whether your computer uses Windows XP or Windows 7/Vista.

NOTE! Throughout the rest of this book, Window 7, Windows Vista, and Windows XP will be referred to as Win 7, Win Vista, and Win XP, respectively.

Win 7/Vista

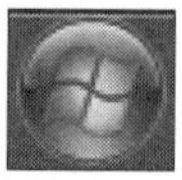

Win XP

The program icon that opens the Word program window is in the Microsoft Office folder, which appears when you click the All Programs menu after clicking the Start button.

HANDS-ON 1.1 Start Word

In this exercise, you will start Word using the Start button on the taskbar and the All Programs menu.

1. If necessary, start your computer.

   The Windows Desktop appears.

2. Follow these steps for your version of Windows (Win 7/Vista or Win XP) to start Word 2010:

   NOTE! The location of items on the menus will likely vary from one computer to another, so the following figures may not exactly match the menus on your computer.

Win 7/Vista

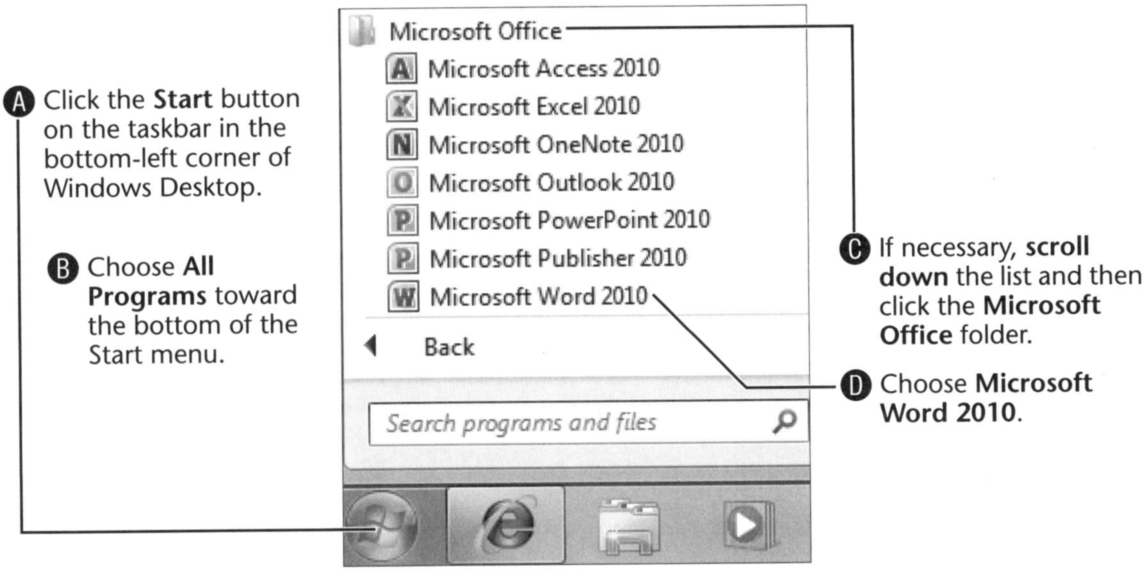

If you use Win 7/Vista, skip the Win XP portion of this step and continue with the next step.

Win XP

Ⓐ Click the **Start** button on the taskbar in the bottom-left corner of Windows Desktop.

Ⓑ Choose **All Programs** toward the bottom of the Start menu.

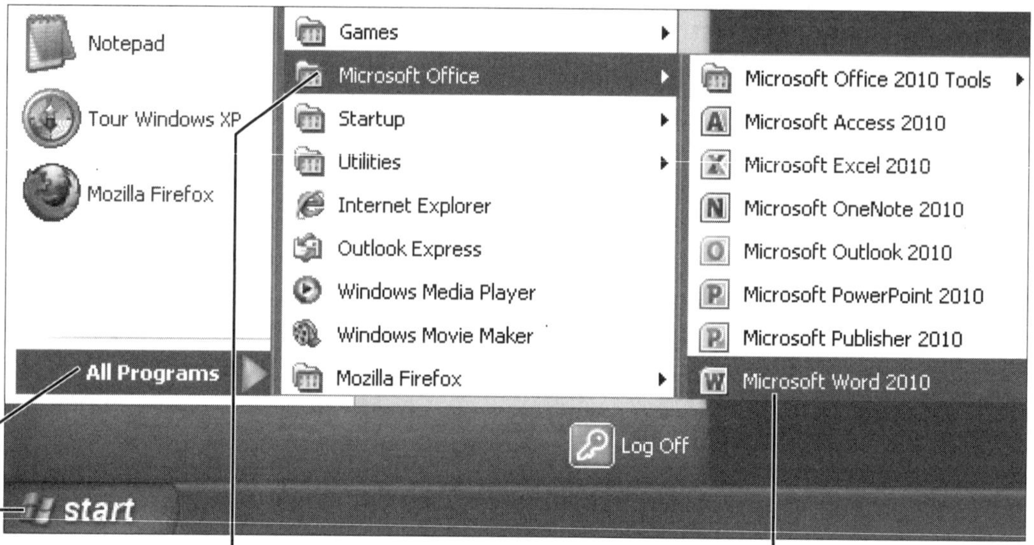

Ⓒ If necessary, **scroll down** the list and then click the **Microsoft Office** folder.

Ⓓ Choose **Microsoft Word 2010.**

There is a pause as the Word program starts. The Word window may or may not fill the screen. If not, the next command maximizes the Word window.

3. If necessary, click the **Maximize** button in the upper-right corner of the Word window.

Exploring the Word Window

Following is an illustration of the Word window when it first opens. Do not be concerned if your document window looks a bit different from this example. The Word screen is customizable.

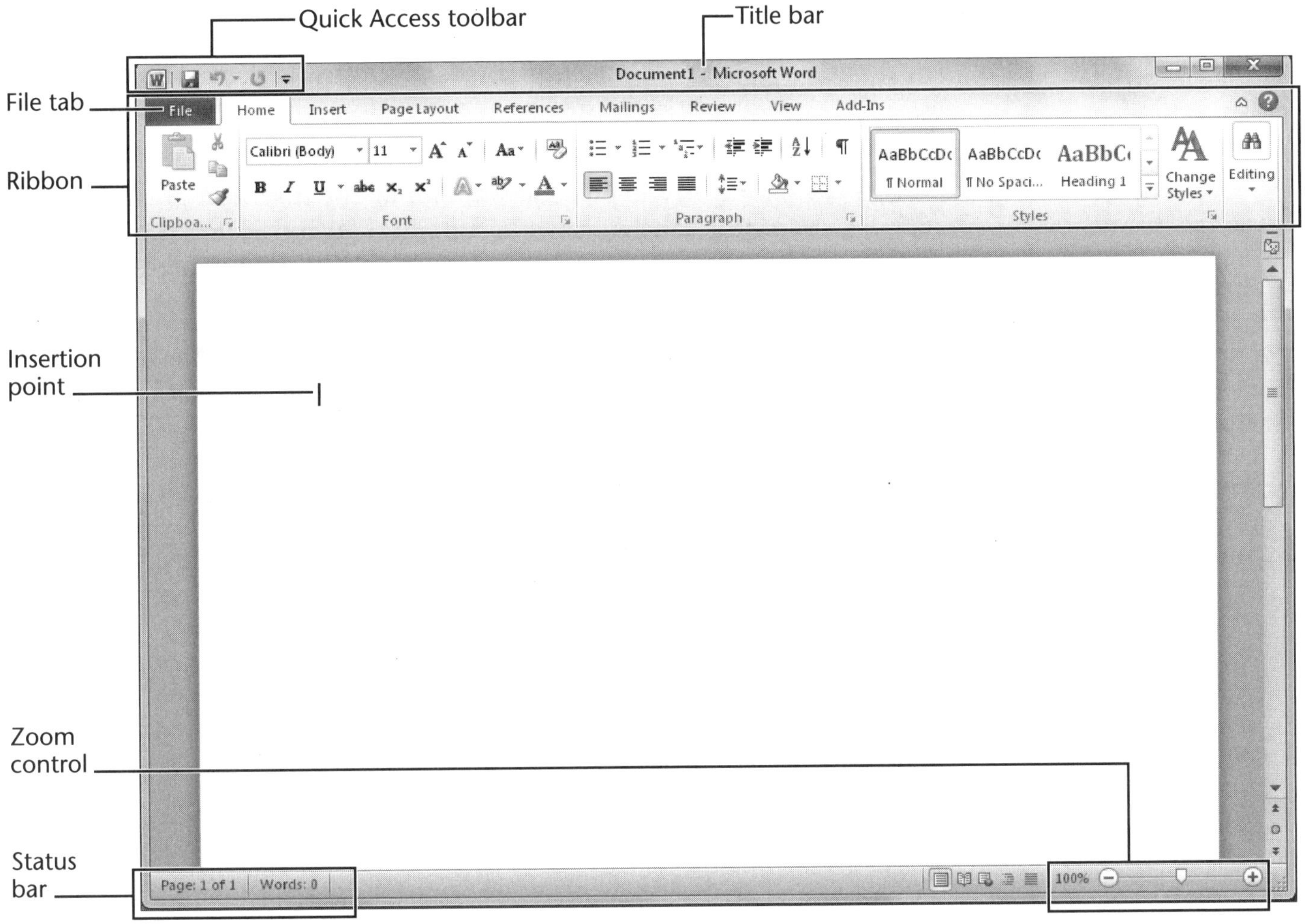

Element	Description
Ribbon	This is control central, where you find the tools you need to create, format, and edit your documents.
File tab	This tab displays the Backstage view, where you find file-management tasks, including opening, printing, and saving your work. This view also provides information about the document and options to change Word's default settings.
Quick Access toolbar	Frequently used commands appear on the Quick Access toolbar; you can add your own favorites.

Element	Description
Title bar	The name of your document appears on the title bar. You see a generic filename, Documentx (where "x" stands for the document number), until you save and name your document.
Insertion point	This is where the action is. When you type, the characters appear at the flashing insertion point. The insertion point is sometimes referred to as the cursor.
Status bar	The status bar tells you what page contains the insertion point. In the preceding example, the insertion point is on page 1 of a one-page document. It also tells you the number of words in your document. In this example, there are no words typed in the document.
Zoom Control	Dragging the Zoom control or clicking the buttons allows you to zoom in or out on the document.

Introducing the Ribbon

The band running across the top of the screen is the Ribbon. This is where you find the commands you need to create, format, and edit your documents.

The Ribbon consists of three main elements:

- Tabs
- Groups
- Commands

The tabs include Home, Insert, Page Layout, and so on. A group contains related commands within a tab. Groups on the Home tab, for example, include Clipboard, Font, Paragraph, Styles, and Editing. An example of a command in the Font group is the Bold command.

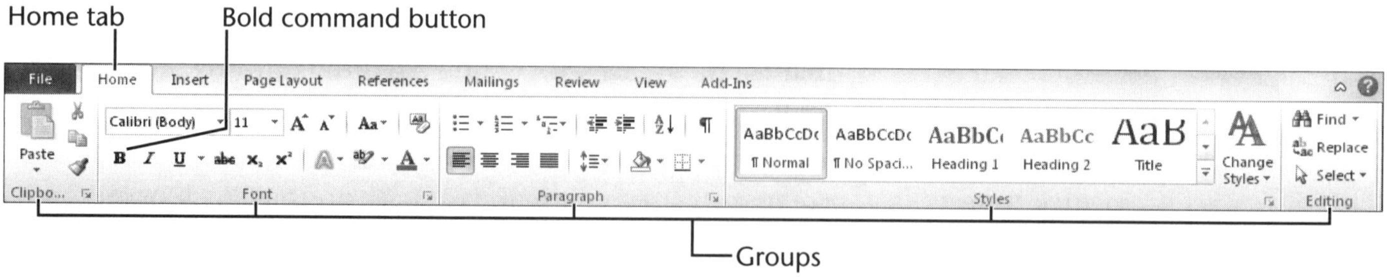

ToolTips

When you hover the mouse pointer over commands on the Ribbon, ToolTips may appear. These are little balloons that contain command descriptions, and they often contain keystrokes that you can use instead of selecting the commands with the mouse. In the following example, you see the ToolTip for the Bold command. You can use Ctrl+B to execute the command rather than clicking the Bold button if you wish.

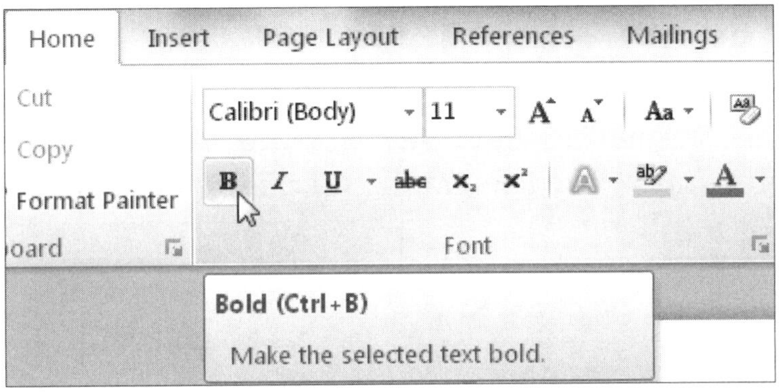

Contextual Tabs

Contextual tabs appear in context with the task you are performing. For example, if you are working with tables, the Table Tools tabs, Design and Layout, appear, as shown in the following figure. You'll learn more about this in Lesson 2, Word – Writing a Letter and a Resume.

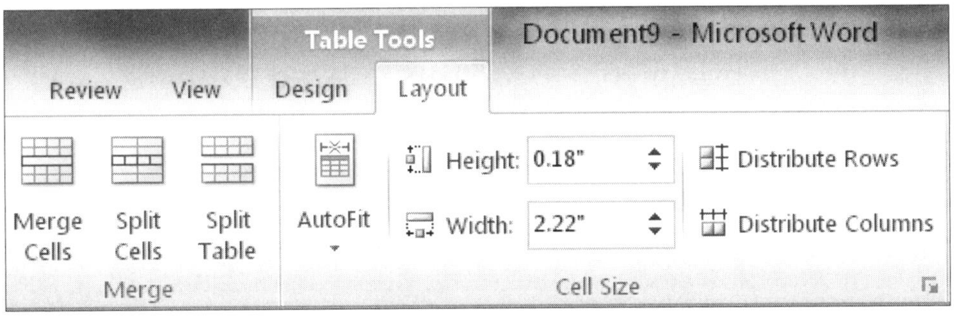

If you are working with clip art, the Picture Tools Format tab appears. You'll learn more about this in Lesson 4, Word – Encouraging Recycling with Flyers.

Varying Button Arrangements

Be aware that the arrangement of buttons on the Ribbon can vary depending on your screen resolution and how the Word window is sized. Following are two examples of how the Paragraph group might appear on the Ribbon.

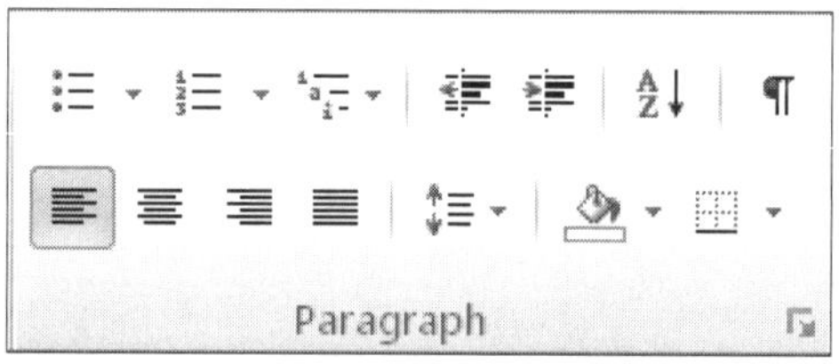

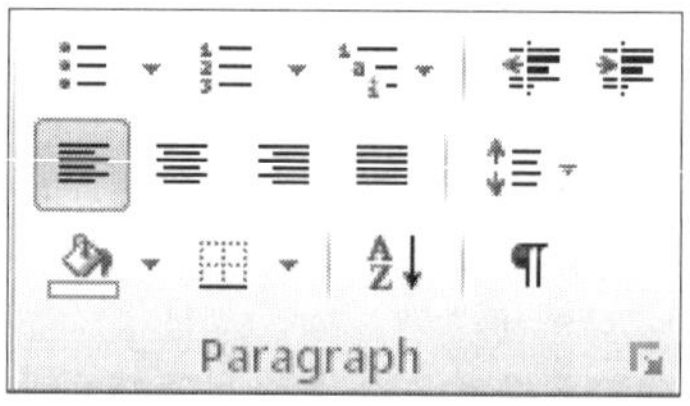

TIP! It's usually a good idea to maximize the program window so the Ribbon buttons always appear the same way.

Introducing the Toolbars

There are two important toolbars in Word 2010: the Quick Access toolbar and the Mini toolbar.

The Quick Access Toolbar

The Quick Access toolbar in the upper-left corner of the screen contains frequently used commands. It operates independently from the Ribbon.

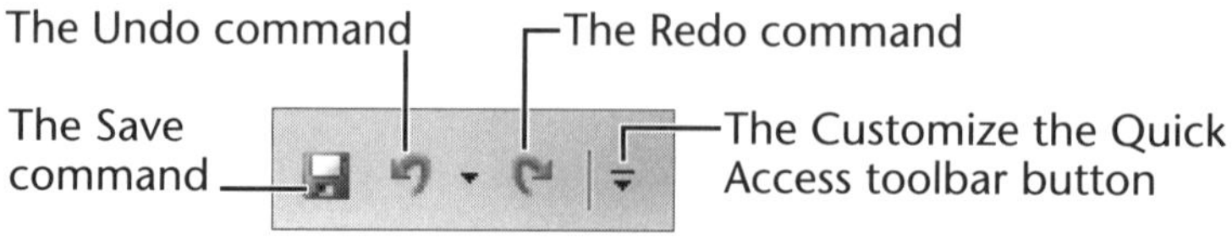

The Mini Toolbar

This toolbar contains frequently used formatting commands such as Bold and Italic. When you select (highlight) text, the Mini toolbar fades in. You will use the Mini toolbar when you learn about formatting in Lesson 4, Word – Encouraging Recycling with Flyers.

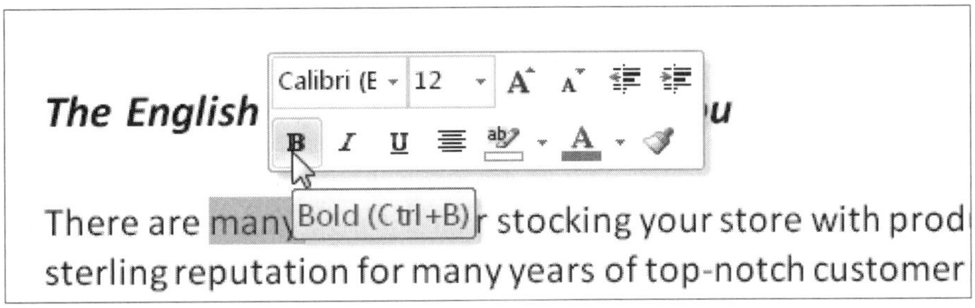

The Mini toolbar appears when you select (highlight) text.

HANDS-ON 1.2 Explore Tabs and Groups on the Ribbon

In this exercise, you will explore various tabs and groups on the Ribbon.

Display the Insert Tab

1. Click the **Insert** tab on the Ribbon to display the commands available in that category.

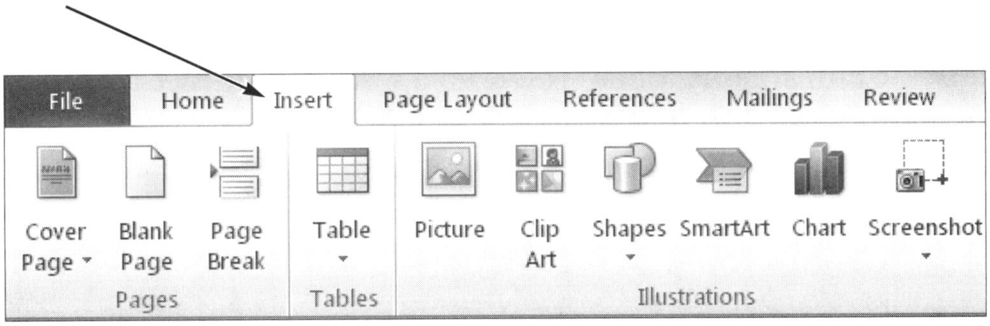

Notice the Pages, Tables, and Illustrations groups on the Insert tab.

2. Click the **Page Layout** tab.
   This tab displays commands for arranging text on the page.
3. Feel free to examine more tabs on the Ribbon.
4. Click the **Home** tab.

Opening Documents

The Open command on the File tab displays the Open dialog box, where you can navigate to a storage location and open previously saved documents. Once you open a document, you can edit or print it.

Downloading and Storing Exercise Files

Throughout this book, you will be referred to files in your "file storage location." You can store your exercise files on various media, such as on a USB flash drive, in the Documents (My Documents in Win XP) folder, or to a network drive at a school or company. While some figures may display files on a specific drive, it is assumed that you will substitute your own location for that shown in the figures. See Storing Your Exercise Files for additional information on alternative storage media. Storing Your Exercise Files is available on the student web page for this book at **labyrinthelab.com/ wtmo10**.

If you have not yet copied the student exercise files to your local file storage location, follow the instructions in Storing Your Exercise Files, located on the student web page for this book.

Opening Documents Created in Earlier Versions of Word

If you open a document created in a previous version of Word, it opens in Compatibility Mode. The term appears in the title bar, as shown in the following illustration. Older Word documents do not understand the new features in Word 2010, so those features are limited or disabled.

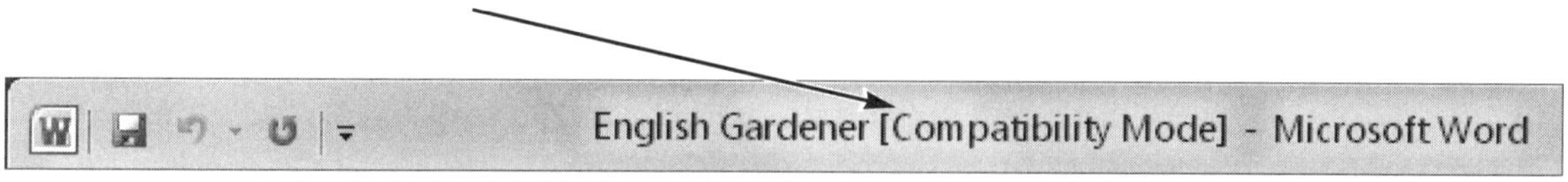

This is an example of a document created in Word 2003 and opened in Word 2010.

TIP! When you open a document created in an earlier version, a Convert command appears in the central panel of Backstage view. You can use the command to upgrade the file and make the new features of Word 2010 available to the document.

HANDS-ON 1.3 Open a Document

In this exercise, you will open an existing document through the Open dialog box.

Before You Begin: If you have not downloaded your exercise files, navigate to the student web page for this book at **labyrinthelab.com/wtmo10** and see the Downloading the Student Exercise Files section of Storing Your Exercise Files for instructions on how to retrieve the student exercise files for this book and to copy them to your file storage location.

1. Follow these steps to open a document:

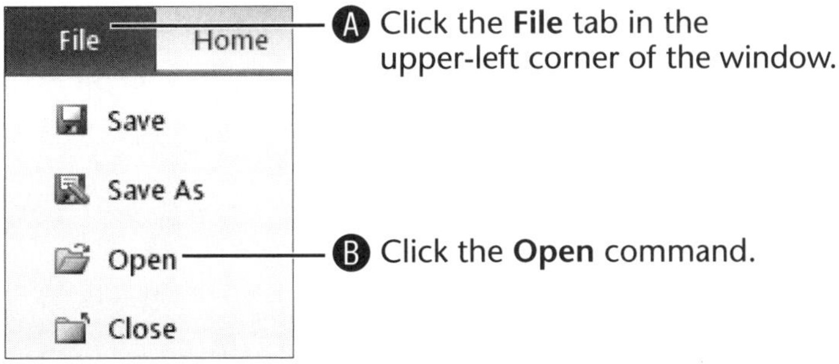

NOTE! Later in this lesson, the preceding steps will be written like this: Click the File tab and choose *Open* from the menu.

2. Follow these steps to open the English Gardener document:

Ⓐ Navigate to the Lesson 01 folder in your file storage location.

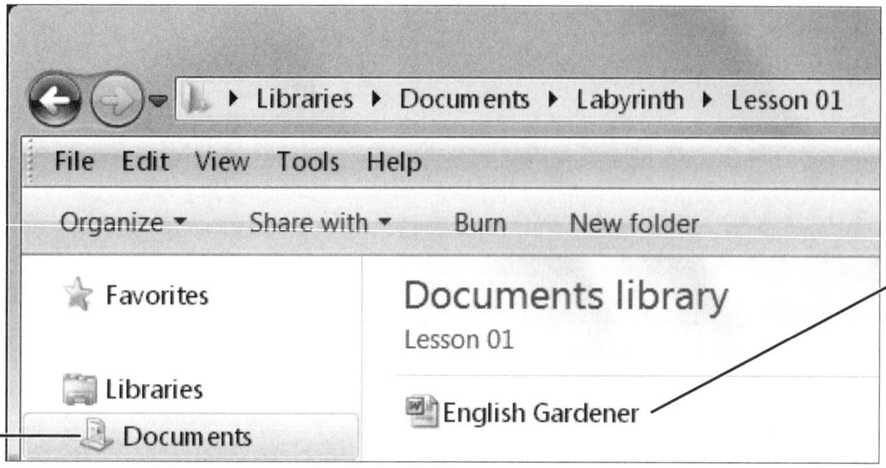

Ⓑ Click the **English Gardener** filename to select (highlight) it.

Ⓒ Click the **Open** button in the bottom-right corner of the dialog box.

Navigating in a Word Document

If you are working in a multipage document, it is helpful to know about various techniques for moving through documents. You can navigate using the scroll bar located at the right side of the screen, or you can use keystrokes.

Navigating with the Scroll Bar

The scroll bar lets you browse through documents; however, scrolling does not move the insertion point. The Previous Page and Next Page buttons at the bottom of the scroll bar do move the insertion point. The following illustration shows the components of the scroll bar.

Recognizing Different Mouse Pointer Shapes

The mouse pointer must be shaped like an I-beam I when you want to position the flashing insertion point using the mouse. (You click the left mouse button to place the insertion point at the position of the I-beam.) The mouse pointer appears as an I-beam when it is between the document margins.

The mouse pointer appears as a right-tilting white arrow when it is in the selection bar, which is located in the document's left margin. The white arrow is used to select (highlight) text in a document. You will learn more about selecting text in Lesson 3, Word – Editing the Business Etiquette Column.

HANDS-ON 1.4 Scroll and Position the Insertion Point

In this exercise, you will use the scroll bar to move through a document. Then you will reposition the insertion point in the document.

1. Follow these steps to scroll in the document:

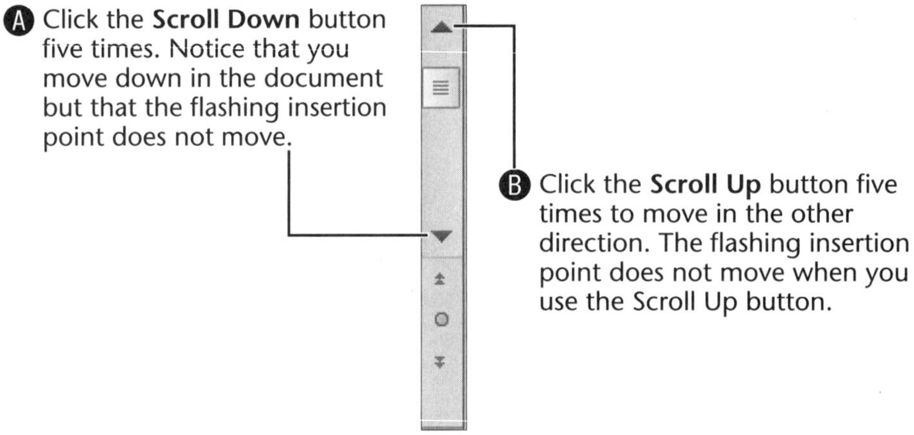

2. Slide the **I-beam** mouse pointer in the body of the document.

   The mouse pointer looks like an I-beam when it's between the document margins.

Position the Insertion Point

3. Click the **I-beam** mouse pointer anywhere in the document to position the blinking insertion point.

   If the background is highlighted, you accidentally selected the text. Deselect by clicking the mouse pointer in the document background.

4. Move the **mouse pointer** into the left margin area.

   The white arrow shape is now visible.

5. Position the **I-beam** mouse pointer in the first line of the first paragraph and click.

   The insertion point appears just where you clicked.

6. Click the open part of the **scroll bar** below the scroll box to move down one screen.

Use the Scroll Box and the Next Page/Previous Page Buttons

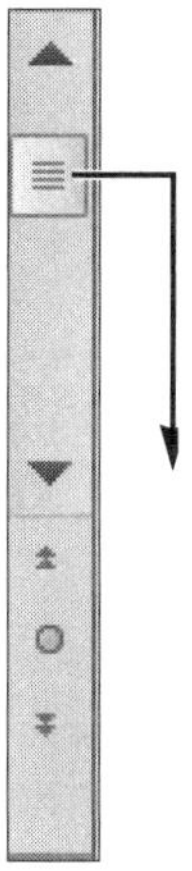

7. Drag the **scroll box** down with the mouse pointer until the end of the document is visible.
8. Click the **I-beam** mouse pointer at the end of the text to position the insertion point on the last page.
9. Drag the **scroll box** to the top of the scroll bar; then, click the **I-beam** mouse pointer in front of the first word of the first paragraph.
10. Click the **Next Page** button to move to the top of page 2.

    The insertion point moves with you when you use the Next Page and Previous Page buttons.
11. Click the **Previous Page** button to move to the top of page 1.

Navigating with the Keyboard

Whether you use the mouse or the keyboard to navigate through a document is a matter of personal preference. Navigating with the keyboard always moves the insertion point so it will be with you when you arrive at your destination.

The following Quick Reference table provides keystrokes for moving quickly through a document.

QUICK REFERENCE: Navigating with the Keyboard

Press	To Move
→	One character to the right
←	One character to the left
Ctrl+→	One word to the right
Ctrl+←	One word to the left
↓	Down one line
↑	Up one line
PageDown	Down one screen
PageUp	Up one screen
Ctrl+End	To the end of the document
Ctrl+Home	To the beginning of the document

QUICK REFERENCE: Navigating with the Keyboard (Continued)

Press	To Move
[End]	To the end of the line
[Home]	To the beginning of the line

HANDS-ON 1.5 Use the Keyboard to Navigate

In this exercise, you will use the keyboard to move through a document.

Use the Arrow Keys

1. Click the **I-beam** I mouse pointer in the middle of the first line of the second paragraph.
2. **Tap** the right arrow [→] and left arrow [←] keys a few times to move to the right and left, one character at a time.
3. **Tap** the up arrow [↑] and the down arrow [↓] keys a few times to move up and down, one line at a time.

Use Additional Keys

4. **Hold down** [Ctrl] and keep it down, then **tap** [Home] to move to the beginning of the document. **Release** [Ctrl].
5. Use the **arrow keys** to position the insertion point in the middle of the first line of the first paragraph.
6. **Hold down** [Ctrl] and keep it down, then **tap** the left arrow [←] key a few times to move to the left, one word at a time. **Release** [Ctrl].
7. **Hold down** [Ctrl] and keep it down, then **tap** the right arrow [→] key several times to move to the right, one word at a time. **Release** [Ctrl].
8. **Tap** [Home] to move to the beginning of the line.
9. **Tap** [End] to move to the end of the line.
10. Spend a few moments navigating with the keyboard. Refer to the preceding Quick Reference table for some additional keystrokes.

Closing Documents

You close a file by clicking the File tab and choosing the Close command from the menu. If you haven't saved your document, Word will prompt you to save it.

HANDS-ON 1.6 Close the Document

In this exercise, you will close your file.

1. Click the File tab and choose **Close** from the menu.
2. Click **Don't Save** if Word asks if you want to save changes.
3. If a blank document is on the screen, use the same technique to **close** it.
   The document window below the Ribbon is completely blank when all documents are closed.

Starting a New Blank Document

When all documents are closed, you can click the File tab and choose the New command from the menu to open a new blank document. You can also open a new document using the keyboard shortcut Ctrl+N.

QUICK REFERENCE: Opening, Closing, and Starting a New Document

Task	Procedure
Open a document	• Click the File tab. • Choose Open from the menu. • Navigate to your storage location. • Click the file you want to open. • Click the Open button.

QUICK REFERENCE: Opening, Closing, and Starting a New Document (Continued)

Task	Procedure
Close a document	• Click the File tab. • Choose Close from the menu.
Start a new document	• Click the File tab. • Choose New from the menu. • Double-click the Blank Document icon or click the Create button in the right-hand Backstage view panel. *or* • Press [Ctrl]+[N].

HANDS-ON 1.7 Start a New Document

In this exercise, you will open a new blank document.

Before You Begin: No documents should be open in the Word window at this time.

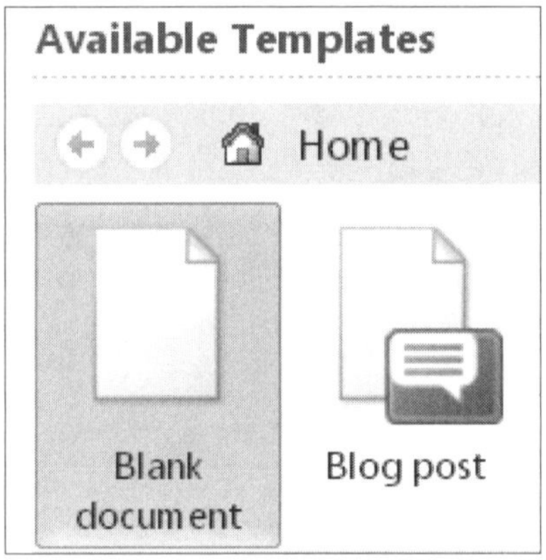

1. Click the File tab and choose **New** from the menu.

   Notice that Blank Document is highlighted in the center Backstage view panel.

2. **Double-click** the **Blank Document** button to open a new document.

   Now you will close the new document and try using the shortcut keystrokes to start another new document.

3. Click the File tab and choose **Close** from the menu.

4. **Hold down** [Ctrl] and **tap** [N] on your keyboard to open a new document.

   Leave the document open.

Getting Help in Word 2010

The Microsoft Word Help button appears in the upper-right corner of the Word screen. Clicking the Help button opens the Word Help window, where you can browse through the Table of Contents, click links to access a variety of topics, or type a term in the Search box and let the system find the answer for you.

HANDS-ON 1.8 Use Word Help

In this exercise, you will work with several Help techniques.

1. Click the **Microsoft Word Help** button in the upper-right corner of the Word window.
2. Click the **Show Table of Contents** button to display the Table of Contents on the left side of the window.

3. Follow these steps for an overview of Word Help:

Ⓐ Hover your **mouse pointer** over the buttons to see ToolTips descriptions of the buttons.

Ⓑ Click in the **Search box** to position the insertion point and type **`printing`**.

Ⓒ Click the **Search** button to display related topics on the right side of the window.

Ⓓ Explore the Table of Contents by clicking the **Getting Started with Word** book icon to display its related topics.

Ⓔ If necessary, **scroll down**, and then click the **Introducing Backstage** link to display the topic on the right side of the window. Read the first three paragraphs of Introducing Backstage.

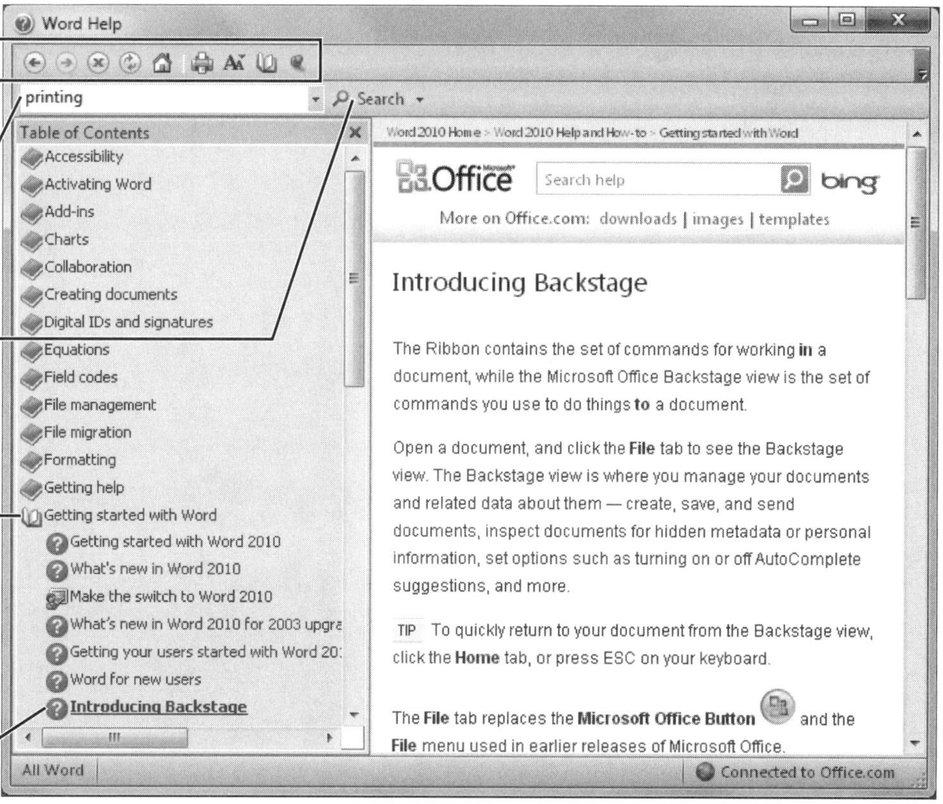

4. Click the **Close** [X] button in the upper-right corner of the Word Help window.

Exiting from Word

Clicking the [File] tab then clicking the Exit [X] button on the menu closes the Word program. It's important to exit Word in an orderly fashion. Turning off your computer before exiting Word could cause you to lose data.

HANDS-ON 1.9 Exit from Word

In this exercise, you will practice exiting from Word. Since the blank document on the screen has not been modified, you won't bother saving it.

1. Click the [File] tab.
2. Click the **Exit** [X] button at the bottom of the menu.
3. Click **Don't Save** if Word prompts you to save changes.
   Word closes and the Windows Desktop appears.

Concepts Review

To check your knowledge of the key concepts introduced in this lesson, complete the Concepts Review quiz on this and the next page. Or, you can take the quiz online by going to the URL **labyrinthelab.com/wtmo10**.

True/False Questions

			Page number
1. The insertion point automatically repositions when you scroll through a document using the scroll bars.	**true**	**false**	_______
2. The mouse pointer looks like a white arrow when placed in the left margin of a document.	**true**	**false**	_______
3. The Quick Access toolbar contains commands for positioning the insertion point.	**true**	**false**	_______
4. The arrangement of buttons on the Ribbon can vary depending on how the Word window is sized.	**true**	**false**	_______
5. The File tab provides access to file-management tasks, such as saving, opening, and closing a document.	**true**	**false**	_______
6. You find the commands you need to create and edit your documents on the Ribbon.	**true**	**false**	_______

Multiple Choice Questions

7. Which shape does the mouse pointer have when it is in the text area?

Page number: ______

- **a.** Right-pointing arrow
- **b.** I-beam
- **c.** Left-pointing arrow
- **d.** Four-headed arrow

8. The Open dialog box is where you can _____.

Page number: ______

- **a.** save newly created documents
- **b.** convert documents created in older versions of Word to Word 2010 documents
- **c.** choose to start a new blank document
- **d.** navigate to a storage location and open previously saved documents

9. The Ribbon consists of three primary areas, which are _____.

Page number: ______

- **a.** tabs, groups, and the selection bar
- **b.** the Quick Access toolbar, commands, and groups
- **c.** tabs, groups, and commands
- **d.** the Quick Access toolbar, the status bar, and groups

10. When you add text to a document, _____.

Page number: ______

- **a.** the existing text moves out of the way to make room for it
- **b.** the mouse pointer is shaped like a white arrow
- **c.** the Mini toolbar appears in case you want to format text
- **d.** the existing text collapses to close the gap

Skill Builders

SKILL BUILDER 1.1 Identify Elements of the Word 2010 Window

In this exercise, you will practice using correct terminology with parts of the Word window. It's important to use the right terms when talking about the Word program. If, for example, you need to discuss an issue with people in your IT department, they can help you faster if they are clear on what you are talking about.

1. Start **Word 2010**.
2. Using the table on the next page, write in the correct terms for items A through E.

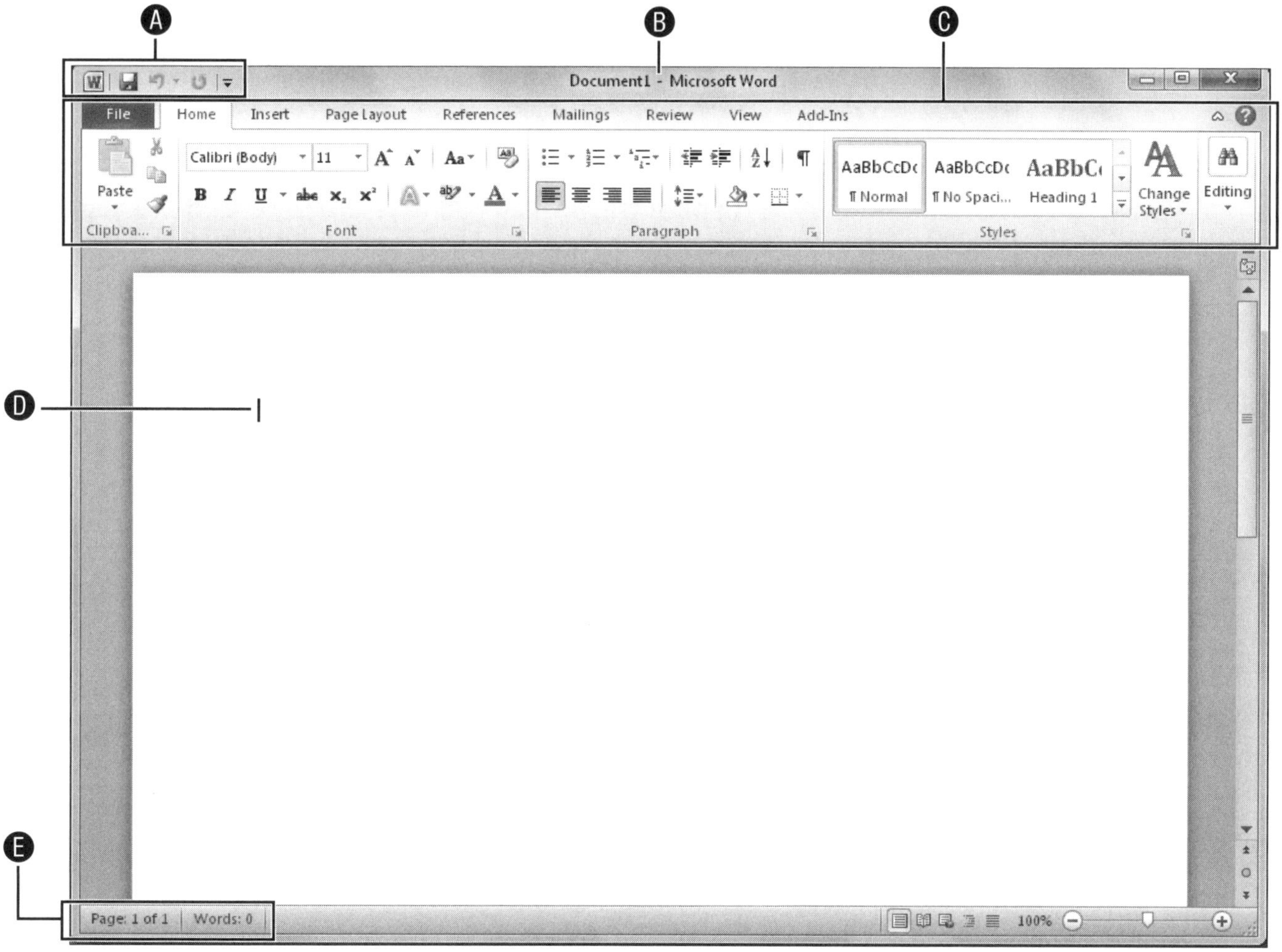

Letter	Term
A	
B	
C	
D	
E	

SKILL BUILDER 1.2 Use Word Help

In this exercise, you will work with the Word Help window to find information that can assist you as you work.

1. Click the **Microsoft Word Help** button in the upper-right corner of the Word window.
2. If necessary, click the **Show Table of Contents** button to display the Table of Contents on the left side of the Word Help window.

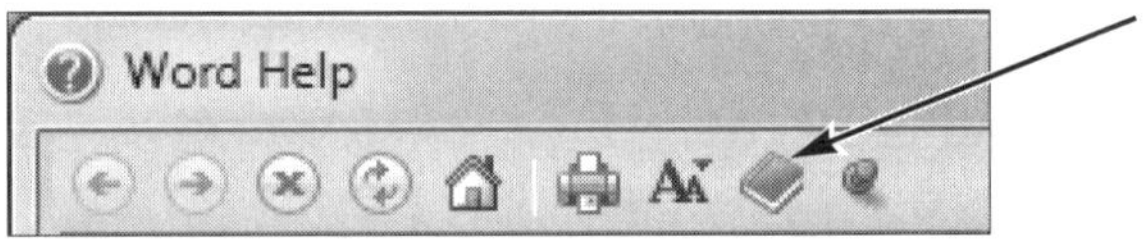

Use the Table of Contents

Now you'll review how you open a new blank document.

3. Click the **book icon** to the left of the **Creating Documents** topic to display its subtopics.
4. Click the **Create a Document** link.

   The subject appears in the right-hand panel.
5. Read the first major topic, **Open a New Document and Start Typing**, to review how you start a new blank document.

Search for Help

In the next lesson, you will work with the line spacing feature. In this lesson, you will search for information on line spacing to get a head start on the subject.

6. Follow these steps to search for help on this topic:

Ⓐ Type **line spacing** in the search box.

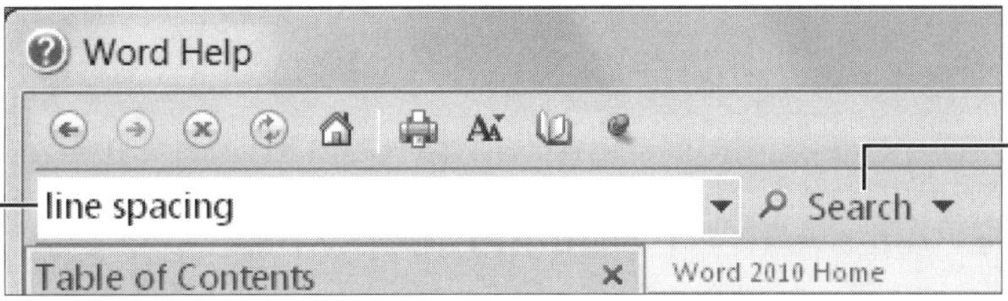

Ⓑ Click the **Search** button.

7. Click the link in the right-hand panel for this topic: **Adjust the Line Spacing between Text or Paragraphs**.

8. Read the topic, **Line Spacing in Word 2010**.

9. Click the **Close** button in the upper-right corner of the Word Help window.

SKILL BUILDER 1.3 Navigate in Word

In this exercise, you will use a report you created for your Oriental Languages class to practice navigating in Word.

1. Click the File tab and choose **Open** from the menu.

2. If necessary, navigate to your **file storage location** and open the Lesson 01 folder.

3. **Double-click** to open the file named sb-Heart Report.

Navigate with the Scroll Bar

4. Click the **Next Page** button at the bottom of the scroll bar to move to the top of the second page.

5. Click the **scroll bar** below the scroll box to move down one screen.

6. Drag the **scroll box** to the top of the document and then position the **insertion point** at the beginning of the document.

7. Click the **Scroll Down** button and hold the mouse button down for a few seconds to scroll quickly through the document.

8. Click the **Previous Page** button to return to the top of the document.

Navigate with the Keyboard

9. **Tap** the down arrow [↓] key enough times to position the insertion point in the first line of the first paragraph on the second page.

10. **Tap** [End] to move the insertion point to the end of the line.

11. **Tap** [Home] to move to the beginning of the line.

12. **Tap** [Ctrl]+[End] to place the insertion point at the end of the document.

13. **Tap** [Ctrl]+[Home] to move to the top of the document.

    If you press and hold the arrow keys, they quickly move the insertion point through the document.

14. **Press and hold** the [↓] key long enough to move the insertion point to the first line of the first paragraph on the second page.

15. **Hold down** [Ctrl] and **tap** [→] three times to move to the right, one word at a time.

Close the Document

16. Click the File tab and choose **Close** from the menu.

17. Click **Don't Save** if a message appears asking if you want to save changes.

Exit from Word

18. Click the File tab.

19. Click the **Exit** button at the bottom of the menu.

LESSON 2

Word – Writing a Letter and a Resume

In this lesson, you will change line and paragraph spacing. Then you will type a letter using AutoComplete to add the date to your letter, and you will insert bullet points to draw the reader's attention to important items. You will also save and print your letter and learn about Word Wrap and when to use the [Enter] key. Then you will use Word's Table feature to help you lay out a resume and, finally, you will create an envelope for mailing your letter and resume.

LESSON OBJECTIVES

After studying this lesson, you will be able to:

- Work with line and paragraph spacing
- Automate tasks with AutoComplete
- Use Word Wrap and the [Enter] key to lay out paragraphs
- Add bullet points in your document
- Create a table
- Save and print documents
- Type an envelope

Student resources ***labyrinthelab.com/wtmo10***

Case Study: Using a Table to Organize a Resume

Victor Gomez just completed his degree in sales and marketing. He is now ready to begin his career! He is interested in a Customer Support position at Goodspeed Industries.

Using Word 2010, Victor creates a professional looking cover letter. He uses Word's Bullets feature to point out pertinent information he wants to draw the hiring manager's attention to.

February 10, 2010

Mr. Anthony Williams, Hiring Manager
Goodspeed Industries
456 Apple Blossom Lane
Windy Hills, CA 94491

Dear Mr. Williams:

Your ad for a Customer Support Representative in this Sunday's Chronicle caught my attention. I believe I can offer Goodspeed Industries a blend of skills and enthusiasm that will help you maintain a satisfied client base.

- Principles of good salesmanship and clear, effective communication skills have been the focus of my studies for the last four years.
- A double major in Sales and Communications demonstrates that I can take on above-average challenges and responsibilities. I am not afraid of hard work, which is demonstrated by my 3.9 grade point average.
- The positions I have held in student government demonstrate my leadership abilities and my interest in people's needs and challenges.
- To finance my education, I worked in a hospital call center where I demonstrated the skill to quickly gain rapport and to efficiently assist patients with their billing questions.

I am excited about starting my professional career, and I would appreciate the opportunity to add to Goodspeed Industries' success. I will call you in the near future to see if we can schedule a time to meet.

Best regards,

Victor Gomez

Enclosure

Typing a Cover Letter

In this part of the lesson, you will type a cover letter. Later you will create a resume and an envelope.

TIP! If you Google *cover letter*, you will find many websites that provide good ideas for cover letters designed to grab the attention of a hiring manager.

Text is always inserted at the flashing insertion point. As you type, the insertion point moves along in front of the text.

Line and Paragraph Spacing

Word 2007, the version prior to Word 2010, introduced new default (preassigned) line spacing. Rather than a default of single spacing (1.0), which has been the standard for word processors from the beginning, Word 2007 introduced 1.15 line spacing. This new line spacing default continues with Word 2010.

The additional white space between lines can make your documents easier to read. The new spacing also includes an extra 10 points of space at the end of paragraphs. (That's a little over an eighth of an inch.) Rather than tapping [Enter] twice at the end of a paragraph, just tap [Enter] once and Word adds the extra spacing.

Apply Traditional Spacing Using the Line and Paragraph Spacing Button

When writing business-oriented letters, a traditional, more compact look (without the additional spacing) is still considered appropriate. Therefore, when you begin a letter, you may wish to switch to single (1.0) spacing and remove the extra space after paragraphs by choosing the options shown in the following figure.

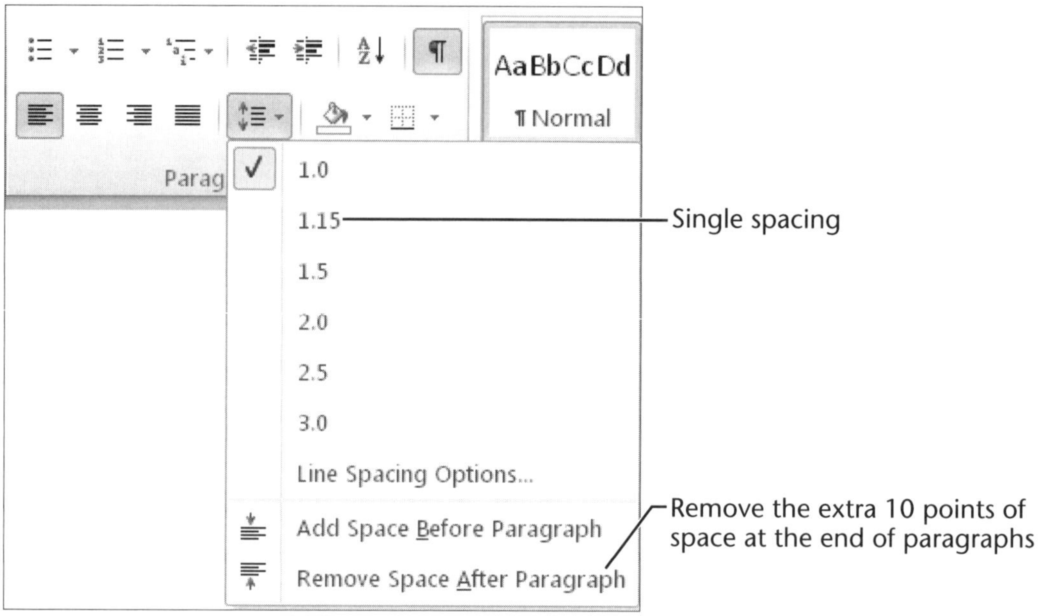

Apply these settings when you wish to type a more compact, traditional letter.

TIP! Another way you can eliminate extra spacing at the end of a paragraph is to tap [Shift]+[Enter] rather than just [Enter].

Nonprinting Characters

The Show/Hide [¶] button on the Ribbon displays nonprinting characters. Word has a number of nonprinting characters that are not visible unless you turn on the Show/Hide feature. Nonprinting characters do not appear on the printed page even when the characters appear on the screen.

The [Enter] and [Spacebar] keys, as well as several others, create nonprinting characters. Being able to see these characters can help you make sure the spacing is correct in your document.

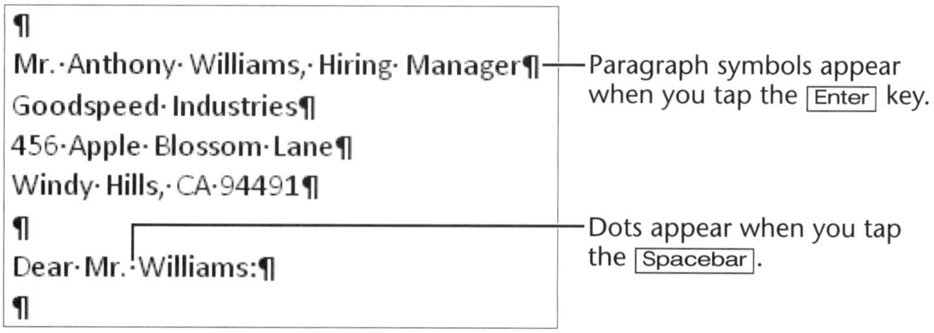

Paragraph Symbols Carry Formatting in Them All new, blank documents contain a paragraph symbol; you don't see it if you don't turn on the Show/Hide feature. Paragraph symbols carry formatting in them. For a new document, formatting includes default spacing of 1.15 lines and extra space at the end of a paragraph.

You can select (highlight) a paragraph symbol and reformat it, thereby changing the default format for the document.

NOTE! Formatting paragraph symbols in this lesson provides a quick introduction to formatting. You will learn a lot more about formatting documents in Lesson 4, Word – Encouraging Recycling with Flyers.

AutoComplete

AutoComplete can do some of your typing for you. It recognizes certain words and phrases, such as names of months and days of the week, and offers to complete them for you. You accept the phrase that AutoComplete proposes by tapping [Enter].

Using AutoComplete to Insert the Entire Current Date If you are typing a month with a long name, keep typing until you finish the name of the month, and then Word will offer to enter the entire current date.

If you are typing a month with a short name, such as June, Word doesn't offer to complete the month. However, when you finish typing the month, Word offers to enter the full current date.

HANDS-ON 2.1 Change Spacing and Use AutoComplete

In this exercise, you will display nonprinting characters, select (highlight) the embedded paragraph symbol, change the default line spacing to 1.0, and remove additional space after the paragraph. Then you will use AutoComplete to insert the date in the document.

Display Nonprinting Characters

1. Start **Word** and make sure the Word window is **maximized**.
2. Follow these steps to turn on the Show/Hide feature:

Ⓐ If necessary, click the **Home** tab.

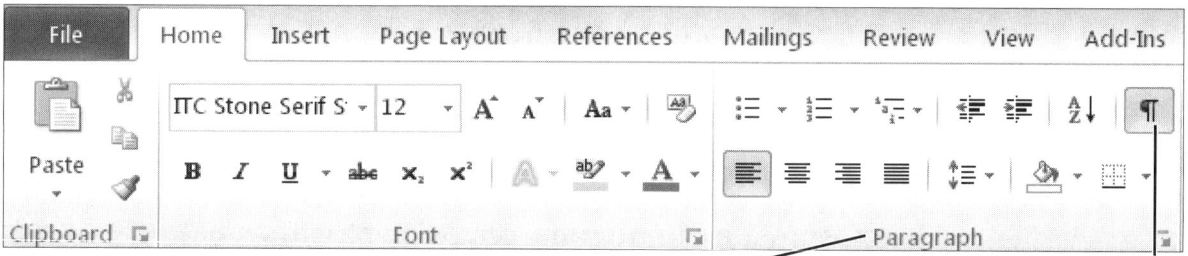

Ⓑ Locate the **Paragraph** group.

Ⓒ Click the **Show/Hide** button.

A paragraph symbol now appears on the page.

NOTE! Later in the book, the preceding steps will be written like this: Choose Home→Paragraph→Show/Hide ¶ from the Ribbon.

Format the Paragraph Symbol for Single Spacing

3. Follow these steps to select (highlight) the paragraph symbol.

Ⓐ Position the **mouse pointer** in the margin to the left of the paragraph symbol. (The mouse pointer should look like a white, right-pointing arrow.)

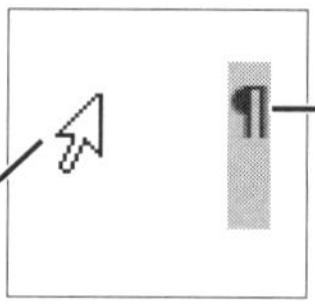

Ⓑ Click the **left mouse button** to select the paragraph symbol.

4. Choose **Home→Paragraph→Line and Paragraph Spacing** from the Ribbon.

5. Follow these steps to change line spacing to single space and remove the extra space after a paragraph:

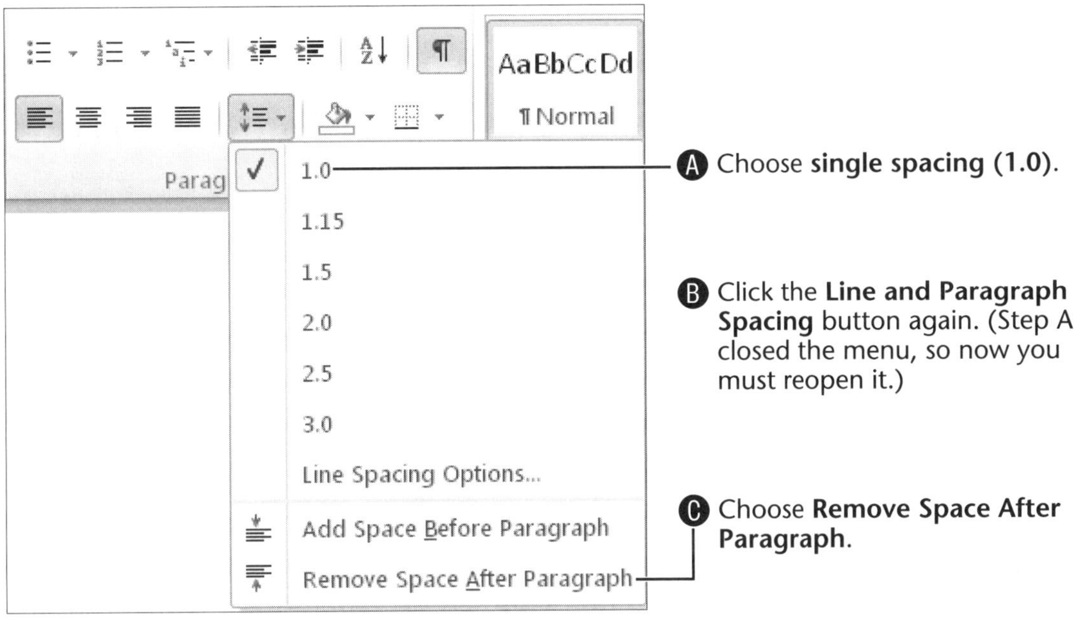

Enter the Date Using AutoComplete

6. **Tap** [Enter] six times to place the insertion point about 2 inches from the top of the page.

7. Start typing **`Febr`** but stop when AutoComplete displays a pop-up tip.
   AutoComplete suggests the word it thinks you are typing and offers to complete it.

8. **Tap** [Enter] to automatically insert *February* into the letter.

9. Finish **typing** the date as **`February 10, 2011`**.

TIP! If you make a typographical error (typo), use the [Backspace] key (deletes characters to the left of the insertion point) or the [Delete] key (deletes characters to the right of the insertion point) to delete it, and then continue typing.

You can also click the Undo button on the Quick Access toolbar to undo mistakes, starting with the most recent error. (You will learn more details about the Undo feature in the next lesson.)

Leave the document open. You will continue to use it throughout the lesson.

The Enter Key and Word Wrap

Tap the [Enter] key at the end of a short line that must remain short. The greeting line in a letter is a good example; it consists of a short line.

Dear Mr. Williams: [Enter]

You can also use the [Enter] key whenever you need to create blank lines, such as between paragraphs.

When Not to Use the Enter Key When you type along a line and reach the right-hand margin, Word automatically wraps down to the next line. You *should not* tap the [Enter] key at the ends of lines *within* a paragraph. If you do, it can make your life very difficult when it is time to make editing changes. Just let it wrap!

TIP! As you complete the exercises in this lesson, the text on your screen may not begin a new line at the same locations as the illustrations show. Don't be concerned; just let the text wrap at the end of the line and use [Enter] at the locations indicated.

HANDS-ON 2.2 Use the Enter Key and Word Wrap

In this exercise, you will use the [Enter] key to create blank lines. You will also use [Enter] to force the inside address lines and the greeting line to remain short, and then you will let Word Wrap take care of the line endings in the main paragraphs.

Don't be concerned if you see squiggly red or green underlines. They indicate possible spelling or grammatical errors, which you'll learn more about in a later lesson. Meanwhile, if you know you made a typo, just use [Backspace] or [Delete] to delete it and keep typing.

1. **Tap** [Enter] four times to generate white space after the date.

   Word inserts a fresh line each time you tap the [Enter] key.

2. **Type** the inside address and greeting line, **tapping** [Enter] as shown:

   Mr. Anthony Williams, Hiring Manager [Enter]
   Goodspeed Industries [Enter]
   456 Apple Blossom Lane [Enter]
   Windy Hills, CA 94491 [Enter]
   [Enter]
   Dear Mr. Williams: [Enter]
   [Enter]

   Next you'll type the first main paragraph of the letter and let Word Wrap do its thing.

Use Word Wrap

3. **Type** the following paragraph, but don't press [Enter] until indicated at the end of the paragraph.

   Don't be concerned if your line widths are not the same as that shown in the following example. Word Wrap will take care of the line endings.

   Your ad for a Customer Support Representative in this Sunday's Chronicle caught my attention. I believe I can offer Goodspeed Industries a blend of skills and enthusiasm that will help you maintain a satisfied client base. [Enter]

Using the Bullets Feature

Use of bullet points makes it easy for your reader to find pertinent information in your document. If you are writing to busy people, such as hiring managers, they will appreciate bullets that focus their attention on the significant points.

You can use the Bullets feature located in the Paragraph group of the Home tab to quickly create bulleted lists.

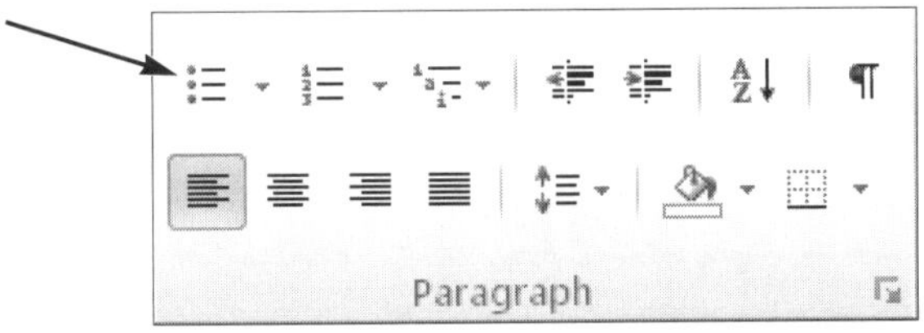

Once you begin a bulleted list, tapping [Enter] generates the next bullet. When you have completed the list, tap [Enter] twice to turn off the feature.

HANDS-ON 2.3 Add a Bulleted List to Your Letter

In this exercise, you will use bullets to draw the hiring manager's attention to the main points that demonstrate why the applicant is qualified for the job.

1. Choose **Home→Paragraph→Bullets** from the Ribbon.
2. **Type** the following paragraph:
   - **Principles of good salesmanship and clear, effective communication skills have been the focus of my studies during the last four years.**

3. **Tap** [Enter] to generate the next bullet.

4. **Type** the following bulleted paragraphs, **tapping** [Enter] where indicated:

   - **A double major in Sales and Communications demonstrates that I can take on above-average challenges and responsibilities. I am not afraid of hard work, which is demonstrated by my 3.9 grade point average.** [Enter]
   - **The positions I have held in student government demonstrate my leadership abilities and my interest in people's needs and challenges.** [Enter]
   - **To finance my education, I worked in a hospital call center, where I demonstrated the skill to quickly gain rapport and to efficiently assist patients with their billing questions.** [Enter]

   Your last [Enter] generated another bullet; a second [Enter] turns off the feature.

5. **Tap** [Enter] again.

   Now you're ready to finish the letter.

6. **Type** the following paragraph and closing:

   I am excited about starting my professional career, and I would appreciate the opportunity to add to Goodspeed Industries' success. I will call you in the near future to see if we can schedule a time to meet. [Enter]

   [Enter]

   Best regards, [Enter]

   [Enter]

   [Enter]

   [Enter]

   Victor Gomez [Enter]

   [Enter]

Saving a Document

When you are working on a document, it is located in your computer's memory. Memory is *temporary* storage, meaning that if you lose power, your computer loses its memory. If this happens, you could lose information.

To avoid this problem, you will save your letter on a storage device, such as a USB flash drive or the hard drive inside your computer. These storage methods are permanent, meaning your data won't be lost in the event of a power failure. You should save frequently—every five to ten minutes is a good idea.

Save Compared to Save As

In Word, you can save a document by issuing one of two commands: Save or Save As. The first time you save a document, you use the Save As command and give the document a name. After that, when you make modifications to a document, you use the Save command to update the file on your storage device.

Word's DOCX File Format A file format is a technique for saving computer data. Early versions of Word saved documents in the *doc* format. Word 2007 introduced a new file format: *docx*. Word 2010 uses the same docx format. This is important because users of earlier versions of Word cannot read Word files in the new docx file format without installing special software.

TIP! Users of early Word versions can download the Compatibility Pack from the Microsoft website. This allows users of previous versions of Word to open, edit, and save files created in the new docx file format.

The Save As Dialog Box When you save a document for the first time, the Save As dialog box appears. The following illustration describes some significant features of the Save As dialog box.

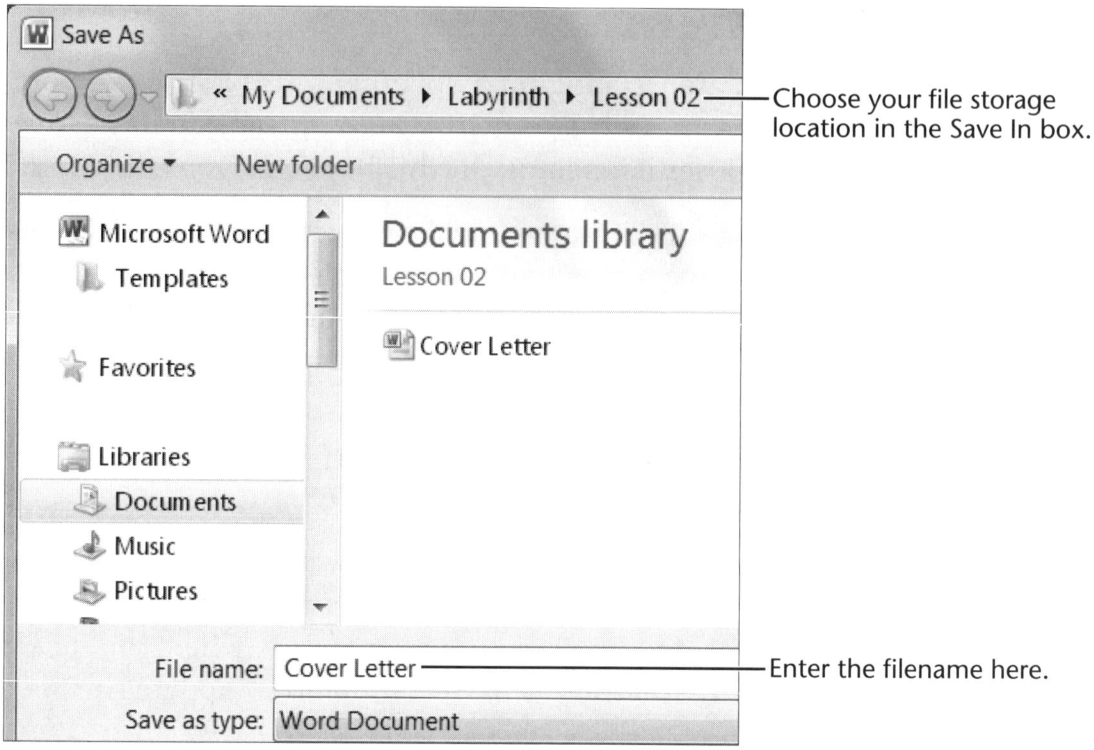

Save a Word 2010 Document in an Earlier Version You can save a document created in Word 2010 in the earlier *doc* version if you want to share it with someone who uses Word 2003 or an earlier version.

The Save As Type list in the Save As dialog box offers this option.

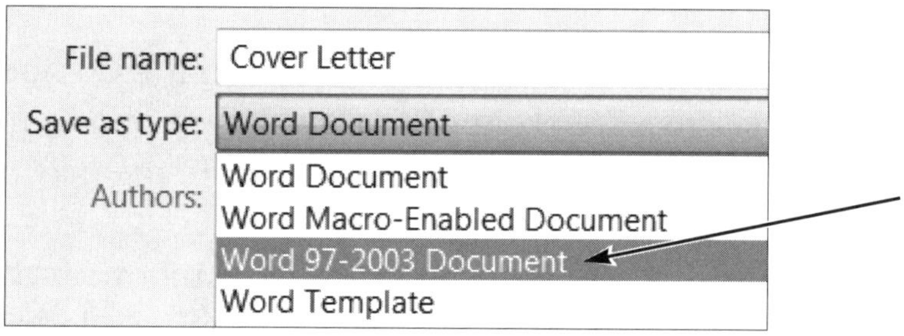

HANDS-ON 2.4 Save Your Cover Letter

In this exercise, you will save the cover letter you created in the previous exercise. This way, if there is a power failure, your letter will be saved.

1. Follow these steps to begin saving the letter:

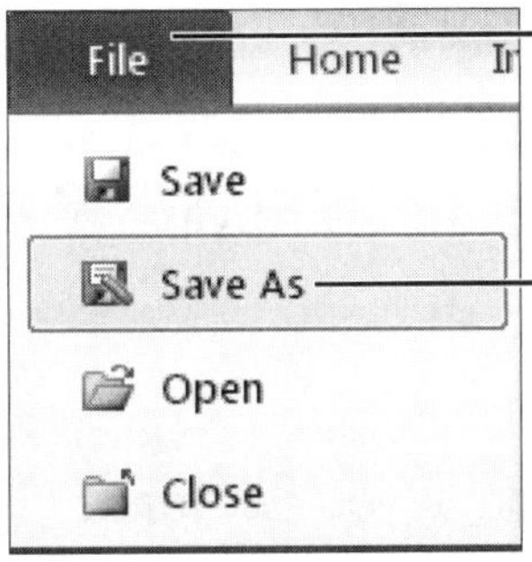

Ⓐ Click the **File** tab.

Ⓑ Choose the **Save As** command.

The Save As dialog box appears.

2. Choose your **file storage location.**

   Notice that Word automatically suggests the first few words in the document as the filename. You want to use your own filename, so you will just type the new name to replace the suggested name.

3. Type **`Cover Letter`** in the File Name field.

4. Click the **Save** button in the bottom-right corner of the dialog box.

Saving a Modified Document

The first time you save a document, you give it a name. If you make changes to the document after that, you must save it again so the changes are not lost. Once the document is saved and named, you can use the Save command rather than the Save As command.

You can use the Save button on the Quick Access toolbar or the Save command on the File tab to save a modified document. When you use Save versus Save As, no dialog box appears. The Save just happens in the background.

HANDS-ON 2.5 Modify Your Letter and Save It Again

In this exercise, you will add the enclosure notification to the bottom of the letter to notify the reader to check for an additional document in the envelope. Later in this lesson, you will create a resume, which will be the enclosure.

1. If necessary, click at the **bottom of the letter** to position the insertion point.

   Now you will add the enclosure notification to the letter. There should be a blank line separating the enclosure notification from the signature block.

2. If necessary, **tap** [Enter] to place the insertion point on the second blank line below the signature block.

3. **Type** the word **`Enclosure`**.

   Now you'll save the letter again to save the change you just made.

4. Click the **Save** button on the Quick Access toolbar in the upper-left corner of the Word window, as shown in the following figure.

QUICK REFERENCE: Saving Documents

Task	Procedure
Save a document for the first time	• Click the File tab and choose Save As from the menu. • Navigate to your storage location. • Type the filename.
Save a modified document	• Click the File tab and choose Save from the menu. *or* • Click the Save button on the Quick Access toolbar.

Printing a Document

You can print your document by choosing the Print command from the File tab. The File tab displays Backstage view, from where you can choose the Print command from the menu on the left.

Choosing Print opens the printer controls in the center panel (shown at left in the following figure) and a preview of your letter in the right-hand panel.

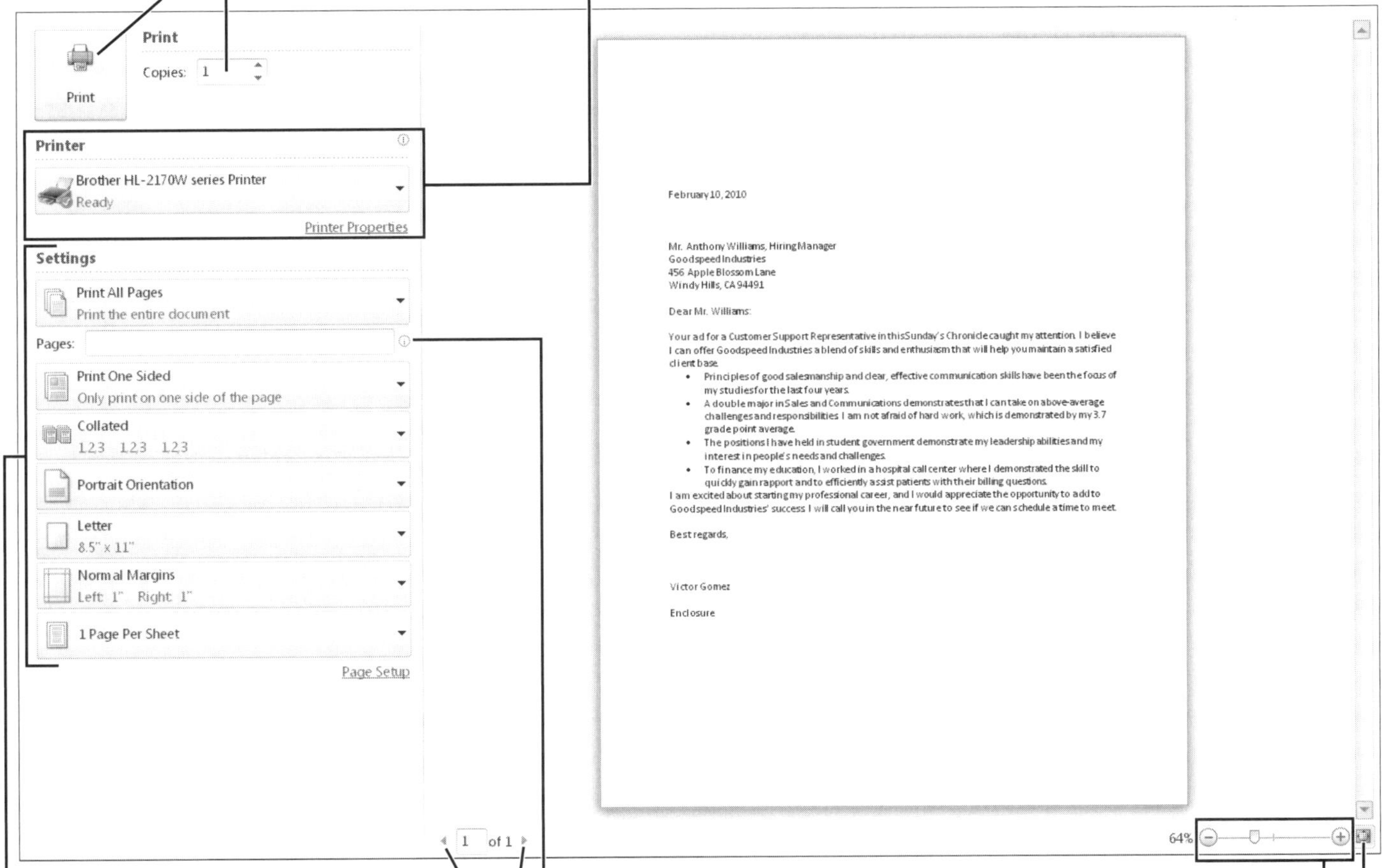

HANDS-ON 2.6 Print Your Cover Letter

In this exercise, you will preview your letter to see how it looks *before* you print. Then you will print your cover letter.

1. Click File and choose **Print** from the menu.
2. Click the **zoom controls** and drag the **slider** in the bottom-right corner of the preview panel a few times to zoom in and out of the letter.

3. Click the **Zoom to Page** button to the right of the zoom controls to fit the page to the preview panel.
4. At the top of the Backstage center panel, click the top part of the **spinner button** once to change the number of copies to 2, as shown in the following figure.

5. Click the **Print** button at the top of the center panel to print two copies of your letter.
6. Click File and choose **Close** from the menu.

Using a Word Table to Organize a Resume

A table is one of Word's most useful tools. Tables are a powerful means of communicating information, yet they are flexible and easy to use. In this part of the lesson, you will use a table to create a resume.

TIP! If you Google *resume*, you will find helpful guidelines for creating a resume that's targeted to the job you are applying for.

Using the Table button on the Insert tab allows you to create a new table.

NOTE! The rectangles that make up the table are referred to as *cells*.

Drag the mouse pointer to select the number of columns and rows you want in the table. Notice the indicator showing the number of columns and rows you selected (3x3 in this example).

Word's Live Preview feature displays what the table will look like before you insert it in the document.

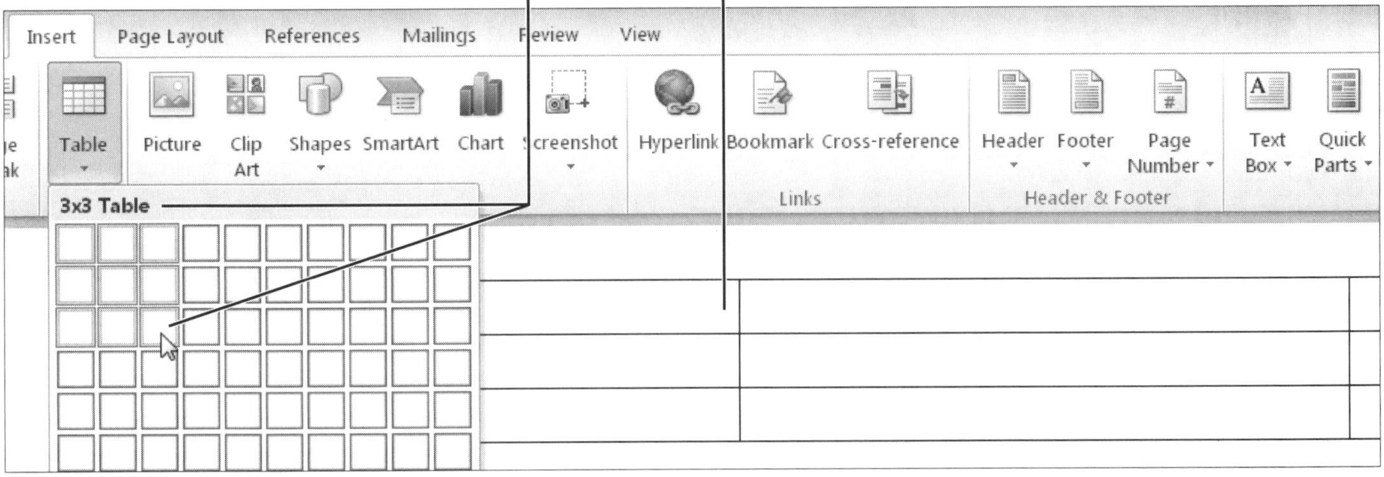

Merging Cells and Centering Data in a Cell

Frequently the first row of a table contains a title describing the contents of the table. In the case of a resume, it's likely the first row would contain the job applicant's contact information. Merging the cells together and centering the information within that cell gives your resume a polished look.

Victor Gomez 123 Cherry Blossom Lane Windy Hills, CA 94941 415-555-1212 victor@yahoo.com	
Objective	A challenging career where I can use my sales and communications skills
Qualifications	• Proven ability to close sales • Superb communication and presentation skills • Ability to quickly gain client rapport

The Table Tools Contextual Tabs: Design and Layout You will use the Table Tools' contextual Layout tab to merge and center-align the first row of the table.

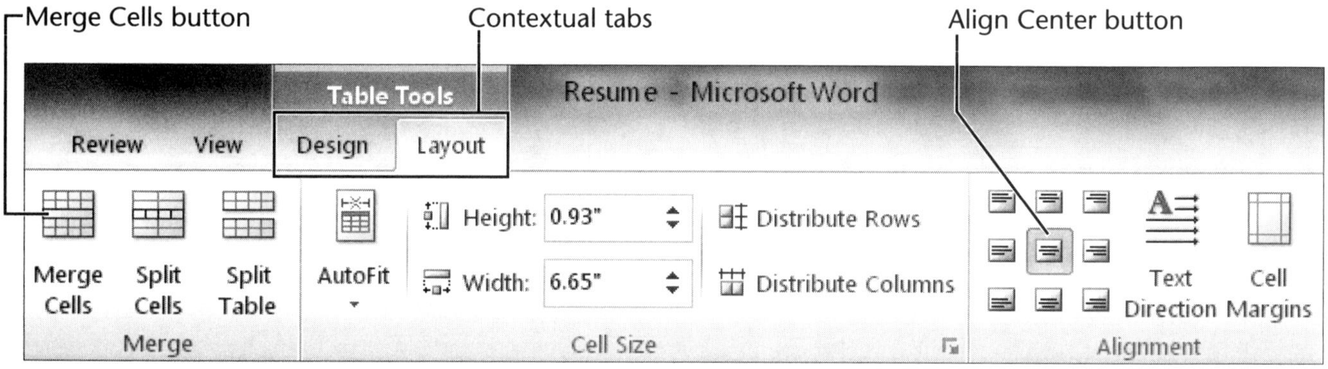

HANDS-ON 2.7 Create a Table for Your Resume

In this exercise, you will create a table. Then you will merge and center-align the cells in the first row of the table.

1. Click File and choose **New** from the menu.

   The Blank Document button is highlighted in the center Backstage view panel.

2. **Double-click** the **Blank Document** button to open a new document.

3. **Tap** Enter three times so the resume will be centered top-to-bottom on the page.

   You are now ready to create the table for your resume.

4. Choose **Insert→Tables→Table** from the Ribbon.

5. Follow these steps to create a two-column, seven-row table:

TIP! Remember, if you make a mistake, you can always click the Undo button on the Quick Access toolbar.

Ⓐ Position the **mouse pointer** in the first cell in the upper-left corner of the grid; then, hold down the **mouse button** and drag to the right to select two columns. Keep the mouse button down.

Ⓑ Drag the **mouse pointer** down seven rows.

Ⓒ Release the **mouse button**.

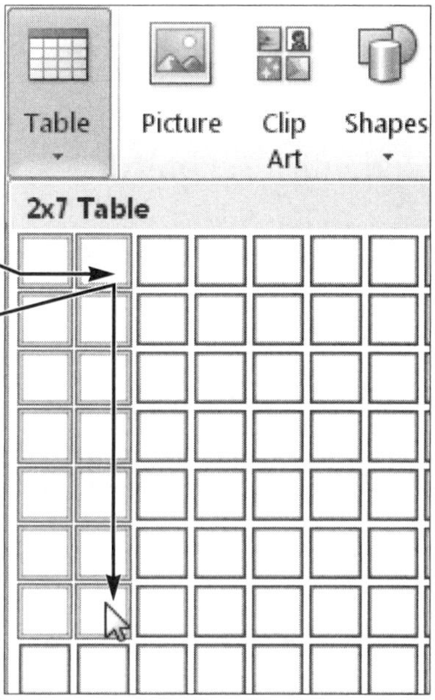

A 2x7 table appears in your document.

Merge and Center the Cells in the First Row

6. Follow these steps to merge and center the first row of the table:

Now you will merge the cells in the first row and apply the Align Center feature in preparation for entering contact information in the first row of the resume.

Ⓐ Position the **mouse pointer** in the margin to the left of the first row of the table. (The mouse pointer appears as a white, right-pointing arrow.)

Ⓑ Click the **mouse button** to select (highlight) the first row.

Ⓒ The Mini toolbar appears whenever you select something in Word. You can ignore it for now; it will fade away.

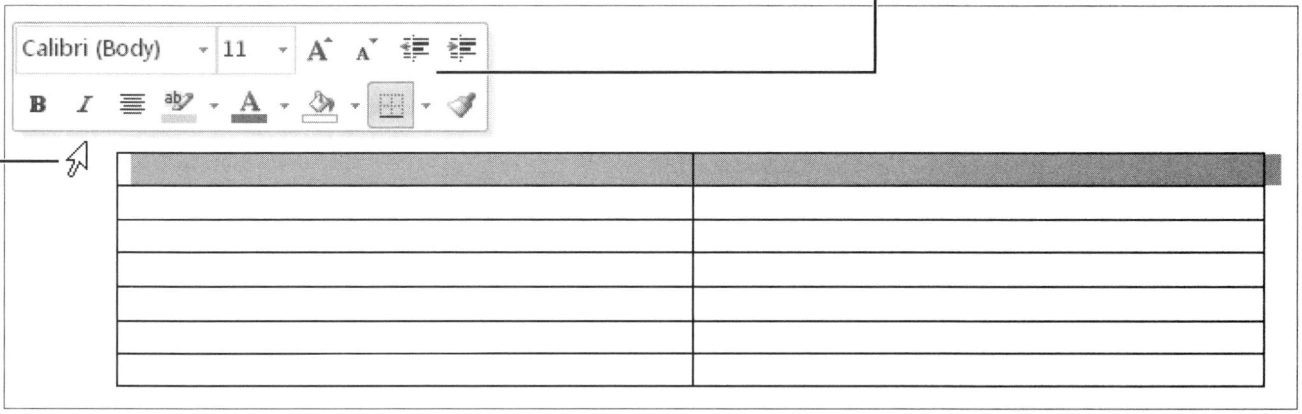

Notice the Table Tools with the Design and Layout contextual tabs that now appear on the Ribbon. They will appear whenever your table is active in the document.

7. Choose **Layout→Merge→Merge Cells** from the Ribbon.

8. Choose **Layout→Alignment→Align Center** from the Ribbon.

TIP! If necessary, hover the mouse pointer over the alignment buttons on the left side of the Alignment group to display ToolTips to help you identify the button.

Now when you type in the first row, the text will be center-aligned.

9. Click anywhere else in the table to deselect the first row.

Navigating in Tables and Adding Rows

You can position the insertion point in a cell simply by clicking it. However, it is often more efficient to use the keyboard to move between cells. You use the Tab key to move forward one cell and Shift+Tab to move back one cell.

If the insertion point is in the last cell of the table, tapping Tab adds a new row to the bottom of the table.

Resizing Column Widths and Row Heights

The Table button inserts tables with equally spaced columns. In many instances, such as typing a resume, you would likely prefer to vary column widths. Word's Table feature makes changing column widths a snap. Row heights adjust automatically to fit the text you enter.

The resize pointer +||+ appears when you place the mouse pointer on a column gridline. You can then adjust the column width by dragging the gridline.

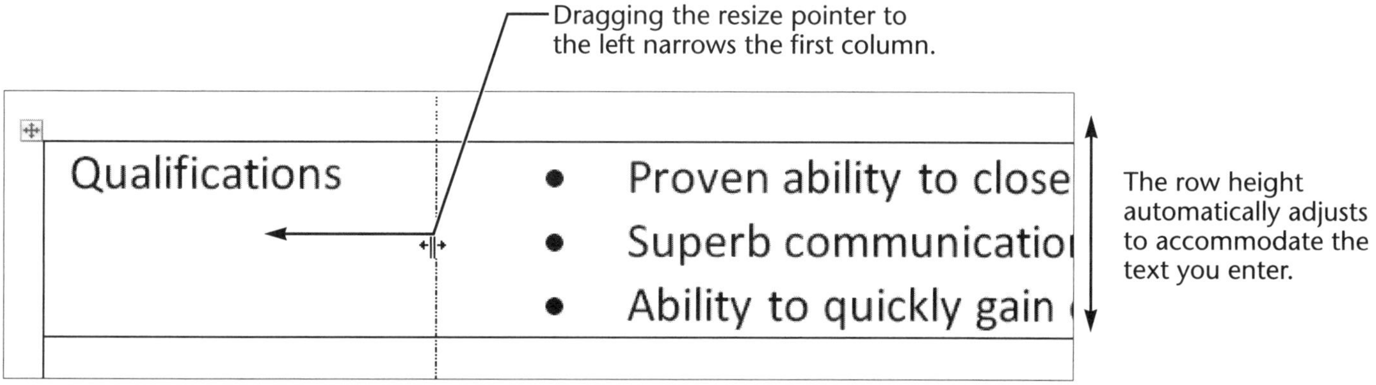

NOTE! Make sure no cells are selected (highlighted) when you drag the column gridline. Otherwise, you might only change the width of the selected column.

HANDS-ON 2.8 Adjust Column Widths and Enter Text

In this exercise, you will narrow the first column to accommodate the headings in your resume. When you enter background information in the second column, you will see that the rows grow taller as you continue to add text. You will realize when you reach the end of the table that you should have created more rows. Not a problem. When the insertion point is in the last cell, you will simply tap [Tab] to generate a new row.

1. Follow these steps to narrow the first column:

Ⓐ Position the **mouse pointer** on the vertical line between columns. The mouse pointer changes to a double-headed arrow (resize pointer) with the arrows pointing right and left.

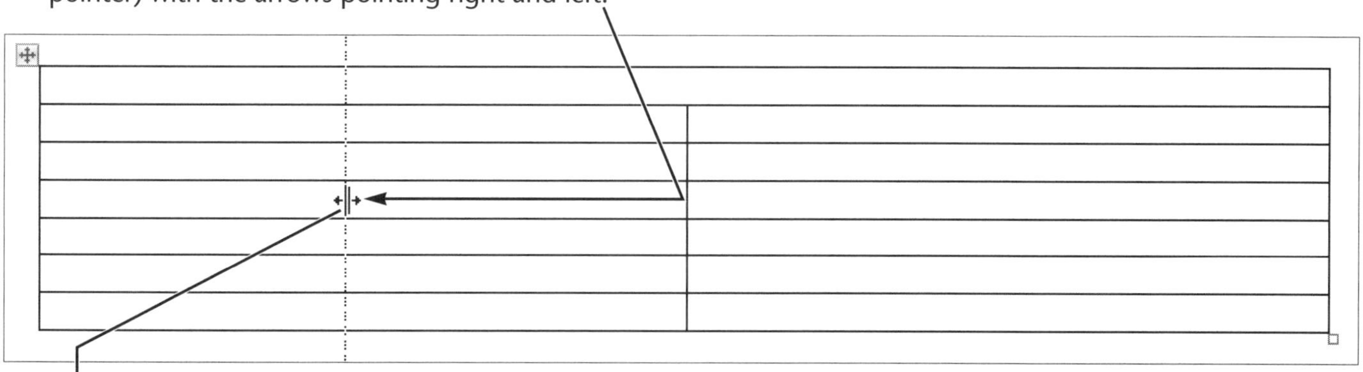

Ⓑ Press and hold down the **mouse button**, and drag to the left until the first column is approximately an inch and a half wide. (Don't worry about being exact. You can always resize the columns again if necessary.)

Now you'll enter the contact information in the first row.

2. Click the **insertion point** in the first row.

3. Type **`Victor Gomez`** and **tap** [Enter].

4. **Type** the rest of the contact information as shown in the following illustration, **tapping** [Enter] at the end of each line except the last line.

   If your Show/Hide button is still turned on, you will see the paragraph symbols at the end of each line when you tap [Enter]. You can feel free to turn Show/Hide on and off as you prefer.

Victor Gomez 123 Cherry Blossom Lane Windy Hills, CA 94941 415-555-1212 victor@yahoo.com

5. **Tap** [Tab] to move to the first cell of the second row.

   Notice when you tap [Tab] following Victor's email address that it becomes blue and underlined. This is an email link. If you were to email your resume, the recipient could click the link to open a new email with Victor's email address in the To line.

Skip a Row in the Table

Now you will skip a row to add white space between the contact information in row one and the first line of the resume.

6. **Tap** [Tab] two more times to move to the first cell in the third row.

7. Type **`Objective`** in the first cell of the third row.

8. **Tap** [Tab] to move to the next cell and type the following: **`A challenging career where I can use my sales and communications skills`**.

   The information you just typed should fit on one line and not Word Wrap. If it did wrap, don't worry. You can adjust the columns when you're done if necessary.

   Again, you will leave a blank row so there's white space between the text entries in the resume. This makes the resume easier to read than if the text were densely packed.

9. **Tap** [Tab] three times to leave a blank row and to move to the first cell of the fifth row.

10. Type **`Qualifications`** and **tap** [Tab] to move to the second cell of the fifth row.

Add Bullets in the Table

Now you will add bullet points to the information in the second column to make it easy for the recipient to locate the important points about Victor's background. You apply bullets in a table the same way you do in the rest of a Word document.

11. Choose **Home→Paragraph→Bullets** from the Ribbon to insert a bullet in the cell.
12. Type **`Proven ability to close sales`** and **tap** [Enter].

    Tapping [Enter] generates the next bullet.
13. Type **`Superb communications and presentation skills`** and **tap** [Enter] to generate the next bullet.
14. Type **`Ability to quickly gain client rapport.`** Don't tap [Enter] this time.

    You are now ready to move down two rows in the table.
15. **Tap** [Tab] three times.
16. **Type** the information shown in the following illustration. Do not tap [Enter] after the third item in the second column.

- B.S. Sales and Marketing, Windy Hills University, 2010
- B.S. Communications, Windy Hills University, 2010
- 3.9 Grade Point Average

Add a Row to the End of the Table

17. **Tap** [Tab] to add a new row to the table.

    When you use [Tab] to add a row to the table, the new row takes on the formatting of the previous row. This row should be completely blank with no bullet.
18. **Tap** [Tab] to move to the second cell of the row.
19. Choose **Home→Paragraph→Bullets** to turn off the bullet in the new row.
20. **Tap** [Tab] to add another new row.

21. **Type** the rest of the information in the table as shown in the following illustration. Remember to **tap** [Enter] to generate a new bullet and **tap** [Tab] to move from cell to cell and to add new rows at the end of the table. Turn bullets on and off as needed. Feel free to adjust the column widths to your satisfaction.

TIP! Remember, you can always click [Backspace] or [Delete] or use Undo if you make a mistake.

Computer Skills	• Microsoft Word, Excel, PowerPoint, and Access • Contact Management Software
Work Experience	• Waiter, family restaurant, summers during high school • Customer Support Assistant, Windy Hills Community Hospital, summers and weekends during college
Student Government	• Student Body President, Senior Year • Class President, Junior Year • Student Council, Membership Coordinator, Sophomore Year

Removing Borders from a Table

The table borders make it easy to see where you are working as you add text to a table; however, a resume might look sleeker if you remove the borders.

You'll use the Borders button in the Table Styles group of the Design tab to remove the table borders.

NOTE! You need to click the menu ▾ button on the Borders button to open the menu. Clicking directly on the button face applies the border style that was last chosen from the menu.

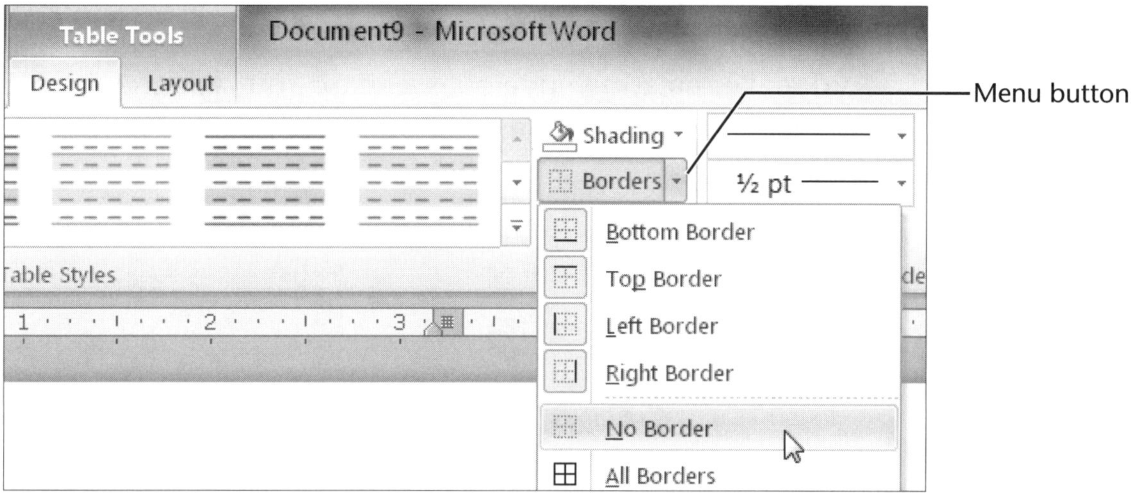

HANDS-ON 2.9 Remove Table Borders

In this exercise, you will remove the borders from the table. Then you will print and save the resume.

1. Position the **mouse pointer** in the margin to the left of the first row of the table.
2. Press and hold the **mouse button** down and drag down in the margin to the last row of the table.

   This selects the entire table.
3. Choose **Design→Table Styles→Borders** menu ▾ button to display the border choices.
4. Choose **No Border** from the menu.

   The grid lines are still visible, but they are not the same as borders. They will not print.

Print, Save, and Close the Resume

5. Click File and choose **Print** from the menu.
6. Click the **Print** button in the Backstage view center panel.
7. Click File and choose **Save As** from the menu.
8. Navigate to your **file storage location**.
9. Type `Resume` in the File Name box toward the bottom of the Save As dialog box.
10. Click the **Save** button.
11. Click File and choose **Close** from the menu.

Creating an Envelope

Word makes creating envelopes a snap. You type the recipient's address and your return address in the Envelopes and Labels dialog box.

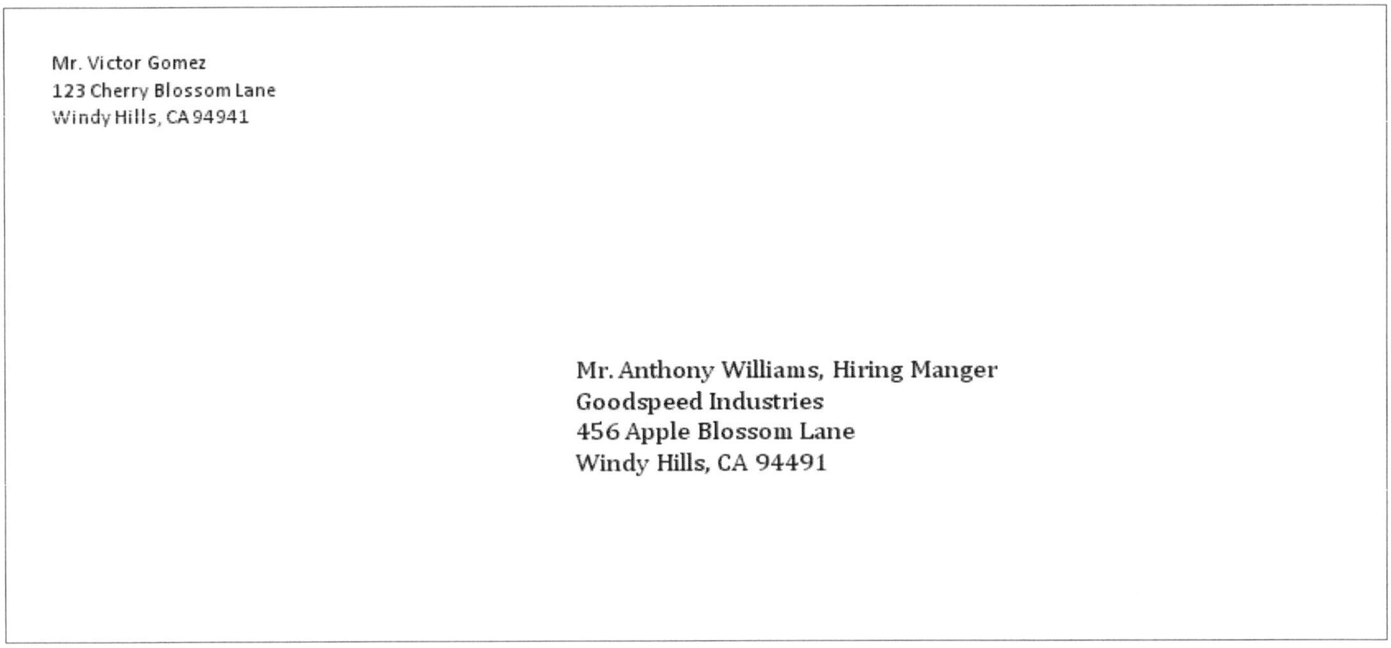

The Envelopes and Labels Dialog Box

The Envelopes and Labels dialog box is where you type the information necessary to create your envelope.

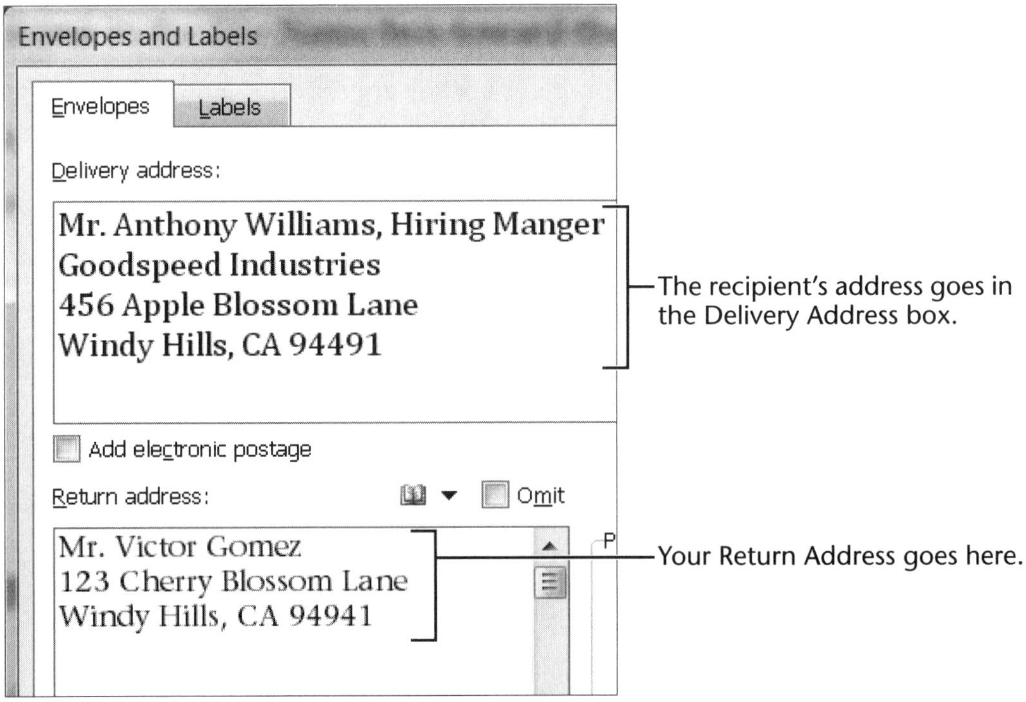

HANDS-ON 2.10 Type an Envelope

In this exercise, you will type an envelope so Victor can send his resume to the hiring manager at Goodspeed Industries.

1. **Press** [Ctrl]+[N] to start a new document.
2. Choose **Mailings→Create→Envelopes** from the Ribbon.
   The Envelopes and Labels dialog box appears.
3. If an address appears in the box, **tap** [Delete] or [Backspace] to remove it.
4. **Type** the following address in the Delivery Address field, **tapping** [Enter] at the end of each line:
   Mr. Anthony Williams, Hiring Manager
   Goodspeed Industries
   456 Apple Blossom Lane
   Windy Hills, CA 94491
5. Click in the **Return Address field** and **type** the following address:
   Mr. Victor Gomez
   123 Cherry Blossom Lane
   Windy Hills, CA 94941
6. Click the **Add to Document button** at the bottom of the dialog box.
7. Click **No** when prompted to save the return address.
8. Click [File] and choose **Save As** from the menu.
9. Navigate to your **file storage location**, if necessary.
10. Type **Envelope** in the File Name box.
11. Click the **Save** button.
    If you are not familiar with printing envelopes, you should consult your printer manual. The steps for loading and printing envelopes can vary from printer to printer.
12. Click [File] and choose **Close** from the menu.

Concepts Review

To check your knowledge of the key concepts introduced in this lesson, complete the Concepts Review quiz on this and the next page. Or, you can take the quiz online by going to the URL **labyrinthelab.com/wtmo10**.

True/False Questions

			Page number
1. Word Wrap is a technique used to keep certain lines, such as a greeting line in a letter, short.	**true**	**false**	_______
2. You made a change to a letter after saving and naming it. To save the new change, you must choose the Save As command.	**true**	**false**	_______
3. You can use the [Enter] key to create blank lines in a document, such as the blank lines following the date in a letter.	**true**	**false**	_______
4. You use the Show/Hide [¶] button to display or hide nonprinting characters.	**true**	**false**	_______
5. AutoComplete recognizes certain words such as names of months and days of the week.	**true**	**false**	_______
6. You should not use the [Enter] key to end lines *within* a paragraph.	**true**	**false**	_______

Multiple Choice Questions

7. The default (pre-assigned) line spacing in Word 2010 is _____.

   Page number: ______

   a. 1.0

   b. 1.15

   c. 2.5

   d. 2.0

8. Which of the following is a characteristic of a Word table?

   Page number: ______

   a. It is made up of cells.

   b. It uses Word Wrap to navigate to the next row.

   c. You cannot adjust column widths.

   d. You cannot remove table buttons.

9. You can add a row at the end of a table by tapping _____.

   Page number: ______

   a. Tab

   b. Enter

   c. Ctrl

   d. Backspace

10. Which of the following keystrokes create nonprinting characters?

    Page number: ______

    a. Enter

    b. Page Up

    c. Delete

    d. Shift

Skill Builders

SKILL BUILDER 2.1 Write a Letter to a Friend

In this exercise, you will conduct online research to find four hints for writing a great resume. Then you will send a letter to a friend who is looking for a job, sharing the information you've discovered. Since this is not a formal business letter, you will use Word's default 1.15 lines spacing.

1. Start a **new blank document**.
2. Fire up **Google** (google.com) or the search engine of your choice.
3. In the Search box, type **`hints for good resumes`** and **tap** [Enter].

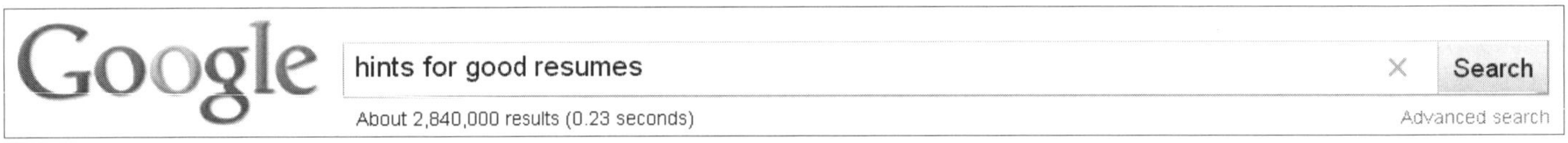

TIP! Ask your instructor for assistance if you are not familiar with web searches.

4. Make a note of the hints you think are most important.
5. Use these guidelines to type the letter in the following illustration:
   - Tap [Enter] four times so the letter will be centered top-to-bottom on the page.
   - Use AutoComplete to enter today's date.
   - Let Word Wrap do its thing. Don't be concerned if your line widths don't match the illustration.
   - Enter the information you found online after the bullets and in place of the word *Hint*.
   - Use the paragraph symbols shown in the letter as a guide for when you should tap [Enter].
   - Use [Backspace] or [Delete] or the Undo button if you make a mistake.
   - Save your letter in your storage location as **`sb-Letter to Martin`**.
   - Print your letter, and then close it.

Today's·Date¶

¶

Dear·Martin,¶

This·is·just·a·quick·note·to·let·you·know·that·I·have·done·some·research·lately·in·preparation·for·creating·my·resume.·I·know·you're·working·on·your·resume·too,·so·I'm·sending·you·some·of·the·good·ideas·I've·discovered.¶

- → Hint¶
- → Hint¶
- → Hint¶
- → Hint¶

Let·me·know·how·the·job·search·is·going.·¶

Good·luck,¶

¶

Harold¶

SKILL BUILDER 2.2 Create an Envelope

In this exercise, you will create an envelope so you can mail the letter to your friend.

1. Start a **new blank document**.
2. Choose **Mailings→Create→Envelopes** from the Ribbon.
3. If there is any address information in the dialog box, delete it by **tapping** [Delete] or [Backspace].
4. **Type** the following address in the **Delivery Address** area of the Envelopes and Labels dialog box:

   Mr. Martin Nguyen
   654 Willow Lane
   Wheeling, West Virginia 26003

5. **Type** the following address in the **Return Address** area:
   `Harold Frost`
   `789 Elm Street`
   `Martins Ferry, OH 43935`
6. Click the **Add to Document** button.
7. Click **No** when prompted to save the return address.
8. **Save** the file in your storage location as **`sb-Envelope for Martin`**.
9. **Close** the envelope document.

SKILL BUILDER 2.3 Manage Your Mysteries with a Table

In this exercise, you will keep track of your mystery novels that are on loan to your friends. You have quite a large collection and keeping track of who has borrowed a book is becoming a mystery to you. You have decided to use Word's table feature to keep track of your books.

1. Start a **new blank document**.
2. Choose **Insert→Tables→Table** from the Ribbon.
   The table grid appears.
3. Position the **mouse pointer** in the upper-left corner of the grid; then, hold down the **mouse button** and drag to the right to select four columns. Keep the **mouse button** down.
4. Drag the **mouse pointer** down six rows, and then release the **mouse button**.
   A 4x6 table appears in your document. Now you will enter the column headings in your table.
5. Make sure the **insertion point** is in the first cell of the first row and type **`On Loan To`**.
6. **Tap** [Tab] to position the insertion point in the second cell of the first row and type **`Title`**.
7. **Tap** [Tab] again and type **`Author`**.
8. **Tap** [Tab] one more time and type **`Main Character`**.
9. **Tap** [Tab] to move the insertion point to the first cell of the second row and type **`Brady`**.

10. Continue entering the information shown in the following table, starting with the second cell in the second row:

On Loan To	Title	Author	Main Character
Brady	Caribbean Mystery	Christie, Agatha	Miss Marple
Opal	The Last Precinct	Cornwell, Patricia	Dr. Kay Scarpetta
Barbara	In the Last Analysis	Cross, Amanda	Kate Fensler
Madden	One for the Money	Evanovich, Janet	Stephanie Plum
Karl	Playing for the Ashes	George, Elizabeth	Thomas Lynley

Your friend, Lucy, just came by to borrow one of your mysteries. Now you'll need to add a row to the bottom of the table.

11. Make sure the **insertion point** is in the last cell of the table.

12. **Tap** [Tab] to add a new row to the bottom of the table.

13. **Type** the following information in the new row, as shown in the following figure.

Lucy	B is for Burglar	Grafton, Sue	Kinsey Millhone

14. **Save** the file in your storage location as **`sb-Mysteries on Loan`**.

15. **Close** the file.

LESSON 3

Word – Editing the Business Etiquette Column

In this lesson, you will learn techniques for selecting text; making editing changes; and using Undo, Redo, and AutoCorrect. You will use AutoCorrect and the Spelling & Grammar Checker, and you will move and copy text. Finally, you will learn to automatically find a word or phrase in a document and, if desired, replace it with another word or phrase.

LESSON OBJECTIVES

After studying this lesson, you will be able to:

- Use a variety of techniques for selecting text
- Edit documents
- Work with Undo, Redo, and AutoCorrect
- Use the Spelling & Grammar Checker
- Move and copy text
- Automatically find and replace text in a document

Student resources ***labyrinthelab.com/wtmo10***

Case Study: Using Word's Spelling & Grammar Checker and Find Feature

Tyrone Williams is on the curriculum committee at Columbia State College, which will be implementing a new Technical Support certificate program. The head of the committee asked Tyrone to write a report about the program and the workshops designed to attract high school sophomores and juniors to the program.

Tyrone finds Word's Spelling & Grammar Checker to be a great aid in helping him write an error-free report. The checker constantly monitors spelling, allowing him to correct errors as he types.

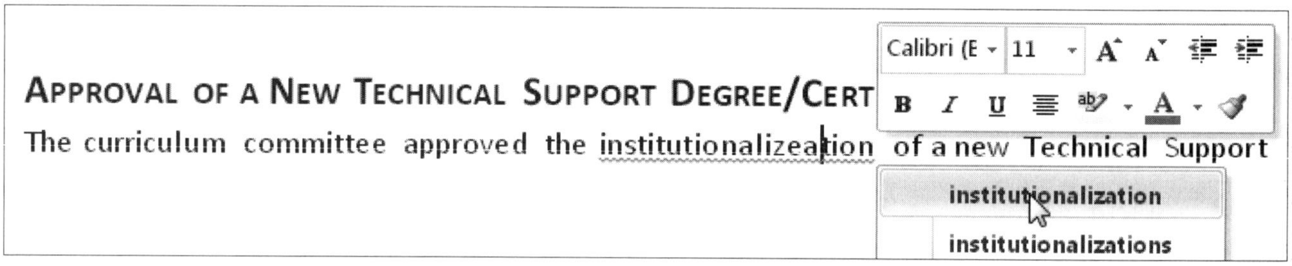

Word's Find feature allows Tyrone to locate all places in the document where workshops are discussed.

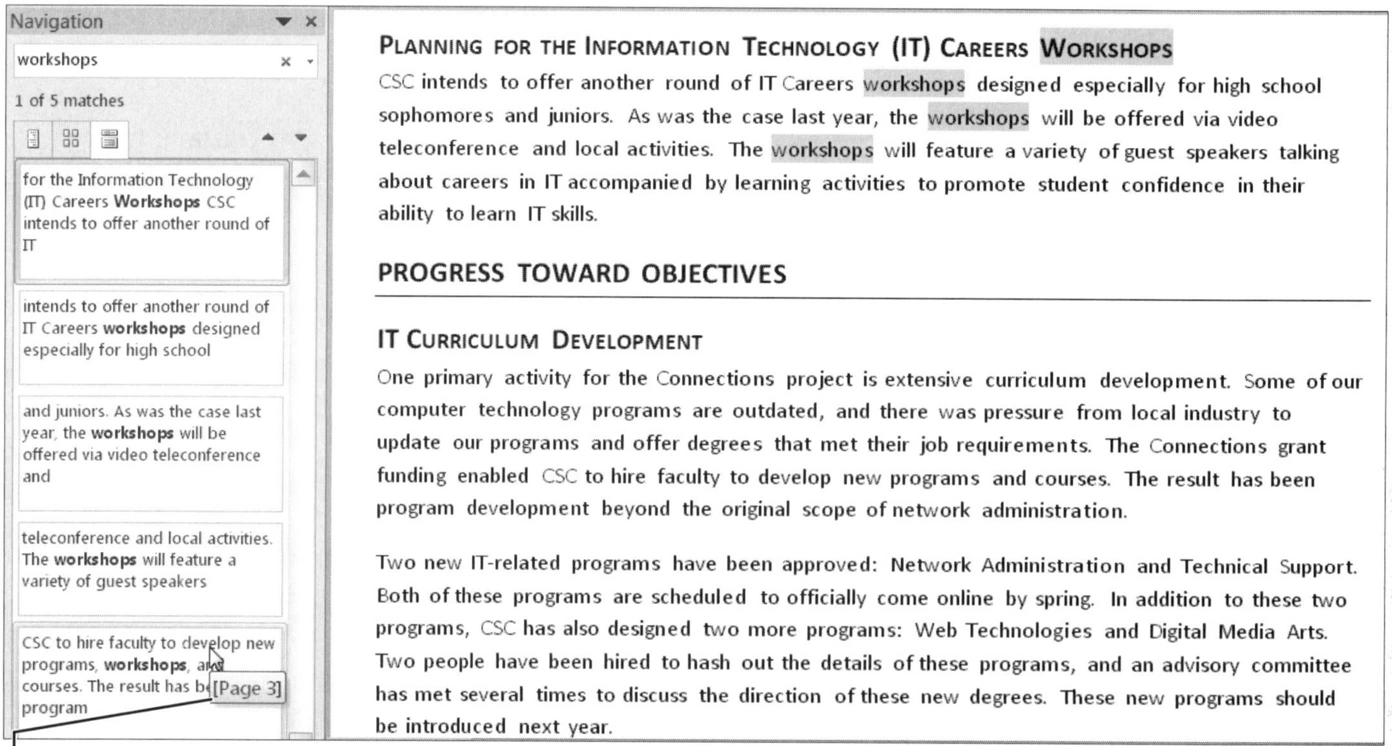

Clicking one of the items in the search results area allows Tyrone to jump directly to that location in the document.

Selecting Text

In Word, you select (highlight) text in order to do something to it. For example, you select text before moving or copying it. You also select text when you want to replace or format it.

You work with two different areas of the screen when selecting text.

- The selection bar (in the left margin of a document)
- The typing area (between the margins)

When you select text, the Mini toolbar appears, as shown in the following illustration. You can ignore it in this lesson. The Mini toolbar contains commands for formatting text, which you will learn more about in Lesson 4, Word – Encouraging Recycling with Flyers.

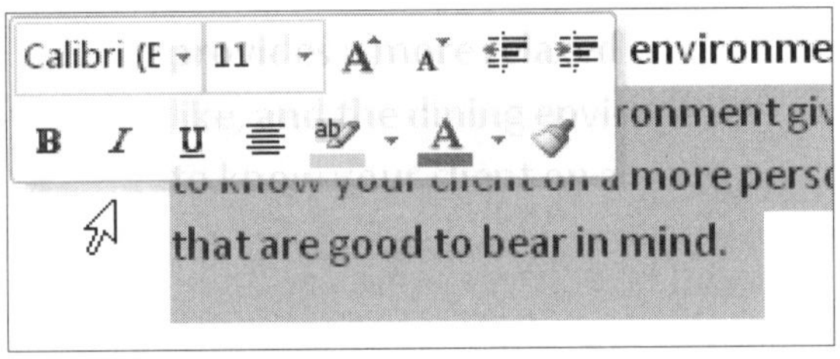

The Selection Bar

The selection bar is in the left margin of a document. When the mouse pointer is in the selection bar, it looks like a right-tilting white arrow.

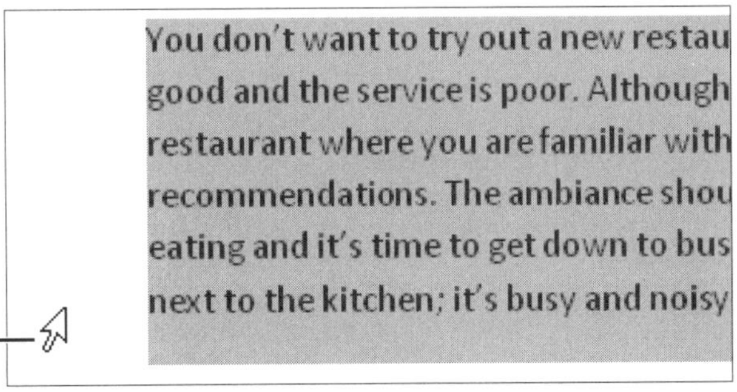

The mouse pointer looks like this in the selection bar.

The Typing Area

The mouse pointer looks like an I-beam I when you select text in the typing area, which is the area between the margins.

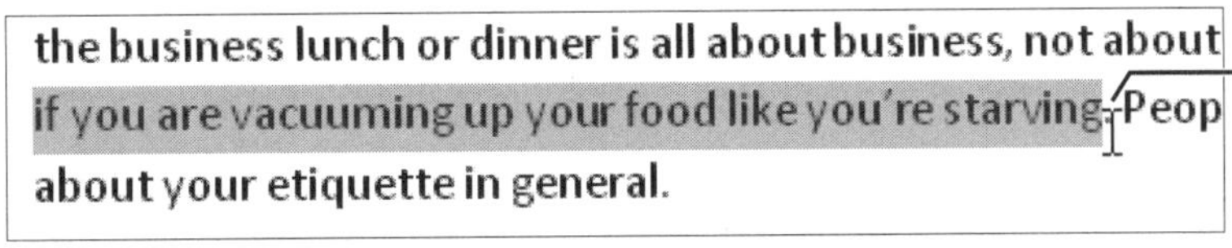

The mouse pointer looks like this when selecting text in the typing area.

Selection Techniques

A basic method for selecting text is to click and drag the mouse pointer. In addition, Word provides mouse and keyboard shortcuts for selecting text. The following Quick Reference table lists several convenient text-selection shortcuts.

QUICK REFERENCE: Selecting Text

Item to Be Selected	Procedure (Mouse)
One word	Double-click the word.
Continuous block of text	Press and hold the left mouse button while dragging the mouse pointer over the desired text.
A line	Place the mouse pointer in the selection bar to the left of a line. Click when the pointer is shaped like an arrow.
A sentence	Hold down [Ctrl] and click the mouse pointer anywhere in the sentence.
One paragraph	Triple-click anywhere in the paragraph, or place the mouse pointer in the selection bar and double-click.
Multiple paragraphs	Drag the I-beam over the desired paragraphs, or position the mouse pointer in the selection bar and drag up or down when the pointer is shaped like an arrow.
Entire document	Triple-click in the selection bar when the mouse pointer is shaped like an arrow, or make sure no text is selected then press and hold [Ctrl] and click in the left margin.
Nonadjacent areas	Select the first block of text then press and hold [Ctrl] while dragging over additional blocks of text.
Item to Be Selected	**Procedure (Keyboard)**
One word	Click at the beginning of the word then press and hold [Shift]+[Ctrl] while tapping [→].
Continuous block of text	Click at the beginning of the text then press and hold [Shift] while tapping any arrow key. You can also click at the beginning of the text, press and hold [Shift], and click at the end of the text to be selected.
A line	Press [Shift]+[End] to select from the insertion point to the end of the line. Press [Shift]+[Home] to select from the insertion point to the beginning of the line.
Entire document	Press [Ctrl]+[A].

HANDS-ON 3.1 Select Text

In this exercise, you will select text from the selection bar and the typing area using both the mouse and keyboard techniques.

You have been asked to write a monthly business etiquette column for the Windy Hills University Review so graduating students can start thinking about human relations skills that are so important in the corporate environment. The editor of the review wants some changes, so it's time to get ready to make edits.

1. Click File and choose **Open** from the menu.
2. Navigate to your Lesson 03 folder and click **Professional Polish** to select it.
3. Click the **Open** button in the bottom-right corner of the dialog box to finish opening the file.

Select Text from the Selection Bar

4. Place the **mouse pointer** in the selection bar at the left edge of the screen just to the left of the first line of the first paragraph.
   The mouse pointer changes to a white arrow.

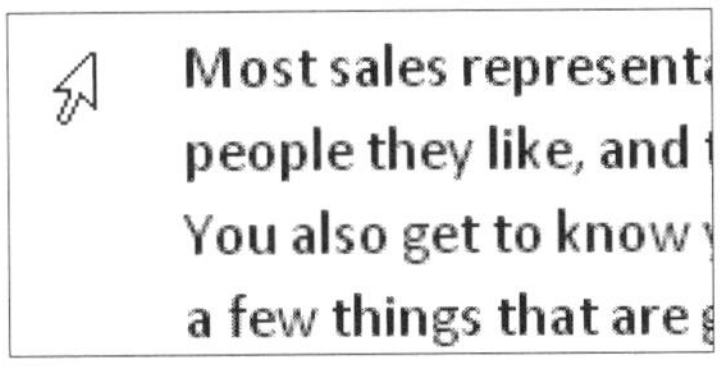

5. Click once to select the **first line**, as shown in the following figure.

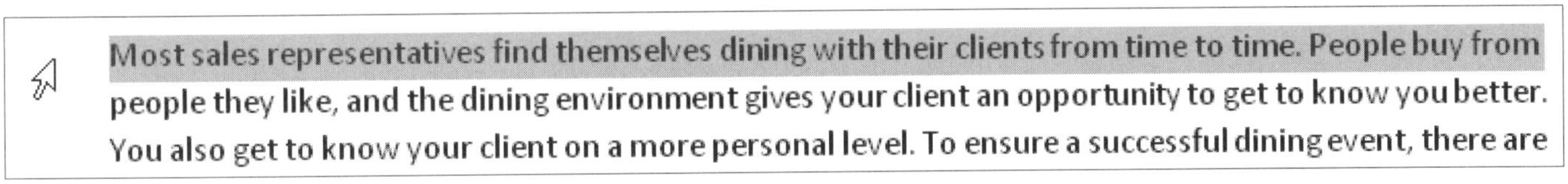

   The Mini toolbar appears when you select text. Ignore it for now; it will fade away.

6. **Double-click** in the **selection bar** to select the entire paragraph.

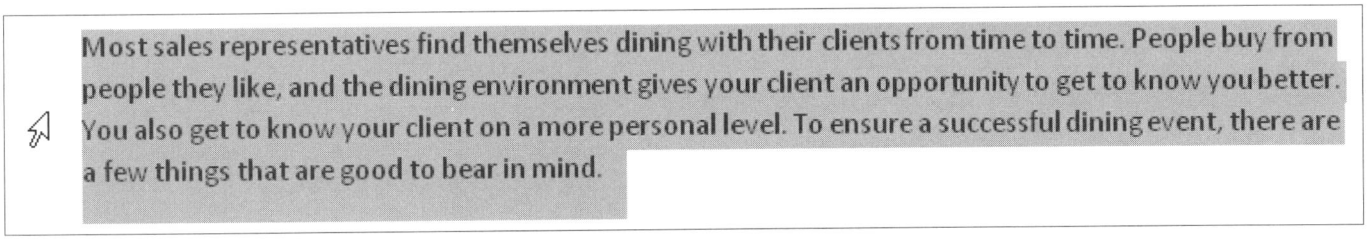

7. **Triple-click** in the **selection bar** to select the entire document.
   If you find triple-clicking difficult, press Ctrl+A to select the entire document.
8. Move the **mouse pointer** into the typing area and click **once** to deselect (remove) the highlighting.

Remember: Clicking once in the selection bar selects an entire line. To remove *all* highlighting you must click in the typing area.

Select Text in the Typing Area

9. Position the **mouse pointer** over the word *Most* at the beginning of the first line of the first paragraph.
10. **Double-click** to select the entire word.

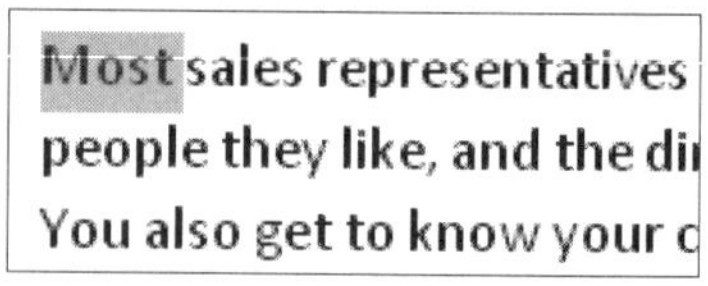

11. Click once in the **typing area** to deselect the text.
12. Position the **mouse pointer** somewhere in the first sentence; **hold down** [Ctrl] and **click**.

    This selects the entire sentence.

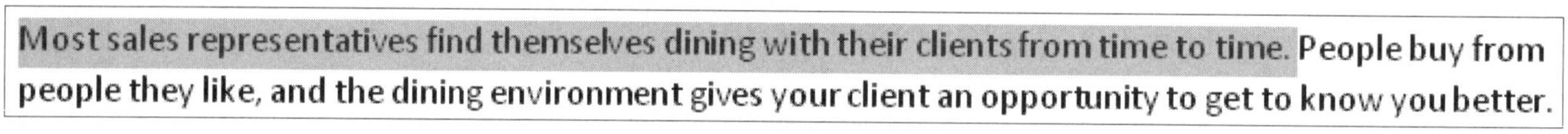

13. Click once in the **typing area** to deselect the highlighted text.

Select Text with the Keyboard

14. Position the **insertion point** at the beginning of the first line of the first paragraph.
15. **Press and hold** [Shift], and then click at the **end** of the paragraph.

    This selects everything from the insertion point to the [Shift]-and-click position.
16. **Release** [Shift], and then click once in the **typing area** to deselect the text.
17. Position the **insertion point** at the beginning of the first paragraph again.
18. **Press and hold** [Ctrl] and [Shift], and then **tap** [→] several times to select one word at a time.
19. **Release** [Ctrl] and [Shift], and then **tap** any arrow key on the keyboard to deselect the text.

    Leave this document open. You will use it throughout the lesson.

Editing Techniques

You know that the Delete and Backspace keys delete one character at a time. Word has several other ways you can edit text, including adding, deleting, and replacing selected blocks of text. Word will even help you edit as you type with its AutoCorrect feature.

Add, Delete, and Replace Text

To add text to an existing document, simply click the insertion point where you want the new text to appear and begin typing. Word will make room for the new text as you type, while Word Wrap keeps the paragraph nicely organized.

You can delete a block of text all at once by selecting the text and tapping Delete. Word Wrap then closes up the gap and rewraps the text.

To replace existing text, select the text you want to replace and type the new text in its place. It doesn't matter if the selected text block is larger or smaller than the text replacing it. The surrounding text expands or collapses to accommodate the new text.

QUICK REFERENCE: Editing Text

Task	Procedure
Add text	Position the insertion point where you want the new text to appear and begin typing.
Delete text	Position the insertion point where you want to delete text then press Backspace to erase characters to the left of the insertion point or Delete to erase characters to the right of the insertion point. Or, select the block of text to be deleted and tap Delete.
Replace text	Select the text to be replaced then type the new text in its place.

AutoCorrect

Word has a wonderful feature called AutoCorrect that automatically corrects misspelled words and typos for you as you type. For example, if you type *aboutthe*, AutoCorrect will change it to *about the*. It corrects other errors too, like incorrect capitalization and accidentally typing with Caps Lock turned on.

HANDS-ON 3.2 Use AutoCorrect and Add, Delete, and Replace Text

In this exercise, you will work with AutoCorrect and add, delete, and replace text. You will begin by adding a bullet point at the end of page 2. You will purposely make mistakes so you can watch Word fix them for you.

AutoCorrect

1. Scroll down to **page 2** and click the **insertion point** at the end of the last bulleted item.
2. **Tap** [Enter] to generate a new bullet.
3. Type **`Turn offf`** and **tap** [Spacebar].
   Word corrects the word *off*.
4. Type **`teh`**, **tap** [Spacebar], and watch Word change it to *the*.
5. Finish **typing** the bulleted item as shown here:
   `Turn off the cell phone. You insult your guests when you indicate that your phone call is more important than they are.`

Add Text

6. **Hold down** [Ctrl] and **tap** [Home] to position the insertion point at the top of page 1.
7. Position the **insertion point** at the beginning of the second sentence in the first paragraph, as shown in the following example.

> Most sales representatives find themselves dining with their clients from time to time. |People buy from people they like, and the dining environment gives your client an opportunity to get to know you better.

8. **Type** the following sentence:
   `Sharing a meal provides a more relaxed environment than the typical conference room.`
9. **Tap** [Spacebar].
   Notice how Word makes space for the new text and how Word Wrap keeps things in order.

Delete Text

10. Follow these steps to select and delete text in the first paragraph:

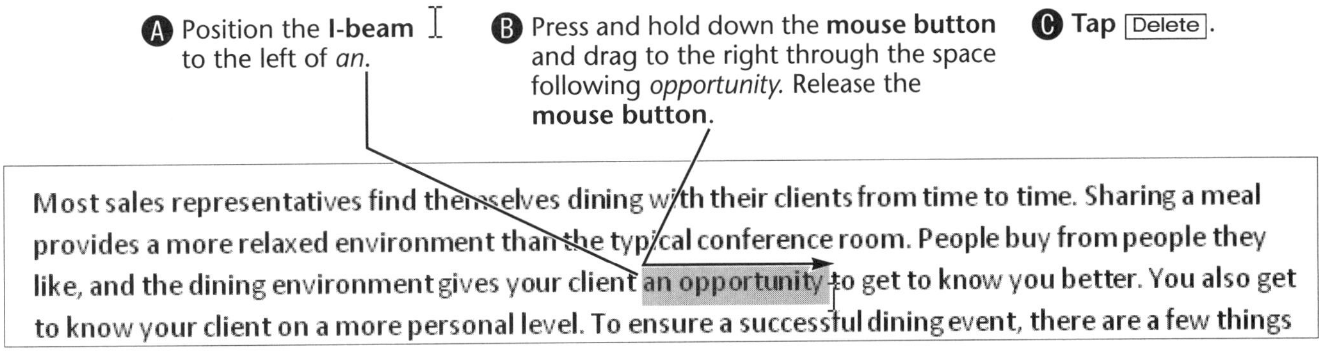

The insertion point should appear to the left of *to,* as shown in the following figure.

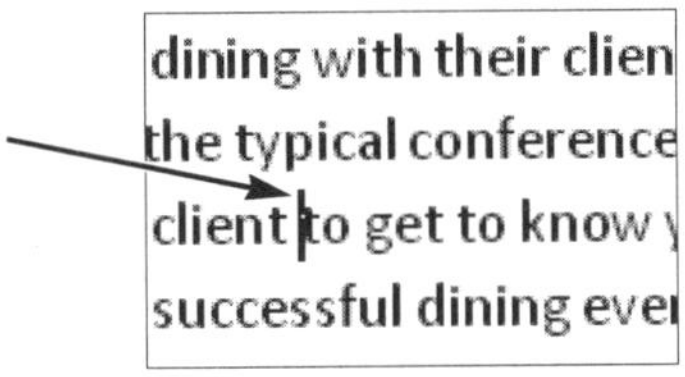

11. Correct the position of the insertion point if necessary.
12. Type **`a chance`** followed by a space in place of the deleted words.

Replace Text

13. Position the **mouse pointer** over the word *perceive* in the first line of the second paragraph.
14. **Double-click** to select the word, as shown in the following figure.

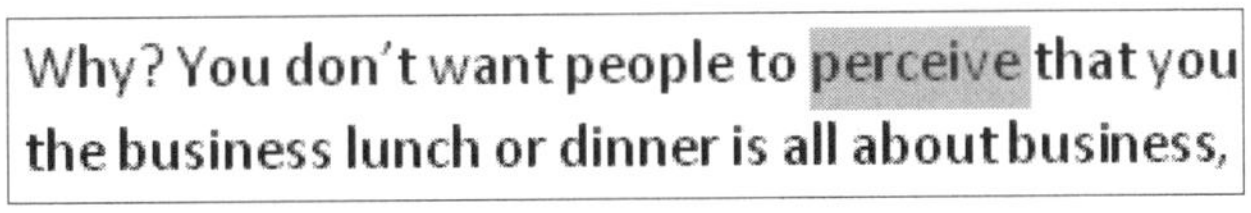

15. Type **`think`**.

    The word you just typed replaced the selected word.
16. Click the **Save** button on the Quick Access toolbar to save your changes.

Spelling & Grammar Checker

Once again, Word helps you with your editing tasks. If you make a typo and AutoCorrect isn't sure how to fix it, the Spelling & Grammar Checker comes to the rescue. It monitors your spelling as you type and underlines words it suspects are misspelled with a squiggly red line. Right-clicking the underlined word displays a pop-up menu with suggestions of possible correct spellings. You only need to choose the correct spelling from the menu, as shown in the following figure.

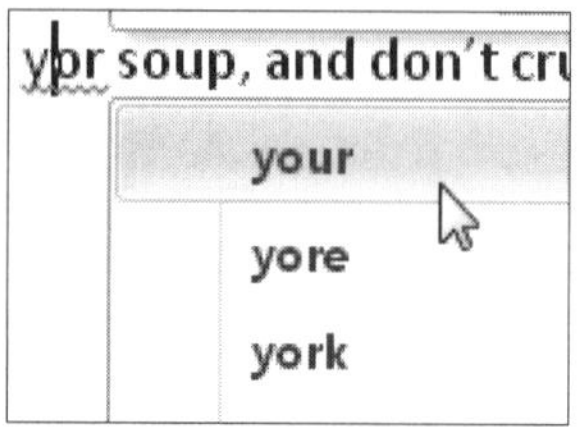

Not Every Misspelling Is Caught Sometimes the Spelling & Grammar Checker marks a word as a possible misspelling when it is correct. Some proper names fall into that category, although the checker has many common proper names in its dictionary and does not mark them. If Word marks a term incorrectly, you can either ignore the underlining (it won't print) or choose Ignore All from the pop-up menu.

Grammar and Context Checking Word also checks for possible grammatical errors and marks them with a green squiggly underline. If you see a blue squiggly underline, it means Word thinks the term is correctly spelled but may not be correctly used in the current context.

Undo and Redo

The Undo and Redo buttons appear on the Quick Access toolbar. You've likely had a little experience with Undo by now. If you undo something and then change your mind, that's where Redo comes in. You can redo what you undid!

How Undo Helps You Clicking Undo reverses your last action. If you click Undo again, the next-to-the-last action is reversed, and then the next-to-the-last from that, and so forth. Essentially, you are backing your way out of the problem. If you go too far or change your mind, just use Redo.

You can get out of most any catastrophe if you click Undo enough times. If you get into a mess, don't try to fix it; just undo it!

What Undo Can and Cannot Undo Undo works for things you do that make modifications to a document: inserting text, editing text, formatting text, and so on. It cannot reverse actions like printing, saving a document, or selecting text. Once you close a document, it's too late to undo. If you want to make changes when you open the document again, you will have to use editing techniques rather than the Undo feature.

HANDS-ON 3.3 Use Spelling & Grammar Checker, Undo, and Redo

In this exercise, you will purposely make some typos so you can see the Spelling & Grammar Checker in action. You will replace a word and then undo the replacement. Finally, you will change your mind and decide that you do want to replace the word, so you use Redo to replace the word again.

Spell Check

1. **Hold down** [Ctrl] and **tap** [End] to move the insertion point to the end of the document.
2. Make sure the **insertion point** is at the end of the last bullet point and **tap** [Enter] to generate the next bullet.
3. **Type** the following sentence and purposely misspell *your* and *saltines,* as shown in the example:

   `Don't dunk bread in yor soup, and don't crush salteens inside the bag and dump them in your soup.`

   Notice the squiggly red lines under *yor* and *salteens*, indicating possible spelling errors.
4. Place the **mouse pointer** over *yor* and click with the **right mouse button** to display the pop-up menu.
   The Mini toolbar appears again and, once again, you can ignore it.
5. Choose the correct spelling of *your* from the menu.
6. Now **right-click** *salteens* and choose *saltines* from the pop-up menu.

Undo and Redo

7. **Press** [Ctrl]+[Home] to return to the top of the document.
8. **Double-click** *representatives* in the first line of the first paragraph to highlight it, as shown at right.

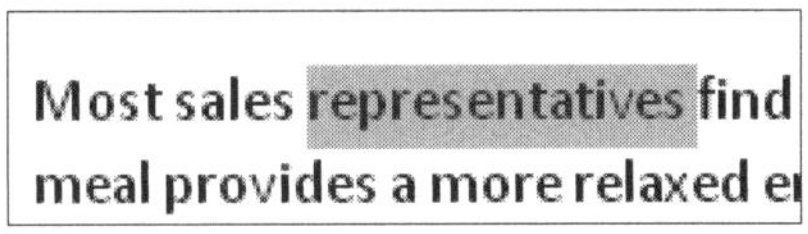

9. Type **`people`** to replace the selected word.
   Hmmm, maybe *representatives* was better.

10. Click the **Undo** button on the Quick Access toolbar one time to return to the original word.

    Now you decide you prefer *people.*

11. Click the **Redo** button on the Quick Access toolbar once to return to *people.*

12. Click the **Save** button on the Quick Access toolbar to save your changes.

Moving and Copying Text

When you move text, you remove it from its original position and place it in a new location. When you copy text, the original text remains intact and a copy is placed in the new location—it's in both places.

Move and Copy Text

You can use the Cut, Copy, and Paste buttons on the Home tab to move and copy text. There are also handy keyboard shortcuts you can use to cut, copy, and paste. The following Quick Reference table describes the steps necessary to move and copy text.

QUICK REFERENCE: Moving and Copying Text

Task	Procedure (Ribbon)
Move text	• Select the text you want to move. • Choose Home→Clipboard→Cut from the Ribbon. • Click the insertion point at the destination. • Choose Home→Clipboard→Paste from the Ribbon.
Copy text	• Select the text you want to copy. • Choose Home→Clipboard→Copy from the Ribbon. • Click the insertion point at the destination. • Choose Home→Clipboard→Paste from the Ribbon.

QUICK REFERENCE: Moving and Copying Text (Continued)

Task	Procedure (Keyboard)
Move text	• Select the text you want to move. • Press Ctrl+X to cut. • Click the insertion point at the destination. • Press Ctrl+V to paste.
Copy text	• Select the text you want to copy. • Press Ctrl+C to copy. • Click the insertion point at the destination. • Press Ctrl+V to paste.

HANDS-ON 3.4 Move and Copy Text

In this exercise, you will move and copy text in your document. You will use both Ribbon and keyboard techniques. You'll start by moving the *Consider Various Tastes* paragraph above the *Eat Before Dinner* paragraph.

Move Text with Ribbon Commands

1. Position the **mouse pointer** in the selection bar to the left of the *Consider Various Tastes* heading, and then press and hold the **mouse button** and drag down to the last line of the paragraph, as shown in the following example.

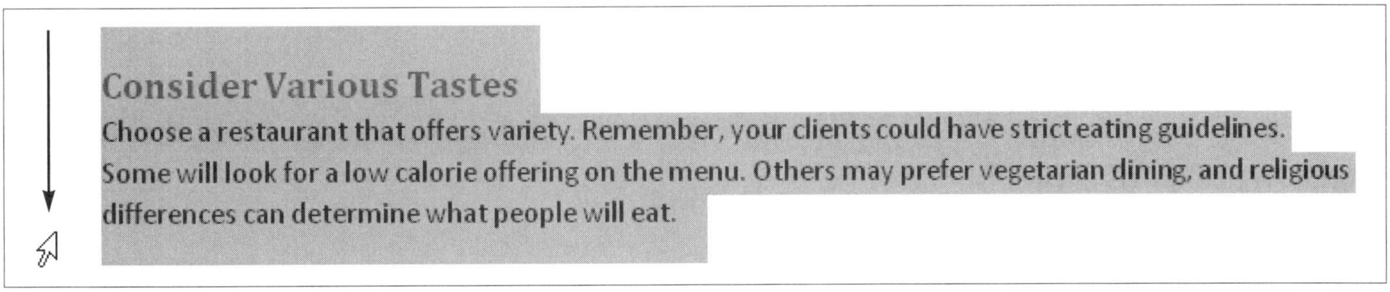

2. Choose **Home→Clipboard→Cut** from the Ribbon.
3. Position the **insertion point** to the left of the *Eat Before Dinner* heading, as shown at right.

4. Choose **Home→Clipboard→Paste** from the Ribbon.

Move Text with the Keyboard

Now you'll use keystrokes to move the *Choose a Familiar Restaurant* paragraph above the *Eat Before Dinner* paragraph.

5. Position the **mouse pointer** in the selection bar to the left of the *Choose a Familiar Restaurant* heading.
6. Press and hold down the **mouse button** and drag down to the last line of the paragraph.
7. **Hold down** Ctrl and **tap** X to cut the paragraph from the document.
8. Position the **insertion point** to the left of the *Eat Before Dinner* heading.
9. **Hold down** Ctrl and **tap** V to paste the paragraph in the new location.

Copy Text with the Mouse

10. Scroll down to the end of **page 2** and place the **insertion point** at the end of the last bullet point.
11. **Tap** Enter three times to set off an area where you will copy information to.
12. Click and drag in the **selection bar** to select the first bullet point.
13. Choose **Home→Clipboard→Copy** from the Ribbon.
14. Position the **insertion point** at the bottom of the page.
15. Choose **Home→Clipboard→Paste** from the Ribbon.
    That information now appears in two places on the page.
16. Position the **mouse pointer** in the selection bar to the left of the second bullet point and **click** to select the line.

Copy Text with the Keyboard

17. **Hold down** Ctrl and **tap** C to copy the information.
18. Position the **insertion point** at the bottom of the page.
19. **Hold down** Ctrl and **tap** V to create a copy of the information.
20. **Hold down** Ctrl and **tap** Home to move back to the top of the document.
21. Click the **Save** button on the Quick Access toolbar to save your changes.

Finding and Replacing Text

What do you do when you need to locate a specific word or phrase in a long document? Let Word locate it for you with the Find feature! There is also a Find and Replace feature, which is one step beyond Find. It lets you find existing text and automatically replace it with new text throughout the entire document. As an example, this is a handy tool if you accidentally misspell a proper noun throughout a document.

The Find and Replace commands appear in the Editing group at the right end of the Home tab.

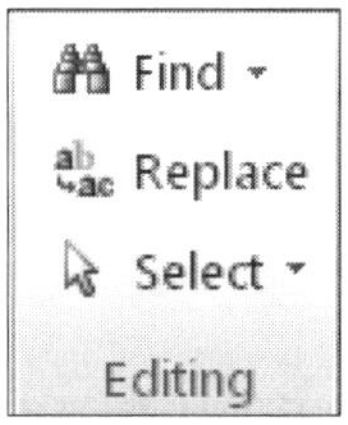

Find with the Navigation Pane

The Find command opens the Navigation pane on the left side of the screen. When you search for a term, the items found conveniently appear in the results list, giving you an overview of everywhere the term appears. Clicking an item in the search results list causes Word to jump to that location in the document. The search terms are also highlighted in the document.

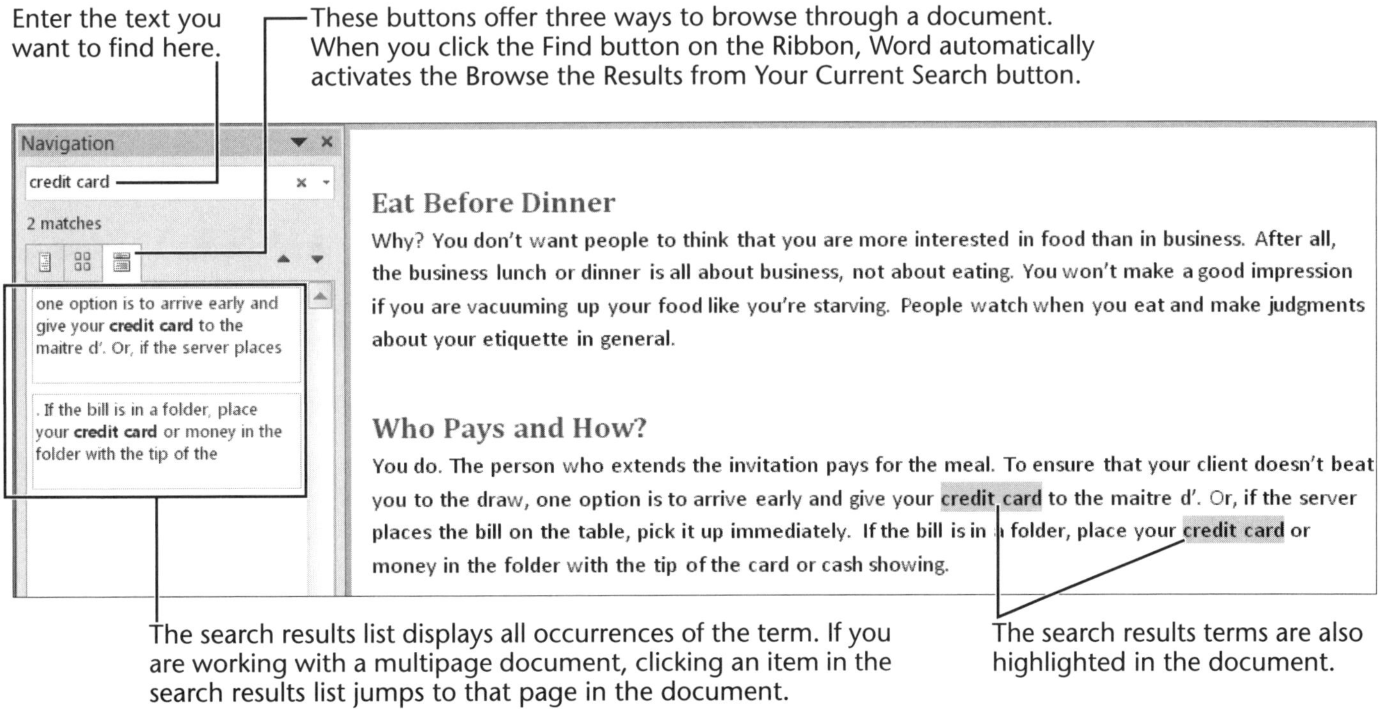

The Find and Replace Dialog Box

The Replace option in the Editing group on the Home tab displays the Find and Replace dialog box, where you can enter the text you want to find and the replacement text. The following figure shows the important parts of the Replace tab in the Find and Replace dialog box.

NOTE! Even though the search term is *client* in the following example, notice that Word found the plural form, *clients*. That's because the word *client* is embedded in the word *clients*. Word will make the replacement, maintaining the plural form when appropriate.

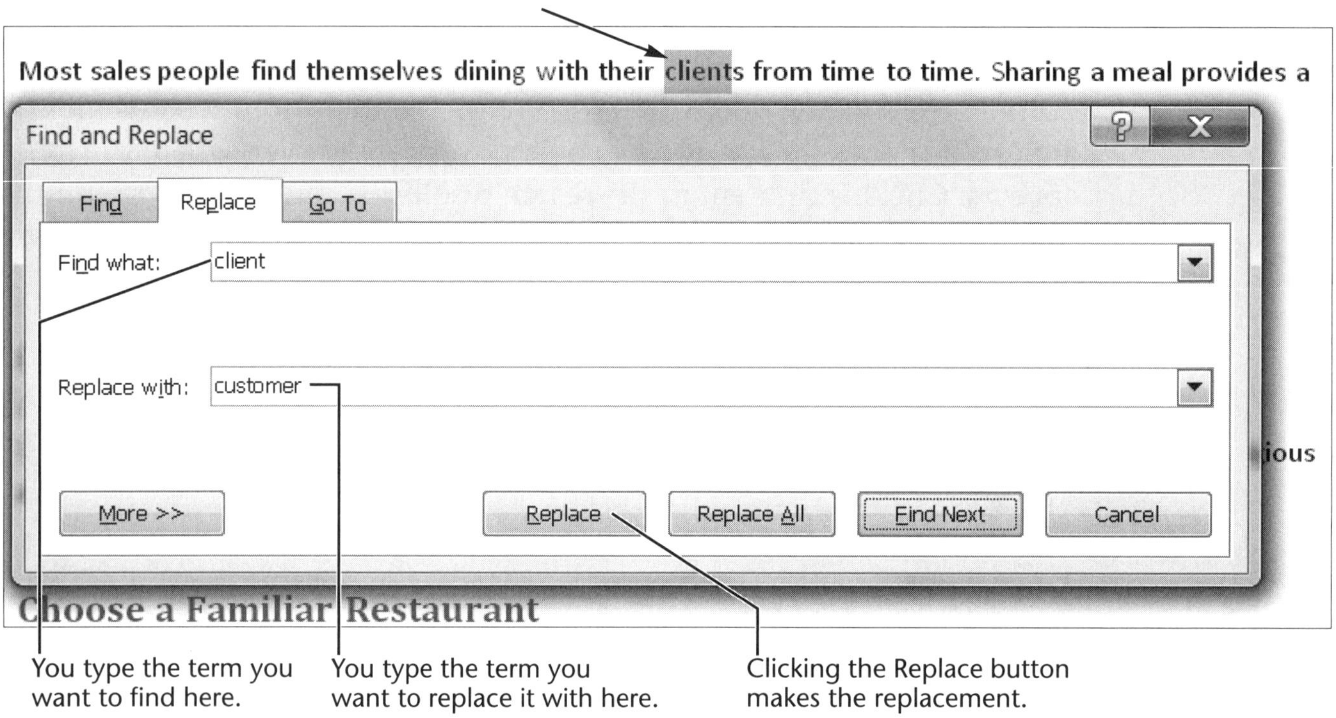

QUICK REFERENCE: Finding and Replacing Text

Task	Procedure
Find text	• Choose Home→Editing→Find from the Ribbon. • Type the search term in the text box at the top of the Navigation pane on the left side of the screen. • If the term appears on multiple pages, click an item in the search results list to scroll the document to that occurrence of the term.

QUICK REFERENCE: Finding and Replacing Text (Continued)

Task	Procedure
Replace text	• Choose Home→Editing→Replace from the Ribbon. • Type the term you are searching for in the Find What box. • Type the term to replace it with in the Replace With box. • Click the Find Next button. • Click the Replace button to replace the first instance of the text or click Find Next to skip to the next occurrence of the search term. *or* • Click the Replace All button to make all replacements at once.
WARNING!	*You should be confident about the changes that will occur when you use Replace All. If you are unsure, you should use the Replace button and monitor each replacement individually.*

HANDS-ON 3.5 Use the Find and Find and Replace Features

In this exercise, you will use the Find feature to locate the part of the document that refers to credit cards, and then you'll use the Find and Replace feature to locate the word *client* and replace it with *customer.*

Use Find

1. Make sure the **insertion point** is at the top of the document.
2. Choose **Home→Editing→Find** from the Ribbon to open the Navigation pane at the left side of the screen.

   TIP! Click directly on the button face of the Find button. If you click the menu ▾ button (the right side of the Find button), it opens a menu, which you will not use in this lesson.

3. Type **`credit card`** in the box at the top of the Navigation pane.

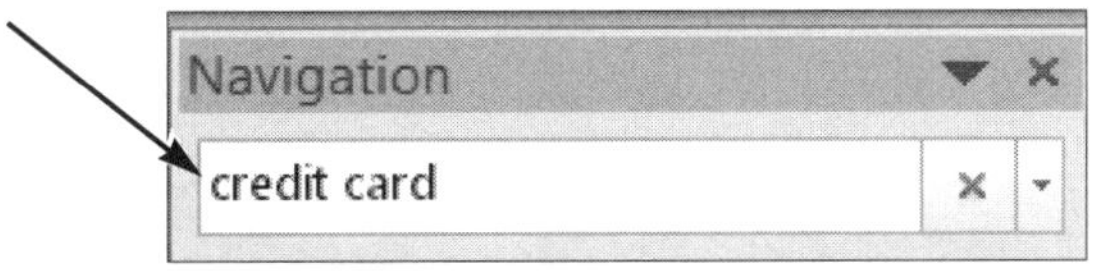

Both occurrences of the term appear in the search results list of the Navigation pane and both terms are highlighted in the document.

4. Click the **Close** button in the upper-right corner of the Navigation pane to close it.

Use Find and Replace

Now you will find the word *client* and replace it with *customer.*

5. If necessary, position the **insertion point** at the top of the document.

6. Choose **Home→Editing→Replace** from the Ribbon.

   The Find and Replace dialog box opens. Word remembers the last term you searched for and placed it in the Find What field. You will just ignore it and type the new term you are searching for over the top of the old search term.

7. Follow these steps to begin replacing *client* with *customer*:

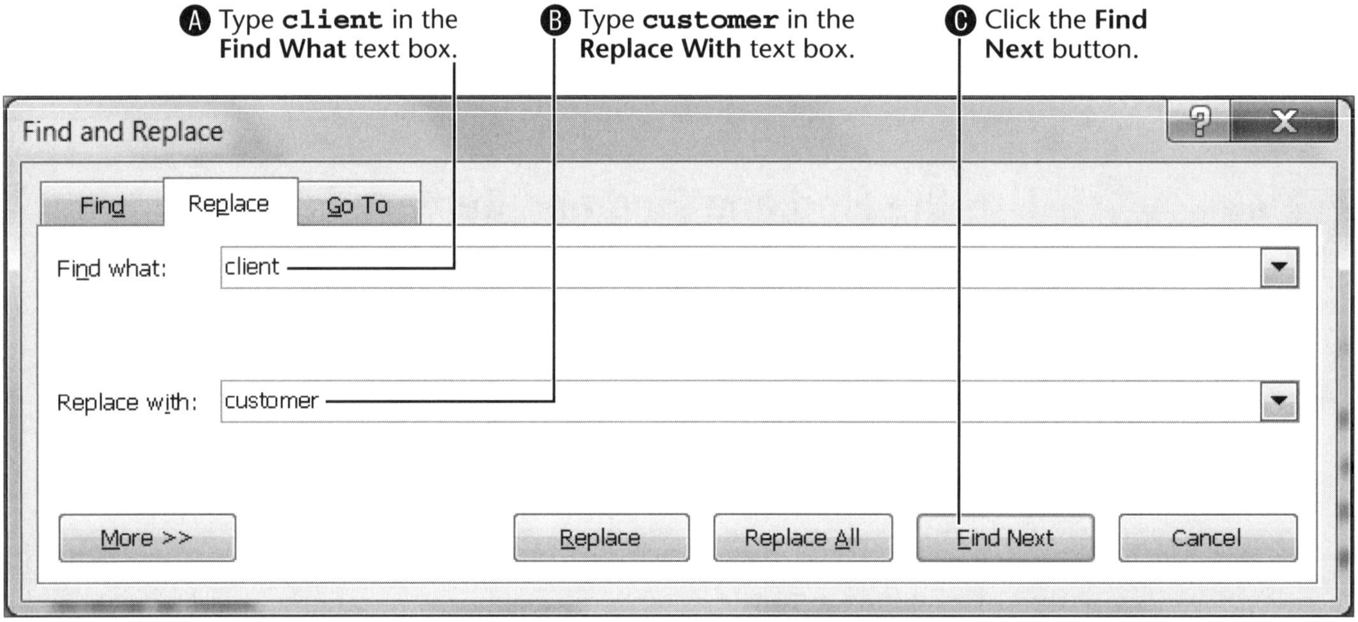

   Word highlights the first occurrence of the word. (You may have to move the Find and Replace dialog box to see the highlighted word. If so, place your mouse pointer on the blue bar at the top of the dialog box, press and hold the mouse button, and drag the dialog box to a new location.)

8. Click the **Replace** button at the bottom of the dialog box.

   Notice that Word made *customer* plural like *clients*, which it is replacing. Word also highlights the next occurrence of the word.

9. Click the **Replace** button again.

10. Continue clicking the **Replace** button as each term is highlighted until you see a message indicting that Word has finished searching the document.

11. Click **OK** to close the message.

12. Click the **Close** button in the Find and Replace dialog box.

13. **Save** and then **close** the document.

Concepts Review

To check your knowledge of the key concepts introduced in this lesson, complete the Concepts Review quiz on this and the next page. Or, you can take the quiz online by going to the URL **labyrinthelab.com/wtmo10**.

True/False Questions

			Page number
1. You select text in order to do something with it, such as move or copy it.	**true**	**false**	_______
2. When you use the Undo feature, you are essentially backing your way out of a problem.	**true**	**false**	_______
3. When you copy text, the original text remains intact and a copy is placed in the new location.	**true**	**false**	_______
4. When you delete a block of text within a paragraph, you must manually rewrap the lines using the [Enter] key.	**true**	**false**	_______
5. When you use the Replace feature, Word always knows the correct replacements to make when you use the Replace All button.	**true**	**false**	_______
6. You can automatically replace text using the Find and Replace dialog box.	**true**	**false**	_______

Multiple Choice Questions

7. The Spelling & Grammar Checker _____.

   Page number: _______

   a. underlines misspelled words with a squiggly green line
   b. corrects all misspelled proper names
   c. is a subset of the AutoCorrect feature
   d. underlines misspelled words with a squiggly red line

8. To select a single word with the mouse, _____.

   Page number: _______

   a. triple-click it
   b. press Ctrl and click the word
   c. double-click it
   d. position the mouse pointer in the selection bar and drag up or down

9. The AutoCorrect feature _____.

   Page number: _______

   a. automatically inserts the date in a document
   b. is located on the Quick Access toolbar
   c. corrects line spacing in your documents
   d. automatically corrects misspelled words and typos

10. Undo works for _____.

    Page number: _______

    a. things you do that make modifications to a document
    b. printing
    c. saving a document
    d. selecting text

Skill Builders

SKILL BUILDER 3.1 Select Text and Use Undo and Redo

In this exercise, you will practice several techniques for selecting text using both the mouse and the keyboard. You will also use the Undo and Redo features.

1. Open sb-Options from your Lesson 03 folder.

Select Text with the Mouse

2. Place the **mouse pointer** in the selection bar to the left of the first main paragraph, and then **double-click** to select the entire paragraph.
3. Place the **mouse pointer** in the typing area, and then click **once** to deselect the text.
4. Select the **paragraph** again, but this time click and drag in the **selection bar** to select it.
5. Click in the **typing area** to deselect the text.
6. **Double-click** the word *option* in the first sentence of the first paragraph to select it.
7. Click in the **typing area** to deselect.

Select Text with the Keyboard

8. Click at the beginning of the **Interest Rate Options** paragraph.
9. **Press and hold** [Shift], then click at the end of the **paragraph** to select the entire paragraph.
10. **Release** [Shift].
11. **Tap** any arrow key on the keyboard to deselect the text.
12. Click at the beginning of the **Interest Rate Options** paragraph. **Press and hold** [Shift], then **tap** [End].
    This selects the entire line.
13. **Tap** any arrow key to deselect the text.

Use the Undo and Redo Features

14. **Hold down** Ctrl and click the first sentence of the **Equity Options** paragraph to select the entire sentence.
15. **Tap** Delete.
16. Click the **Undo** button on the Quick Access toolbar to undelete the sentence.
17. Click the **Redo** button on the Quick Access toolbar to delete the sentence again.
18. Click the **Undo** button again to undelete the sentence again.
19. **Save** the file and leave it **open** for the next exercise.

SKILL BUILDER 3.2 Move and Copy Text

In this exercise, you will practice moving and copying text.

Before You Begin: The sb-Options document should still be open on the screen.

Move Text

First you will move the *Equity Options* paragraph above the *Interest Rate Options* paragraph.

1. Select the **Equity Options** heading and its following paragraph.
2. Choose **Home→Clipboard→Cut** from the Ribbon.
3. **Click** in front of the **Interest Rate Options** heading.
4. Choose **Home→Clipboard→Paste** from the Ribbon to move the text to a new location.
5. Scroll down to **page 2**.

Copy Text

6. Select the **Interest Rate Swap** heading and its following paragraph.
7. Choose **Home→Clipboard→Copy** from the Ribbon.
8. **Press and hold** Ctrl and **tap** End to place the insertion point at the end of the document.

9. Choose **Home→Clipboard→Paste** from the Ribbon to place a copy of the paragraph at the end of the document.
10. Scroll to the top of the page and select the **Interest Rate Swap** heading and its following paragraph again.
11. **Tap** Delete to remove the original paragraph.
12. **Save** and then **close** the file.

SKILL BUILDER 3.3 Add, Delete, and Replace Text

In this exercise, you will open a document and make editing changes to it. You will add, delete, and replace text.

1. Open the sb-Ripe Fruit document from your Lesson 03 folder.

   Locate the paragraph that begins with *Apples, bananas, avocados....* This is where you will make the first few editing changes.
2. Position the **insertion point** between the word *tomatoes* and the comma in the first line of the paragraph.
3. **Tap** Spacebar and **type** the following:

   `(yes, tomatoes are fruits)`
4. Toward the beginning of the next line, **double-click** to select the word *vine* and type **`plant`** in its place.

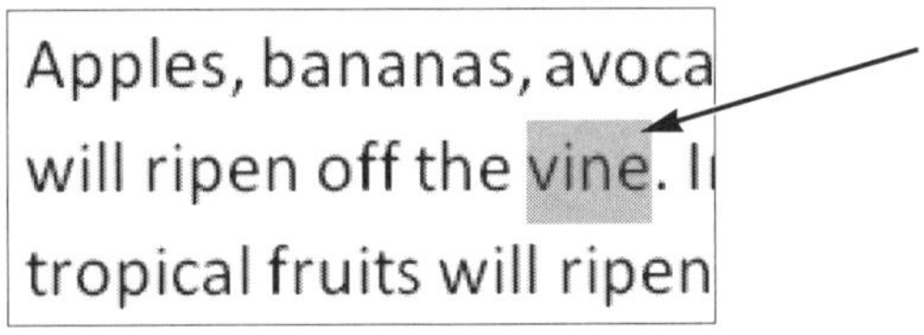

5. Toward the end of the third line, position the **insertion point** right after the word *yields*, **tap** Spacebar, and **type** the following:

   `(but is not mushy)`
6. In the second to last line of the same paragraph, position the **insertion point** between the word *gas* and the comma, **tap** Spacebar, and **type** the following:

   `(ripening agent)`

7. In the last sentence of the paragraph, click to the left of the word *bag* and **type** the word **`paper`** followed by a space.
8. In the first bullet point, **double-click** the word *broken* and replace it with **`split`**.
9. In the second bullet point, **double-click** the word *wrinkled* and replace it with **`shriveled`**.
10. In the second sentence of the fifth bullet point, place the **insertion point** between the word *pull* and the comma.
11. **Tap** [Spacebar] and type **`off`**.
12. In the last sentence of the page, **double-click** the word *usually* and **tap** [Delete].
13. **Save** and then **close** the file.

SKILL BUILDER 3.4 Use Find and Replace

Mrs. Bryan likes to keep busy in her retirement by giving piano lessons to young people in her community. One of her students recently gave her a birthday gift! In this exercise, you will use her thank you note to practice using Find and Replace.

1. Open the sb-Thank You Note file from the Lesson 03 folder.
2. Choose **Home→Editing→Replace** from the Ribbon.
3. Type **`remembering`** in the **Find What** box and **`thinking of`** in the **Replace With** box.
4. Click the **Find Next** button.
   The word *remembering* is highlighted in the note.
5. Click the **Replace** button to replace *remembering* with *thinking of.*
   A message appears to let you know that Word has finished searching the document.
6. Click **OK** to close the message.
7. Type **`doubly`** in the **Find What** box and **`twice as`** in the **Replace With** box.
8. Click the **Find Next** button.
   The first occurrence of doubly is highlighted. You decide that you don't want to replace that one.

9. Click the **Find Next** button again to skip the first occurrence of *doubly.*
   The second occurrence of doubly is highlighted.
10. Click the **Replace** button to replace *doubly* with *twice as.*
   The Word Has Finished... message appears again.
11. Click **OK** to close the message.
12. Click the **Close** button to close the Find and Replace dialog box.
13. **Save** and then **close** the file.

SKILL BUILDER 3.5 Use the Spelling & Grammar Checker

You received a newsy letter as an email attachment from your niece, Gail, updating you about family activities. You want to forward it to other family members, but you noticed a few spelling errors. In this exercise you will correct the spelling errors in Gail's letter.

1. Open sb-Letter from Gail from your Lesson 03 folder.
   Notice the misspelled words as indicated with the red squiggly underlines.
2. **Right-click** the word *suprise* in the second paragraph and select the correct spelling at the top of the pop-up menu.
3. **Right-click** the word *carots* in the third paragraph and select the correct spelling at the top of the pop-up menu.
4. Correct the word *Mexio* in the next paragraph.
5. Correct the remaining misspelled words on your own.
   Notice the *wen tto* error in the fifth paragraph. Word will propose a correction for *tto,* but *wen* is actually a word, so you'll need to take care of that yourself. This points out the fact that the Spelling & Grammar Checker is a *proofreading aid.* No guarantees—you still have to proof your documents.
6. **Save** and then **close** the file.

LESSON 4

Word – Encouraging Recycling with Flyers

In this lesson, you will create a flyer using character formatting, including changing the font type, size, and color. You will work with WordArt to convert ordinary text into graphic objects that you can manipulate with a variety of shapes and colors. You will discover Word's Clip Art gallery, allowing you to add interest to your flyers, and you will control the size and rotation of the images.

LESSON OBJECTIVES

After studying this lesson, you will be able to:

- Apply character formatting from the Ribbon
- Format with the Mini toolbar
- Use Live Preview and galleries
- Change paragraph alignment
- Create and format WordArt images
- Insert and manipulate clip art images
- Create new folders for organizing your documents

Student resources ***labyrinthelab.com/wtmo10***

Case Study: Creating a Recycling Flyer

Suzanne Frost is a student teacher at a local high school. The Earth Sciences students are about to begin a recycling project, and Suzanne wants to create a flyer to attract the students' interest in the project. This is an opportunity for her to practice character formatting and to use some of Word's fun tools like WordArt and clip art.

Formatting with the Ribbon

Character formatting can help you get your message across. Examples of character formatting include:

- Font type
- Font style
- Font size
- Font color

Character format settings take effect from the insertion point forward or until you change them. If you wish to format existing text, you must select the text first, and then format it.

Fonts

The term *font* typically refers to character design, which can vary dramatically. You can apply any font in the Font menu to change the appearance of text.

This is an example of the Calibri font.

This is an example of Comic Sans MS

This is an example of Old English Text Mt

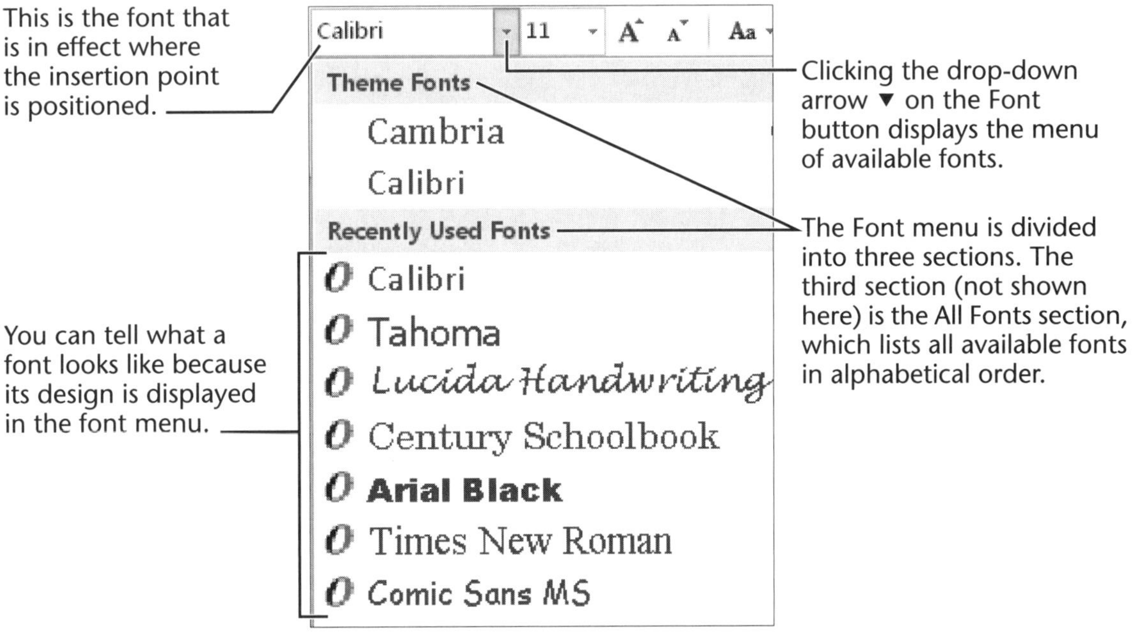

The Font Group

The Font group on the Home tab provides a convenient way to format characters. The following illustration points out some frequently used font attributes.

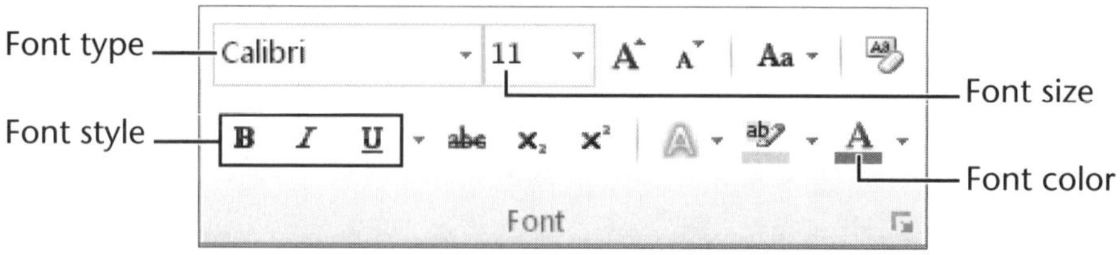

Font Size

Font size is measured in points, and there are 72 points in 1 inch. Frequently used sizes for regular typing (versus headings) are 10, 11, and 12 points.

Formatting with the Mini Toolbar

The Mini toolbar contains frequently used formatting commands. When you select text, the Mini toolbar fades in. After a pause, this shy little toolbar fades away. You can make it reappear by right-clicking the selected text.

In the following example, clicking the Bold button on the Mini toolbar applies bold to the selected text.

Using Live Preview with Galleries

Live Preview shows what a formatting change looks like without actually applying the format. In the following example, selecting a block of text and then hovering the mouse pointer over a font name previews how the text will look. Clicking the font name applies the font to the selected text.

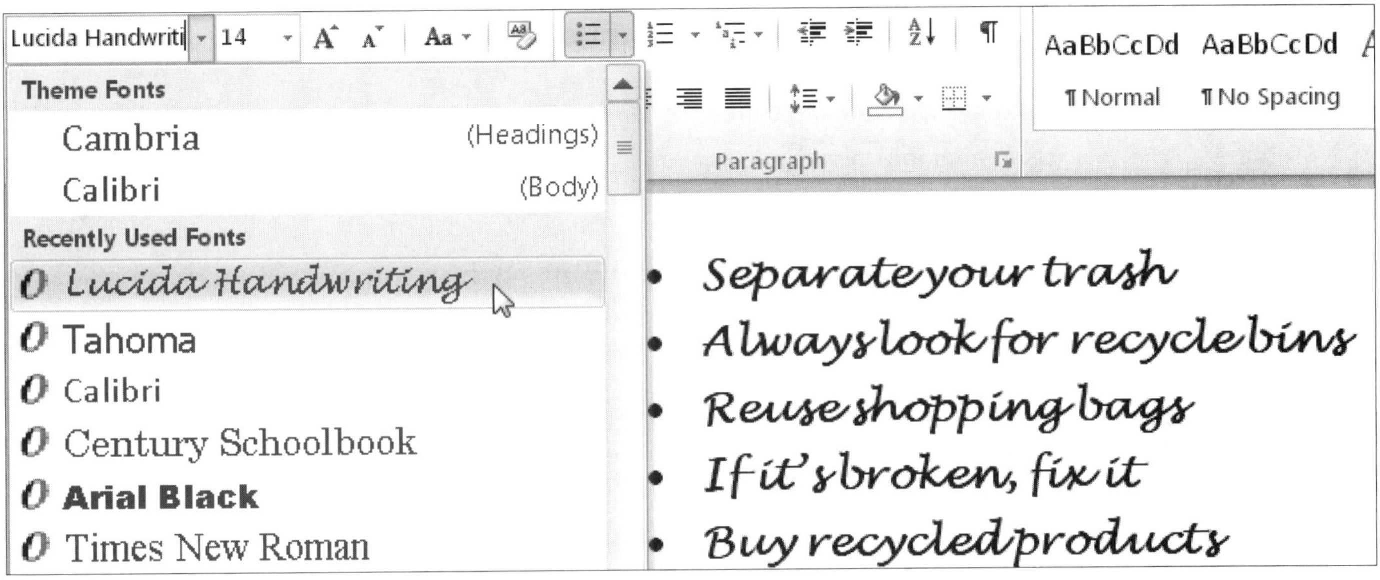

Live Preview of the Lucida Handwriting font

HANDS-ON 4.1 Use Character Formatting

In this exercise, you will type recycling suggestions in your flyer. You will practice formatting characters using the Home tab's Font group and the Mini toolbar.

1. If necessary, start **Word**.
2. If necessary, choose **Home→Paragraph→Show/Hide** [¶] from the Ribbon to display non-printing characters.
3. **Tap** [Enter] four times to move the insertion point down the page.
4. Choose **Home→Paragraph→Bullets** [bullets icon] from the Ribbon.

5. **Type** the following text, **tapping** [Enter] at the end of the line if you need to generate a new bullet.

- Separate your trash
- Always look for recycle bins
- Reuse shopping bags
- If it's broken, fix it
- Buy recycled products
- Take along reusable cups
- Use washable napkins

6. **Tap** [Enter] three times to add blank lines below the text.

   You're adding space because later you will add WordArt at the bottom of the page.

7. Now select the lines you typed.

- Separate your trash
- Always look for recycle bins
- Reuse shopping bags
- If it's broken, fix it
- Buy recycled products
- Take along reusable cups
- Use washable napkins

Use Live Preview with a Variety of Fonts

8. Make sure the **Home** tab is still active.

9. Follow these steps to use Live Preview:

Ⓐ In the **Font** group, click the **menu ▼** button on the Font list.

Ⓑ Scroll down to the **All Fonts** category in the menu. Fonts in this category are in alphabetical order.

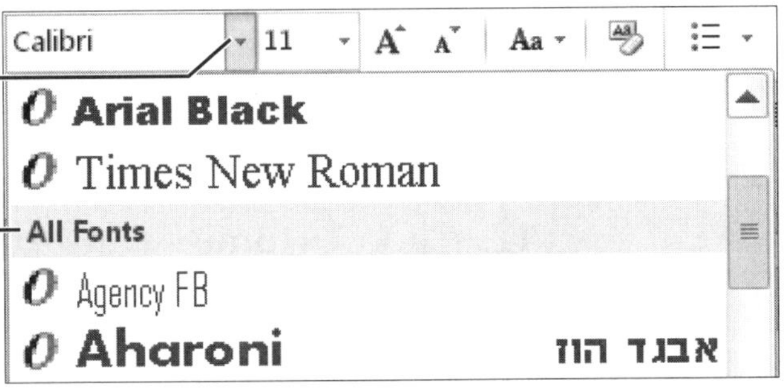

Ⓒ Scroll down to **Comic Sans MS** and hover the mouse pointer over the font to observe a preview of this font. Click **Comic Sans MS** to apply it to the selected lines.

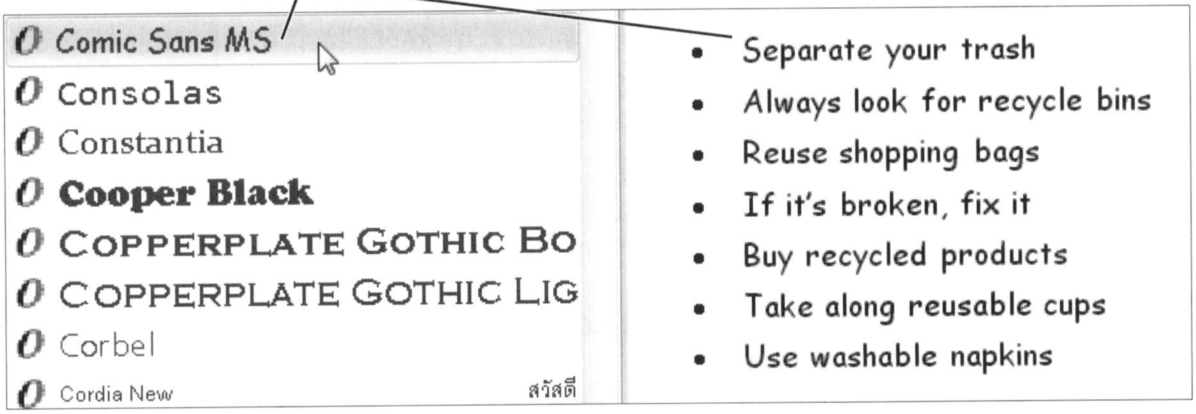

Change the Font Size

10. Make sure the lines are selected, then follow these steps to change the size:

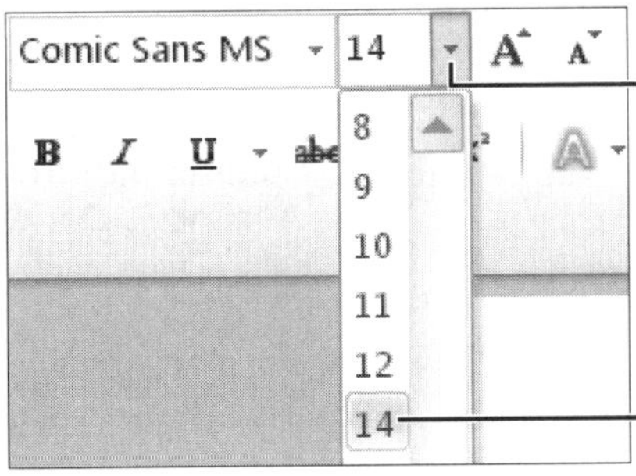

Ⓐ Click the **Font Size menu ▼** button.

Ⓑ Choose **14** points from the menu.

Apply Various Font Styles Using the Ribbon and Mini Toolbar

TIP! The Bold, Italic, and Underline buttons toggle on and off. In other words, you use the Italic button to apply the italic format and you use the same Italic button to remove the format. The same is true for the Bold and Underline buttons.

11. Make sure the lines are still selected; then, choose **Home→Font→Italic** *I* from the Ribbon.
12. Choose **Home→Font→Underline** U from the Ribbon.
13. Now click the **Italic** *I* button again to turn it off.
14. Click the **Underline** U button again to turn it off.
    Next you will use the Mini Toolbar to turn on the Bold feature.
15. Click **once** in the document to deselect the highlighted text.
16. Select the lines again and notice that the Mini toolbar fades into sight.
17. Move the **mouse pointer** toward the toolbar and it continues to fade in.
18. Click the **Bold** **B** button on the toolbar to apply bold to the selected text.

Apply Color to Your Text with the Mini Toolbar

19. Follow these steps to apply a green color to the text:

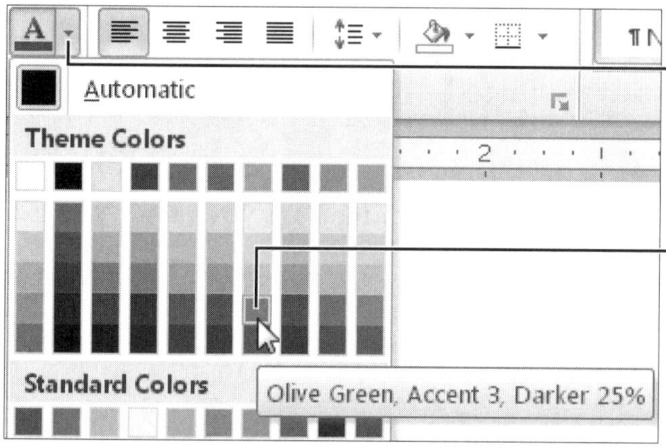

Ⓐ Click the **Font Color menu ▼** button to display the color gallery.

Ⓑ Choose the color in the seventh column, fifth row: **Olive Green, Accent 3, Darker 25%.**

Leave the file open. You will use it throughout the lesson.

Saving a Document to a New Folder

A folder is an electronic location where you store groups of related files. So far, you have been storing files in the folders that relate to a lesson, such as the Lesson 04 folder. You can create folders within folders for organizing your documents. Creating folders is a simple matter with Word 2010.

Creating a New Folder

The Save As dialog box has a toolbar button for creating a new folder. The button varies depending on whether your computer uses Win 7, Win Vista, or Win XP.

The New Folder button in Win 7

The New Folder button in Win Vista

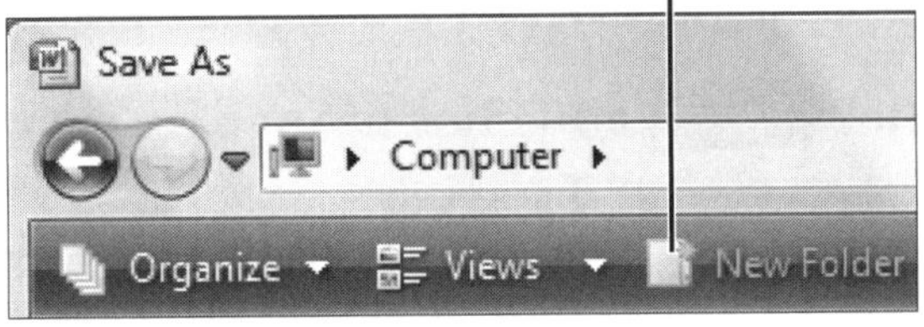

The New Folder button in Win XP

Naming Folders When you click the New Folder button, both Win 7 and Win Vista display a New Folder icon like the one shown in the following figure. The New Folder text is selected so you can just type your new folder's name over the top of the highlighted text.

With Win XP, the New Folder dialog box appears. Here you type the folder name, as shown in the following illustration.

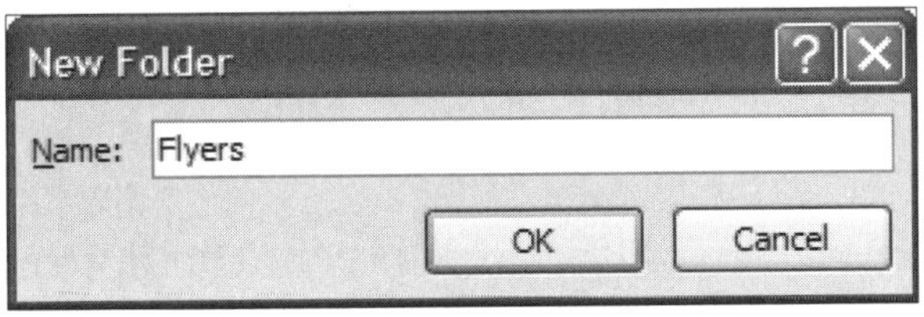

There are certain naming rules you must follow when you create a folder. If you try to name a folder without following the rules, Word displays an error message. The following table lists the rules for naming folders.

QUICK REFERENCE: Naming Folders

Rule	Description
Folder name length	A folder name can contain up to 256 characters.
Characters allowed in folder names	A folder name may contain alphabetic characters, numbers, spaces, periods, commas, semicolons, dashes, apostrophes, and parentheses.
Characters not allowed in folder names	A folder name *cannot* contain the following characters: \ / : * ? " < > |

HANDS-ON 4.2 Create a Folder and Save Your Flyer

You know that it's likely you will want to create more than one flyer for the recycling project. In this exercise, you will create a new folder specifically for saving flyers.

1. Click File and choose **Save As** from the menu.
2. Navigate to your Lesson 04 folder and click the **New Folder** button.
3. Follow the step for your version of Windows:
   - **Win 7/Vista:** Type **`Flyers`** over the top of the highlighted New Folder text and **tap** [Enter].
   - **Win XP:** Type **`Flyers`** in the New Folder dialog box and click **OK**.
4. If you are using Win 7, **double-click** the Flyers folder to place it in the Save In box at the top of the dialog box.

   If you are using Win Vista or Win XP, the new folder automatically jumps to the Save In box at the top of the Save As dialog box. The last folder listed in the Save In box is the active folder, so the document you are saving now will go into the Flyers folder.

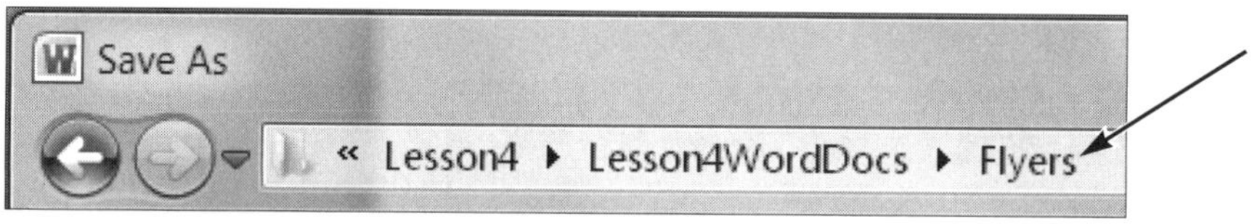

5. Type **`Recycle Flyer`** in the File Name box at the bottom of the Save As dialog box, and then click the **Save** button.

Setting Paragraph Alignment

Typically, you use paragraph alignment to align text between the margins of a document. You can also use it to align clip art and other graphic images.

The Alignment Buttons

Paragraph alignment buttons are located in the Paragraph group of the Home tab. Alignment options include Align Text Left, Center, Align Text Right, and Justify.

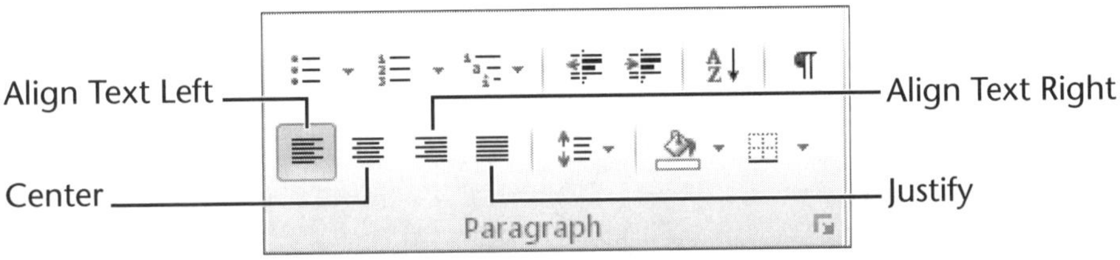

Alignment buttons in the Paragraph group of the Home tab

ALIGNMENT OPTIONS

Alignment	Example	Alignment	Example
The Align Text Left button aligns text with a straight left margin and a ragged right margin.		The Center button centers text between the margins.	
The Align Text Right button aligns text with a ragged left margin and a straight right margin.		The Justify button aligns text with straight left and right margins. This type of alignment typically appears in magazines and newspapers.	

HANDS-ON 4.3 Set Paragraph Alignment

In this exercise, you will use the paragraph alignment buttons in the Paragraph group of the Home tab to align text between the margins.

1. Position the **insertion point** anywhere in a line of text.
2. Choose **Home→Paragraph→Center** from the Ribbon.
   The text is centered between the margins.
3. Choose **Home→Paragraph→Align Text Right** from the Ribbon.
   The text is now aligned with the right margin.
4. Choose **Home→Paragraph→Align Text Left** from the Ribbon to align the text at the left margin.
5. **Save** the file.

Creating WordArt

WordArt is a graphic text image. You can format the image in a variety of shapes and colors. WordArt makes text look flashy—just the perfect thing for a flyer. WordArt also make interesting document headings.

HANDS-ON 4.4 Insert WordArt

In this exercise, you will create a WordArt object by selecting a design from the WordArt gallery and typing the text that will appear in the object.

1. **Press** Ctrl+Home to position the insertion point at the top of the page.
2. Choose **Insert→Text→WordArt** from the Ribbon.
3. Choose the **fifth style** in the **first row** of the WordArt gallery.

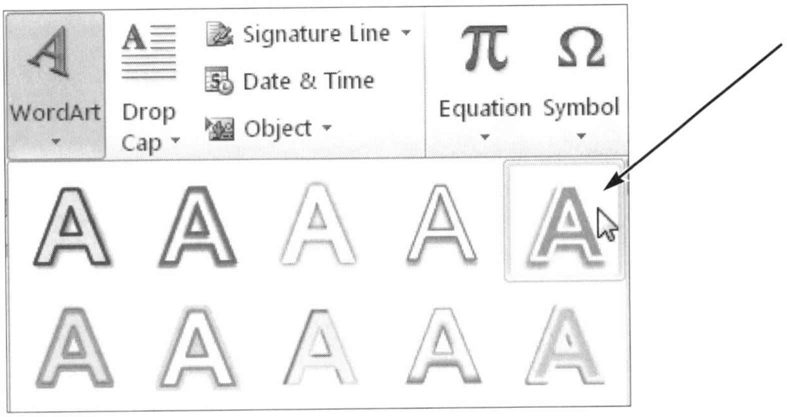

A text box opens where you can type the heading for your flyer. Notice the little square and circular handles that surround the object, indicating that it is selected. You'll learn more about that in the next topic.

4. Type **`Reduce, Reuse, Recycle`** in the text box.

Formatting WordArt

You can format WordArt in a variety of ways. For example, you can change the shape, apply a 3-D style, and add shadow effects.

The following figure shows an example of using Live Preview with the Bevel gallery to test the formatting effect.

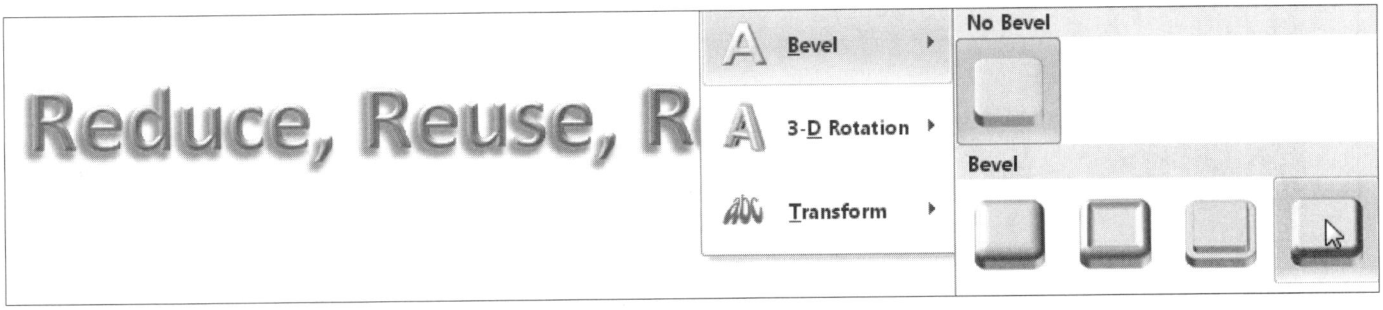

Contextual Tabs on the Ribbon

Contextual tabs appear in context with the task you are performing. When you select a WordArt object, the Drawing Tools' Format tab appears. Here you will find many items to format your WordArt.

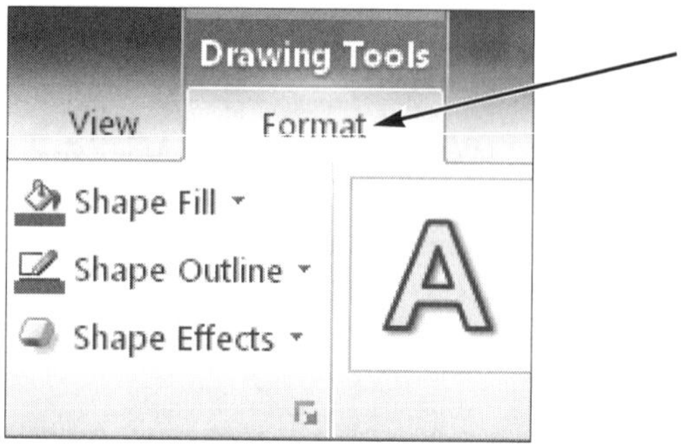

Selecting, Sizing, and Rotating WordArt

When you click a WordArt object, small circles and squares known as handles surround the object. When the insertion point is flashing in a word, only that word is selected and the box surrounding the object is made up of a dashed line. When you click directly on the line, it becomes solid, indicating that all words in the box are selected. Any formatting you do applies to all words.

The green circular handle at the top of the image is the rotate handle, which you can drag with the mouse pointer to rotate the image. You'll learn more about rotating images when you insert clip art later in this lesson.

When you position the mouse pointer on a handle, the pointer changes to a double-headed arrow, which you can drag to increase or decrease the size of the object. Sizing from a corner handle changes the length and width relative to their original proportions.

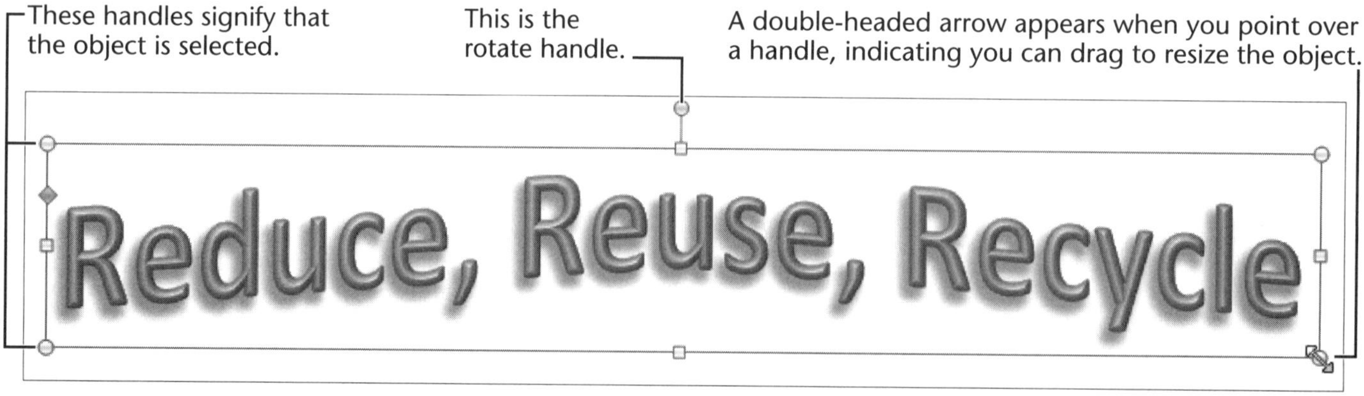

HANDS-ON 4.5 Format WordArt

In this exercise, you will use the contextual Format tab to test a variety of formatting options including applying a Bevel effect.

1. Click the **border** of the WordArt text box.

   The line changes from dashed to solid and the Drawing Tools' Format tab is active.

2. Choose **Format→WordArt Styles→Text Outline** from the Ribbon.

3. Choose the color in the seventh column, fifth row, **Olive Green, Accent 3, Darker 25%.**

   Your heading blends with the bulleted text since you chose the same color for both.

4. Choose **Format→WordArt Styles→Text Effects** from the Ribbon to display text effect categories in the menu.

5. Drag the mouse pointer down to the **Shadow** category, and then hover (don't click) the mouse over several options to see the effects in Live Preview.

6. Use the same technique to explore the other categories.

   Remember: Don't click until you decide what effect you will use.

7. Drag the mouse pointer to the **Bevel** category and click the **last option** in the **first row** (Cool Slant), as shown in the following figure.

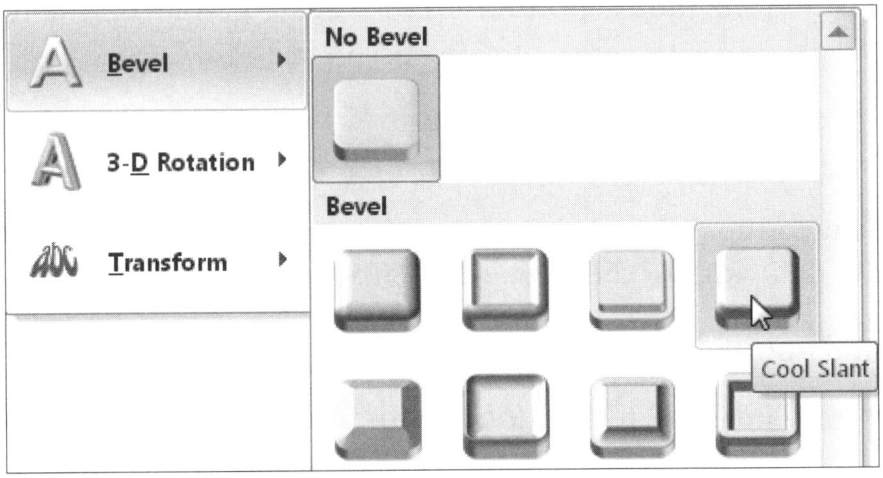

Apply a Transform Effect

8. Choose **Format→WordArt Styles→Text Effects** from the Ribbon.
9. Drag down to the **Transform** category and click **Chevron Up**, as shown in the following figure.

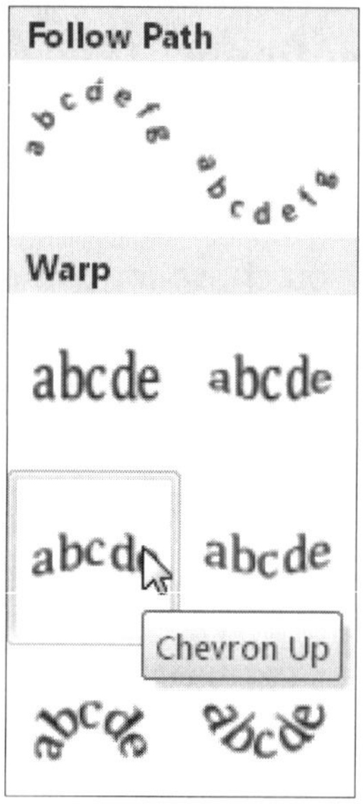

Resize the WordArt Image

10. Position the **mouse pointer** on the square handle on the right side.
    The mouse pointer changes to a double-headed arrow.
11. Press and hold the **mouse button**.
    The pointer changes to a black cross.
12. Drag to the **right** until the right side of the text box is about an inch from the right edge of the page; release the **mouse button**.

Add Another WordArt Image

13. **Press** Ctrl+End to position the insertion point below the bulleted text.
14. Choose **Insert→Text→WordArt** from the Ribbon.
15. Click the **last option** in the **first row**.
16. Type `Do Your Part!` in the text box.
17. Click the **border** of the text box to select the entire object.

18. Choose **Format→WordArt Styles→Text Outline** from the Ribbon.

19. Choose the color in the **seventh column, fifth row.**

20. Choose **Format→WordArt Styles→Text Effects** from the Ribbon.

21. In the Bevel category, choose the **fourth item** in the **first row.**

Resize the WordArt

22. Drag the **right-side handle** until the right edge of the text box is about an inch from the right edge of the page.

    This centers the text between the margins. Don't worry if the overall layout doesn't look right. You still need to add some clip art.

23. **Save** your flyer.

Using Clip Art

Clip Art adds excitement to your documents. Word 2010 includes a clip art collection installed on your hard drive. Even more clip art items are available on a Microsoft website.

Searching for Clip Art

The Clip Art task pane helps you search for clip art to enhance your documents. Each clip has one or more keywords associated with it. When typing a keyword, all clip art images associated with the keyword display. The task pane displays your search results as thumbnail images.

Clip Art Media Types Clip art comes in four different media types.

- **Illustrations:** Images drawn by graphic artists
- **Photographs:** Photographic images
- **Video:** Simple animated pictures or brief video clips
- **Audio:** Sound effects, such as the noise made by a car horn

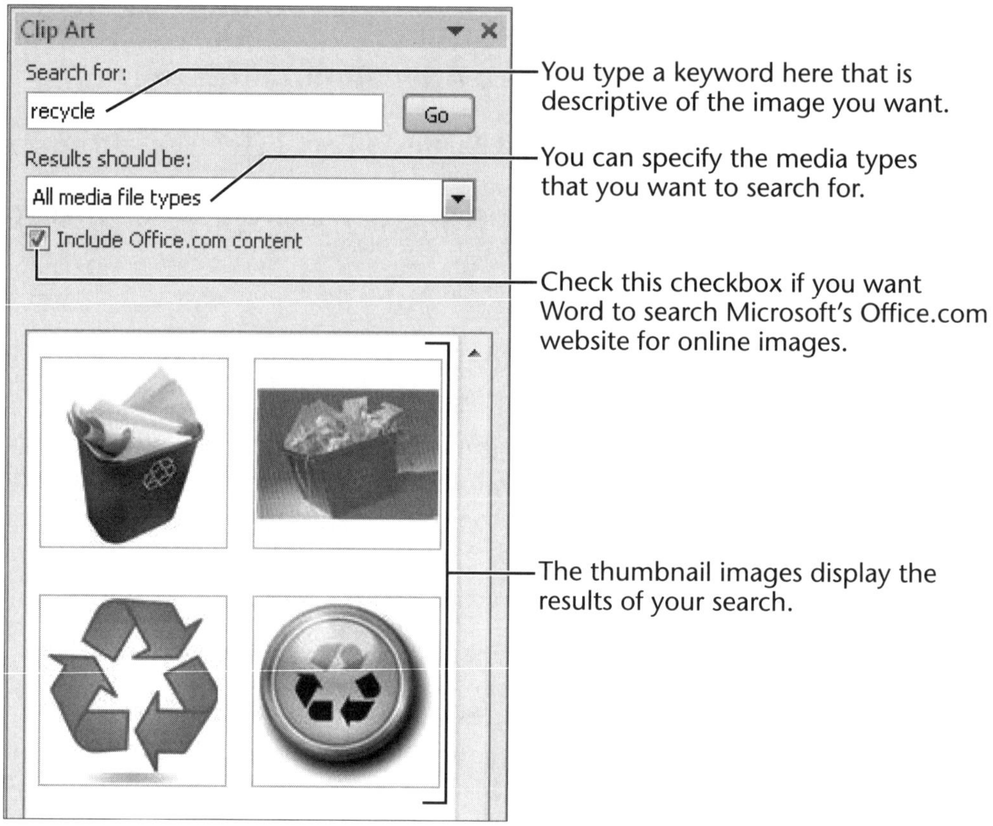

HANDS-ON 4.6 Insert Clip Art

In this exercise, you will search for a clip art image that's appropriate for the recycling project and place it in your flyer.

1. Position the **insertion point** on the line below the flyer's heading.
2. Choose **Insert→Illustrations→Clip Art** from the Ribbon.
   The Clip Art task pane opens on the right side of the screen.

Search for Clip Art

3. Type **`recycle`** in the **Search For** box at the top of the Clip Art task pane.

4. The Results Should Be box should display All Media File Types. If it does not, click the **menu ▾** button and check **All Media Types**; then, click the **menu ▾** button again to close the menu.

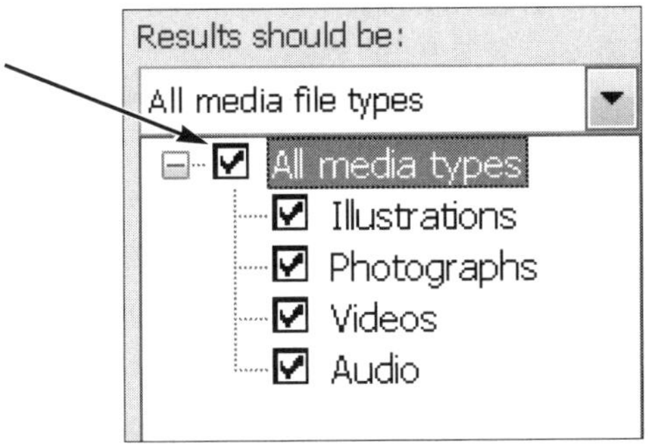

5. Make sure the **Include Office.com Content** checkbox is checked.

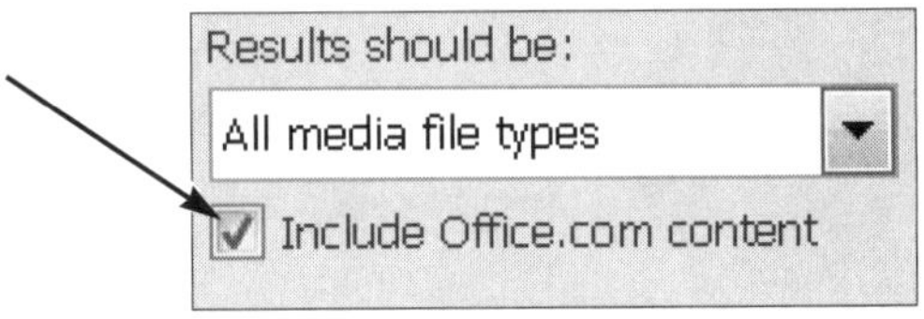

6. Click the **Go** button in the upper-right corner of the task pane to locate clip art related to the keyword *recycle*.

Insert Clip Art

7. Locate the thumbnail image shown in the figure at right. Notice that you are looking for an image that has a small shadow at the bottom. If that image is not available, choose a similar image that reminds you of recycling.

When you hover the mouse pointer over a thumbnail image, a gray button appears on the right side of the image. If you click the button, it displays a menu of options. You do not need to use that button now, so you can just ignore it.

8. Click directly on the **thumbnail image** once to insert the clip art in your flyer.

9. **Save** your document.

Rotating Clip Art

Clip art images have handles that work in a manner similar to WordArt handles. When you position the mouse pointer on the rotate handle, it changes to a circular arrow, as show in the following figure. You can then drag left or right to rotate the image.

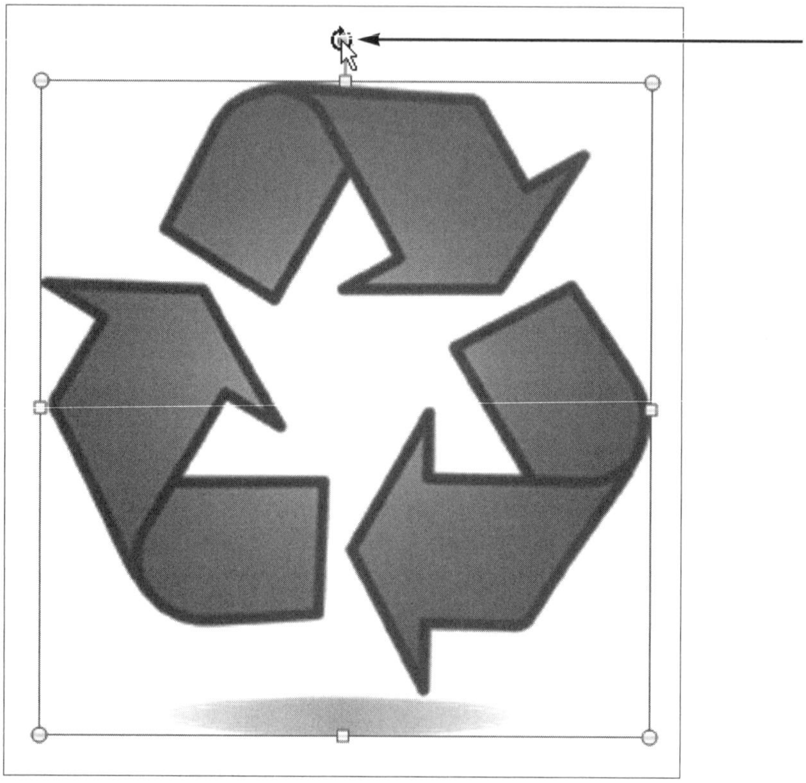

Resizing Clip Art

You can change the size of clip art objects by dragging on their handles like you did to resize a WordArt object earlier in this lesson. When you place the mouse pointer over a handle (other than the rotate handle) the pointer changes to a double-headed arrow. Then you drag to resize the object.

Resizing from a side handle stretches or squeezes an image as you resize it. Resizing from a corner handle changes the height and width proportionally.

HANDS-ON 4.7 Rotate and Resize a Clip Art Image

In this exercise, you will rotate and resize your recycle image.

Rotate the Clip Art Image

1. If necessary, click the **clip art image** once to select it.

   The surrounding circular and square handles are visible when you select the clip art object. Notice the green rotate handle at the top of the image.

2. Position the **mouse pointer** on the green rotate handle, press and hold the **mouse button**, and drag to the **right** to rotate the image as shown here; release the **mouse button**.

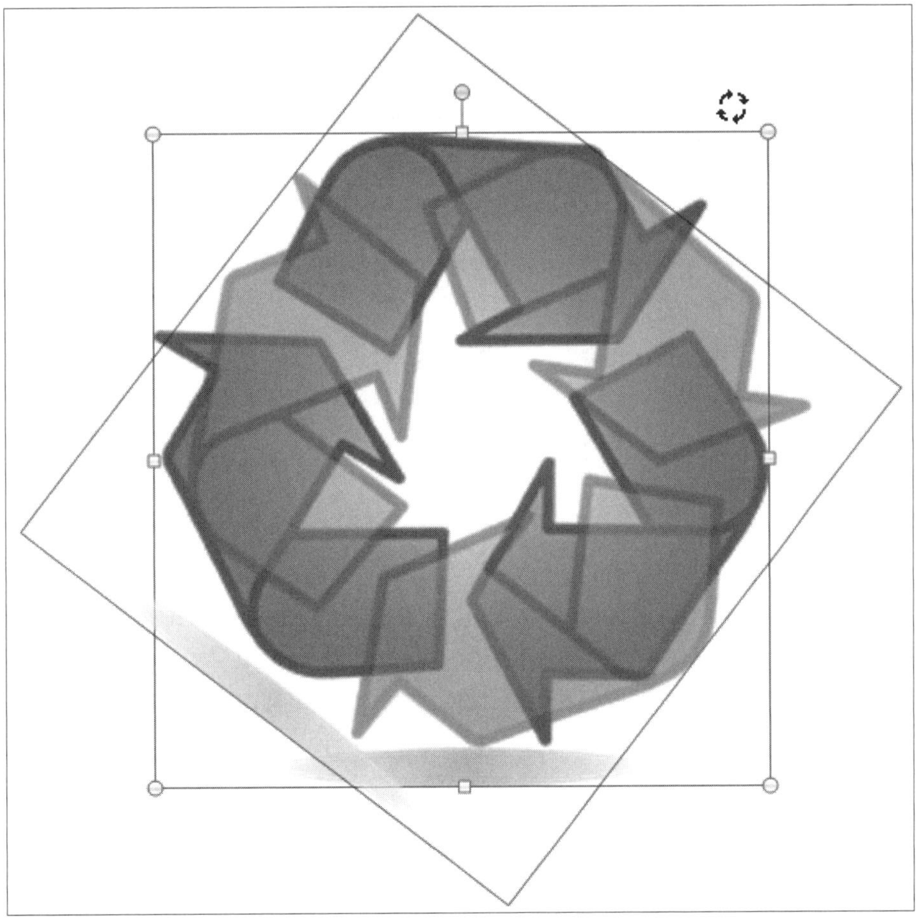

3. Click the **Undo** button on the Quick Access toolbar to undo the rotation.

Resize the Clip Art Image

4. Position the **mouse pointer** on the lower-right corner handle. When the mouse pointer changes to a **double-headed arrow**, drag up and to the left about a half inch to make the image smaller.

   A ghost image previews the clip art as you drag to resize it.

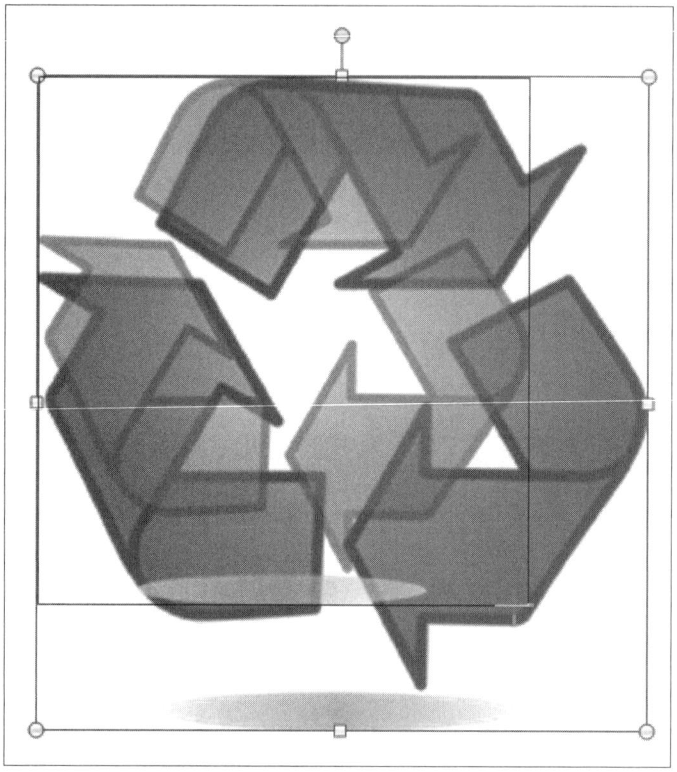

NOTE! If you chose a clip art image other than the one shown, the final image size should be approximately $2\frac{1}{2} \times 2\frac{1}{2}$ inches. Don't be overly concerned about the size. You can feel free to modify the size to your satisfaction at any time.

5. **Save**  the file.

Wrapping Text

Wrap Text provides text tools that allow you to wrap text around graphic images such as clip art. A variety of wrapping options are available. When you choose a wrapping style other than the default, In Line with Text, it's easy to drag the image with the mouse pointer to position it on the page.

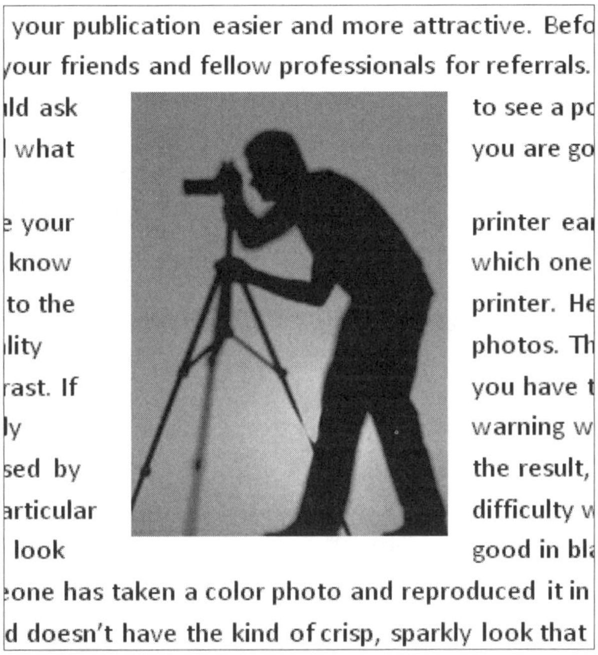

Square wrapping causes the text to wrap around the object.

Behind Text wrapping places the text on top of the image.

Positioning an Image

The Position options on the Ribbon are preset wrapping locations that you choose from a gallery. The following illustrations show the same image positioned at top left, top center, and top right.

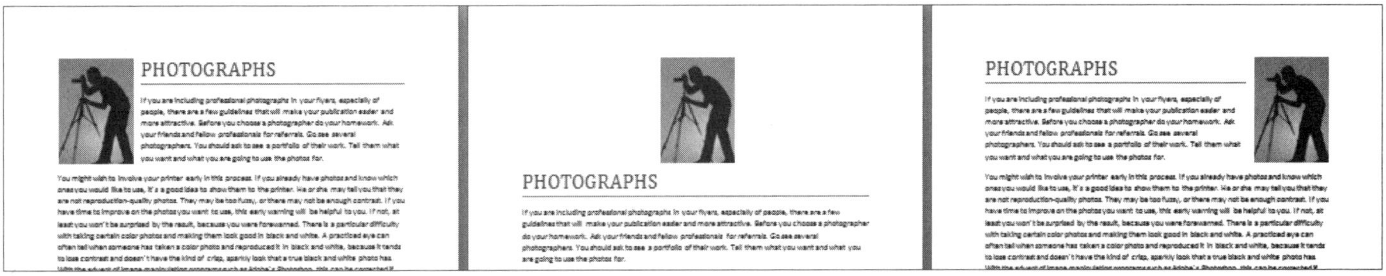

Preset wrapping styles chosen from the Position galley

Cropping Clip Art Images

Cropping allows you to hide parts of a picture. You simply choose the Crop tool and drag on one of the image's cropping handles to hide any unwanted portion of the picture.

Cropping an image does not affect the original image. The area hidden by cropping is not deleted; you can un-crop an image if necessary.

The recycle clip art with the before image at left and the after image at right. The shadow was cropped from the bottom of the image on the right.

HANDS-ON 4.8 Wrap Text, Position an Image, and Crop an Image

In this exercise, you will use the Square text wrapping option with your clip art image, and you will experiment with Live Preview and various Position choices. You will practice cropping an image, and then you will center the image and align the text on the page.

1. If necessary, click the **clip art image** to select it.

Work with Wrapping Options

2. Choose **Format→Arrange→Wrap Text** from the Ribbon.
3. Choose **Square** from the menu so the text wraps to the right side.
4. Choose **Format→Arrange→Position** from the Ribbon.

5. Slide the **mouse pointer** over the menu to see the various effects.

6. Click the mouse in the **document background** to close the menu without choosing a layout option.

7. If necessary, select the **object** and choose **Format→Arrange→Wrap Text** from the Ribbon; then, choose **In Line with Text** from the menu.

Crop and Un-crop the Shadow from the Bottom of the Image

If you chose an image without a shadow, just clip a bit off the bottom of the image.

8. Choose **Format→Size→Crop** from the Ribbon.

9. Position the **mouse pointer** on the bottom-center thick, black handle.

   The mouse pointer looks like a thick black T-shape.

10. Press and hold the **mouse button**, and then drag **up** until the **mouse pointer** is above the shadow; release the **mouse button**.

11. Click in the **document background** to deselect the object and notice the effect of the cropping.

    You've decided you want to keep the shadow. This time you will un-crop the image.

12. Select the **object** again.

13. Choose **Format→Size→Crop** from the Ribbon.

14. Position the **mouse pointer** on the black bottom-center handle.

15. Press and hold the **mouse button** and drag **down** until you think the shadow will be visible again.

16. Release the **mouse button**.

    If the shadow is not completely visible, readjust the image with the Crop tool until you can see the entire shadow.

17. If necessary, choose **Format→Size→Crop** from the Ribbon to turn off the Crop tool.

Align the Image and the Text

18. Choose **Home→Paragraph→Center** from the Ribbon.

    Now you will align the text under the clip art image. You want the text to line up straight on the left, so you won't use the Center button, which would center each line between the margins individually. Instead you will use the Tab key to position the text.

19. Select all **seven lines** of text then **tap** Tab seven times.

    When you select several lines of text, using the Tab key moves all of the lines at once.

20. **Save** and then **close** the file.

Concepts Review

To check your knowledge of the key concepts introduced in this lesson, complete the Concepts Review quiz on this and the next page. Or, you can take the quiz online by going to the URL **labyrinthelab.com/wtmo10**.

True/False Questions

			Page number
1. In the word-processing arena, font size is typically measured in points.	**true**	**false**	_______
2. Live Preview shows how formatting changes look without actually applying the format.	**true**	**false**	_______
3. Once you insert a WordArt image, you cannot change its shape.	**true**	**false**	_______
4. A clip art image has a green rotate handle at the top of the image.	**true**	**false**	_______
5. Word allows you to wrap text around a clip art image.	**true**	**false**	_______
6. Paragraph alignment works for text but not for graphic images.	**true**	**false**	_______

Multiple Choice Questions

7. You know a WordArt image is selected when _____.

   Page number: _______

   a. the handles are visible

   b. it is highlighted

   c. the WordArt task pane appears

   d. it is visible from the Print command in Backstage view.

8. Where do the results appear when you search for clip art?

   Page number: _______

   a. In the document

   b. In the Arrange group on the contextual Format tab

   c. In the Clip Art task pane

   d. In the Clip Art tab

9. Wrap Text allows you to _____.

   Page number: _______

   a. keep typing in a paragraph without tapping [Enter]

   b. wrap text around a graphic image

   c. choose from a predefined gallery of image positions on a page

   d. rotate a graphic image

10. The Mini toolbar _____.

    Page number: _______

    a. contains frequently used formatting commands

    b. is located on the contextual Format tab

    c. always appears at the bottom of the Word window

    d. contains the Wrap Text feature

Skill Builders

SKILL BUILDER 4.1 Create WordArt and Format Text

Your friend, Jack, is in charge of coordinating senior skills classes at the community center. He hears that you are producing some interesting documents with your new computer, and he asks for your help. In this exercise, you will format the senior skills class schedule.

NOTE! Remember, you can turn the Show/Hide button on or off as you prefer.

Create a WordArt Image

1. Open sb-Senior Skills Seminar from your Lesson 04 folder.

   Next you'll use WordArt to format the first line of the document. Since the text is already typed, you can just select it and apply the WordArt style.

2. Select the **first line** in the document.
3. Choose **Insert→Text→WordArt** from the Ribbon.
4. Choose the first WordArt style in the first row, **Fill - Tan, Text 2, Outline - Background 2.**

   Don't worry about the text that pops over to the right of the WordArt; you'll take care of that shortly.

Modify the WordArt Shape

5. Choose **Format→WordArt Styles→Text Effects** from the Ribbon.
6. Drag down to the **Glow** category and choose the **first variation** in the **first row**, as shown in the following figure.

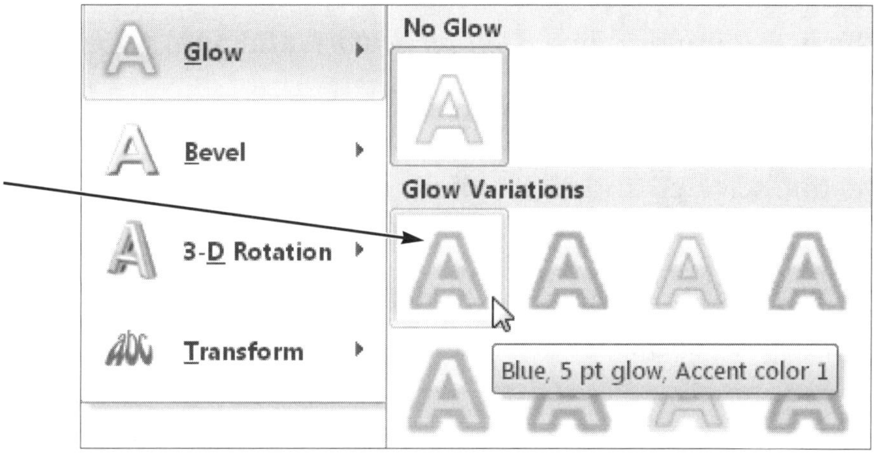

Resize the WordArt Image

When you resize the WordArt, the text to the right of the object will float down below.

7. Place the **mouse pointer** on the right-side handle and drag to the **right** until the right edge of the text box is about an inch from the edge of the page.

Add Fill Color to the Image

8. Choose **Format→WordArt Styles→Text Fill** [A] from the Ribbon.
9. Choose the color in the **fourth column, fifth row.**

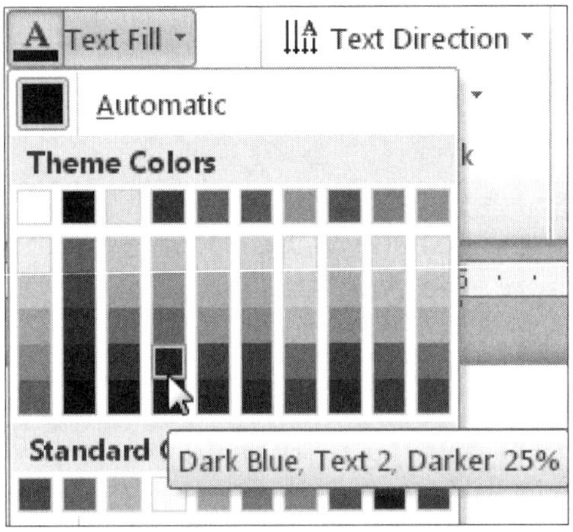

Format Text with the Ribbon

10. Select the next two lines, *Fall Seminar Schedule* and *Course Descriptions.*

    Don't be concerned that the WordArt appears to be selected. It won't interfere with the next steps.
11. Choose **Home→Font→Font Size ▾** from the Ribbon.
12. Change to **16 point** font.
13. Choose **Home→Paragraph→Center** [≡] from the Ribbon.
14. Select the first seminar name, *Golf for Seniors,* and apply **12 point Arial** font.

Format Text with the Mini Toolbar

15. Keep the line selected and **right-click** the selected **text** to display the Mini toolbar.
16. Click the **Bold** [B] button on the toolbar.

    The toolbar remains open.

17. Click the **Font Color** **menu ▾** button and choose a shade of **blue** you think blends well with the WordArt.

> **TIP!** The Font Color button remembers the last color you chose from the menu, and that color appears on the button face. You can repeat the color without opening the menu. Just click the button face.

18. Format the other two seminar names using the same attributes: **12 point Arial**, and the **color** of your choice.

19. Select the first three lines below the *Golf for Seniors* heading and apply the **Arial** font.

20. Repeat that formatting for the first three lines below the other two seminar headings.

21. **Save** and then **close** the document.

SKILL BUILDER 4.2 Work with Clip Art and Create a Folder

It's time for the annual science fair where Suzanne Frost is student teaching. In this exercise, Suzanne works with a student to help him create a flyer to use as a handout for his project.

1. Open sb-Carbon Footprint from your Lesson 04 folder.

2. If necessary, choose **Home→Paragraph→Show/Hide** ¶ from the Ribbon to display non-printing characters.

3. Click next to the **fourth paragraph symbol** below the WordArt heading.

Insert Clip Art

4. Choose **Insert→Illustrations→Clip Art** from the Ribbon.
   The Clip Art task pane appears on the right side of the window. Now you'll search for clip art related to the student's *carbon footprint* project.

5. Type `carbon footprint` in the **Search For** box at the top of the Clip Art task pane.
   Next you will limit the types of media you search for to *Illustrations* and *Photographs*.

6. Follow these steps to limit the media types:

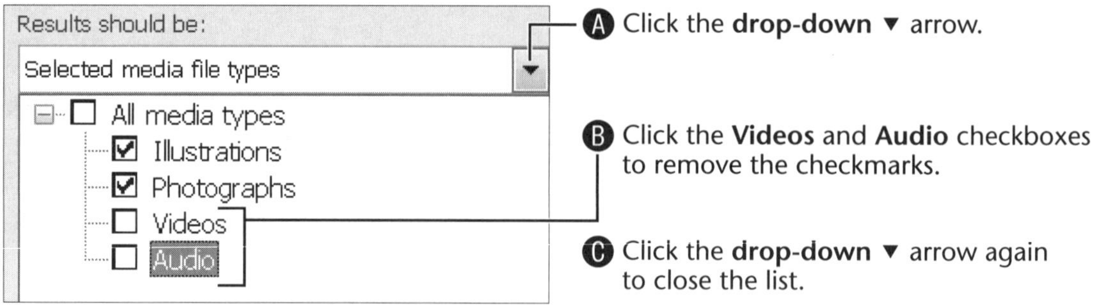

7. Make sure the **Include Office.com Content** checkbox toward the top of the task pane is checked.

8. Click the **Go** button in the upper-right corner to search for clip art.

9. Locate the **thumbprint** clip art image shown in the following figure.

If this clip art is not available, find an image you feel conveys the idea of *carbon footprint*.

10. Click the **image** once to place it in your flyer.

Resize, Rotate, and Center the Clip Art

11. Position the **mouse pointer** on the bottom-right handle of the image.
The mouse pointer changes to a double-headed arrow.

12. Drag **up** and to the **left** about an inch to make the image a bit smaller; release the **mouse button**.

Next you will center the image between the margins.

13. Make sure the **image** is still selected.

14. Choose **Home→Paragraph→Center** from the Ribbon.
Now you will rotate the clip art.

15. Make sure the **image** is selected.
The green rotate handle is visible at the top of the image.

16. Place the **mouse pointer** on the rotate handle.
The pointer changes to a circular arrow.

17. Drag the **handle** to the right approximately the same degree as shown in the following illustration.

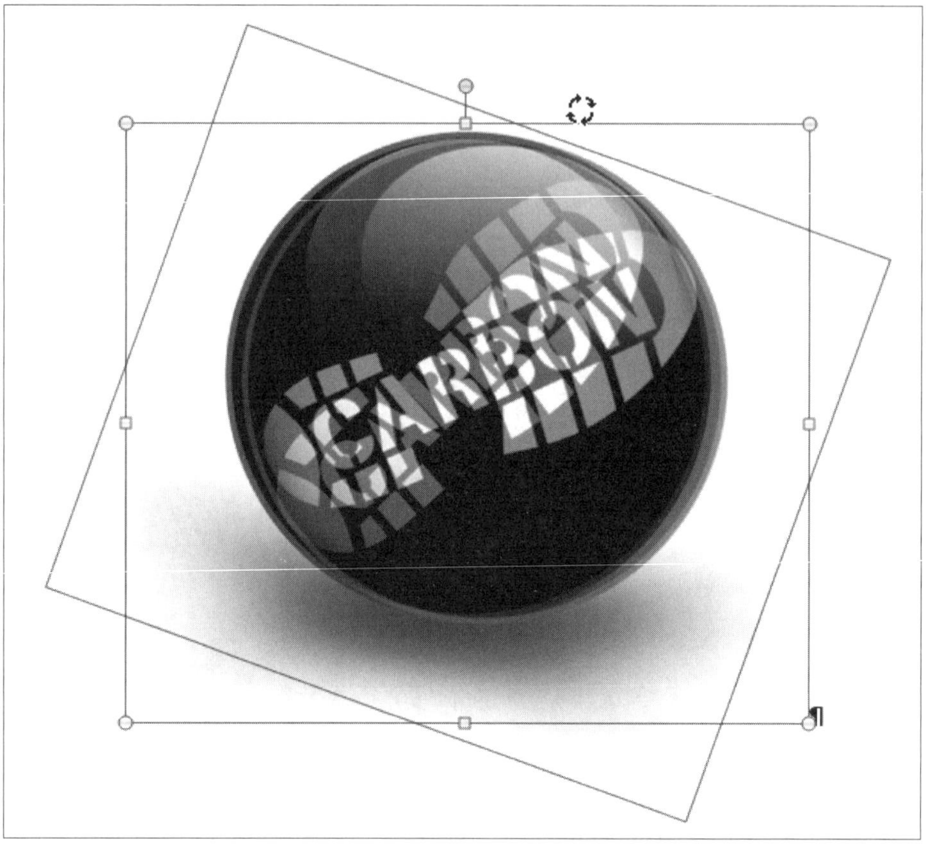

18. If any of the bullet points slip over to a second page, reduce the size of the image enough to place everything back on one page.

Save the Flyer in a New Folder

19. Click File and choose **Save As** from the menu.
20. If necessary, navigate to your Lesson 04 folder.
21. Click the **New Folder** button at the top of the dialog box.
22. Name the folder **`Science Projects`**.
23. If you are using Win 7, **double-click** the Science Projects folder to place it in the Save In box at the top of the dialog box.

    If you are using Win Vista or Win XP, the new folder automatically jumps to the Save In box at the top of the Save As dialog box. The name sb-Carbon Footprint should appear in the File Name box at the bottom of the dialog box.
24. **Save** and then **close** the flyer.

SKILL BUILDER 4.3 Use Wrap Text with Clip Art

In this exercise, you will insert a clip art image in a document and experiment with wrapping text and positioning the image on the page.

1. Open the sb-Photographs document from your Lesson 04 folder.
2. Click the **insertion point** at the beginning of the first main paragraph.

Insert Clip Art

3. Choose **Insert→Illustrations→Clip Art** from the Ribbon if the Clip Art task pane is not open.

   Leave the media type choices as they were in the last exercise; only Illustrations and Photographs should be selected.
4. Type **`photographer`** in the **Search For** box in the Clip Art task pane and click the **Go** button.
5. Locate the following **thumbnail image** in the search results or choose a different photographer image if this one is not available.

6. Click the **image** to insert it into the document.
7. Click the **Close** button in the upper-right corner of the Clip Art task pane to close it.
8. Resize the image to about a quarter of its original size. (If you chose a different image, size it to approximately 2 inches high by $1^{1}/_{2}$ inches wide.

Apply Text Wrapping

9. Make sure the **image** is selected.
10. Choose **Format→Arrange→Wrap Text** from the Ribbon.

    Notice that the icon for In Line with Text is highlighted, meaning it is the default wrapping style.
11. Choose **Square** from the menu.
12. Try out several other wrapping options, and then finally choose the **Square** wrapping style.

Test Various Positions

13. Choose **Format→Arrange→Position** from the Ribbon.
14. Hover the **mouse pointer** over several different positions to preview the various options.
15. Choose the **Top Right** position, as shown in the following figure.

16. **Save** and then **close** the file.
17. **Click** File and choose **Exit** from the menu.

LESSON 5

Excel – Tracking Firefighter Training

In this lesson, you will learn the basics of Excel 2010. You will enter and edit information in a spreadsheet, modify the spreadsheet by adding and deleting columns and rows, discover many convenient techniques for navigating in a spreadsheet, and learn a method for making column and row headings static so they won't scroll off the page when examining a spreadsheet that's longer or wider than your screen. Finally, you will copy, move, and sort data.

LESSON OBJECTIVES

After studying this lesson, you will be able to:

- Identify important parts of the Excel window
- Define spreadsheet terminology
- Examine mouse pointer shapes in Excel
- Navigate in a spreadsheet
- Freeze panes
- Enter and edit data
- Work with ranges of cells
- Move, copy, and sort data
- Insert, delete, and resize columns and rows

Student resources ***labyrinthelab.com/wtmo10***

Case Study: Creating a Training Database

Hans Gutman is an administrator at a fire department in his county. The chief asked him to set up a training database for the firefighters and emergency personnel. Hans finds that Excel is an excellent tool for the job. He realizes that the ability to sort the database on any column is extremely helpful in organizing data in the various ways the chief requests.

Last Name	First Name	Hire Date	Rank	Shift
Alexander	Martin	3/24/1999	Firefighter/EMT-Paramedic	3
Bryan	Henry	3/13/1996	Firefighter	2
Cooper	Douglas	2/12/2003	EMT-Paramedic	2
Elizondo	Jose	1/27/1992	Firefighter/EMT-Paramedic	2
Ellis	Gregory	8/14/1992	Firefighter/EMT-Intermediate	1
Frost	Suzanne	5/19/1996	Firefighter/EMT-Basic	1

Sorted by Last Name

Last Name	First Name	Hire Date	Rank	Shift
Smith	Anthony	12/16/1991	Firefighter/EMT-Basic	3
Elizondo	Jose	1/27/1992	Firefighter/EMT-Paramedic	2
Ellis	Gregory	8/14/1992	Firefighter/EMT-Intermediate	1
Paulson	Glenn	6/15/1993	Firefighter	1
Jensen	Oliver	8/25/1994	Firefighter/EMT-Intermediate	2

Sorted by Hire Date

Last Name	First Name	Hire Date	Rank	Shift
Ellis	Gregory	8/14/1992	Firefighter/EMT-Intermediate	1
Paulson	Glenn	6/15/1993	Firefighter	1
Malik	Hasan	12/4/1995	Firefighter/EMT-Basic	1
Frost	Suzanne	5/19/1996	Firefighter/EMT-Basic	1
Morgan	Jack	8/1/1996	Firefighter	1

Sorted by Shift

Understanding Excel

Excel 2010 is a spreadsheet (also known as worksheet) program that is part of the Microsoft Office 2010 suite of software programs. A spreadsheet program allows you to organize data in columns and rows, as well as analyze the data and perform calculations on it. There are three kinds of entries in spreadsheets: text, numbers, and formulas.

You can use spreadsheets for a wide variety of tasks, including income statements, financial statements, budgets, databases, and invoices.

Starting Excel 2010

Just like starting Word, you start Excel from the Start button on the taskbar in the bottom-left corner or your Windows Desktop. The appearance of the Start button varies depending on whether your computer uses Win 7, Win Vista, or Win XP.

Win 7/Vista **Win XP**

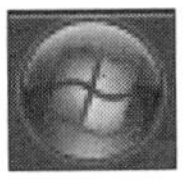

The program icon that opens the Excel program window is in the Microsoft Office folder, which appears when you click the All Programs menu after clicking the Start button.

HANDS-ON 5.1 Start Excel

In this exercise, you will start Excel using the Start button on the taskbar and the All Programs menu.

1. Click the **Start** / button then click the **All Programs** menu.
2. Click the **Microsoft Office folder** that appears in the menu then click **Microsoft Excel 2010**.
3. If necessary, click the **Maximize** button in the upper-right corner of the Excel window.

Exploring the Excel Window

Excel opens with a new blank workbook for you to enter and analyze data and maintain lists of information. There are a number of similarities between the Word window and the Excel window. For example, both windows have a File tab, a Ribbon, and a Quick Access toolbar.

The Suite Advantage Now you're starting to see the advantage of working with a suite of software programs. When you learn one program, you're a step ahead when it's time to learn the next one.

Don't be concerned if your workbook window looks slightly different from the following example. The Excel screen is customizable.

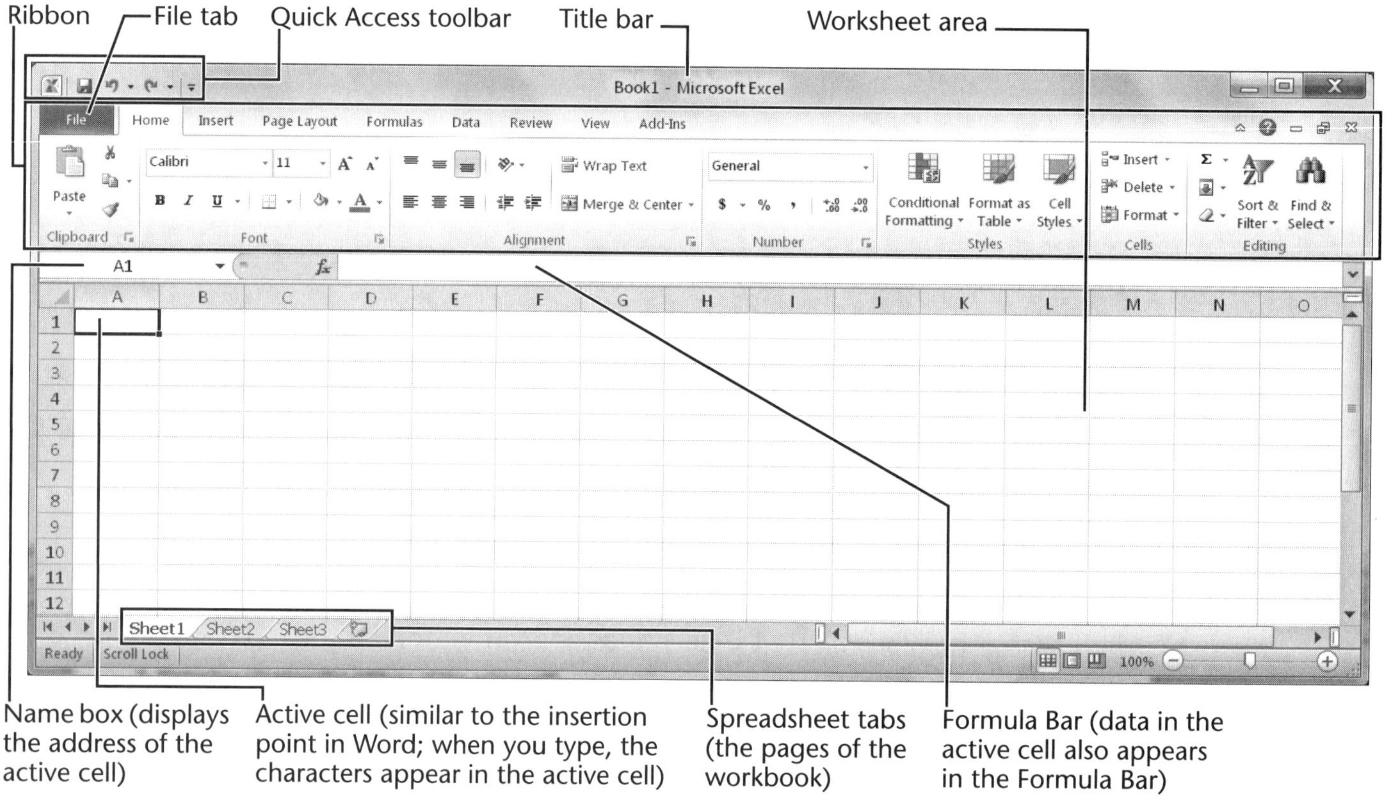

Understanding Workbook Organization

An Excel file is often referred to as a *workbook*. That's because, like a book, it's made up of pages. These pages are known as *spreadsheets* or *worksheets* (see the spreadsheet tabs in the previous illustration).

The Spreadsheet A spreadsheet is made up of a series of columns and rows. The columns are headed with alphabetic characters and the rows are headed with numbers. There are 16,384 columns and 1,048,576 rows. (That's probably more room than you will ever need!) Since there are only twenty-six letters in the alphabet, when Excel gets to column Z, it starts over with AA, AB, AC, and all the way through AZ, and then to moves to BA, BB, BC, and so forth.

Defining Cells A small rectangle appears wherever a column and row intersect. These rectangles are known as *cells*. All cells have addresses that are determined by the column and row indicators. The first cell in the upper-left corner of the spreadsheet—in column A and row 1—is called cell A1. A1 is currently the active cell in the following illustration; the active cell has a dark border around it. When you type data, it automatically goes into the active cell.

The address of the active cell appears in the Name Box at the left end of the Formula Bar.

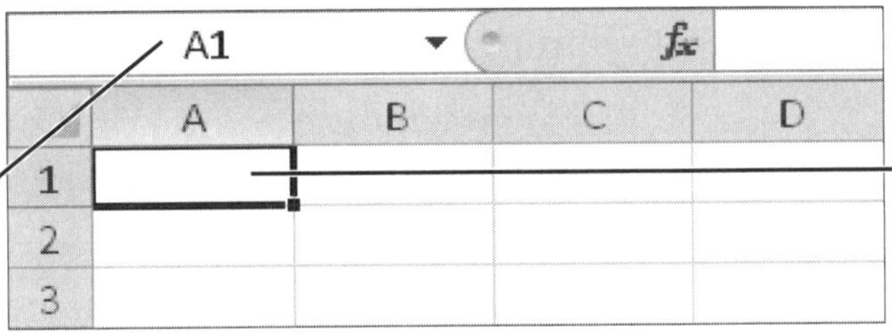

This is the active cell (A1).

Mouse Shapes in Excel

The mouse pointer in Excel takes on many different shapes, depending on what you are doing at the time. Excel behaves differently relative to the mouse pointer shape. The following table describes the mouse shapes and their purposes.

EXCEL MOUSE POINTER SHAPES

Mouse Shape	Purpose
	The thick white cross appears when the pointer is over a cell. Clicking when the pointer is a white cross selects a cell. Clicking and dragging with the white cross selects a range of cells.
	The AutoFill shape appears when you place the mouse pointer on the tiny square (fill handle) in the bottom-right corner of a selected cell. Dragging the fill handle either copies cells or generates a data series to adjacent cells.
	The mouse pointer looks like a white arrow when you move it over the Ribbon or when you use the scroll bars.

EXCEL MOUSE POINTER SHAPES (CONTINUED)

Mouse Shape	Purpose
	The move pointer displays when you hover the mouse pointer over the edge of a cell (except in the bottom-right corner) or a range of selected cells. You can then click and drag to move cells to a new location.
	The mouse pointer changes to the resize pointer when you place it between row or column headers. You can then click and drag to change the size of rows or columns. You can also double-click when the mouse pointer is between columns to make the column as wide as its widest entry.
	When the mouse pointer is on a row header, it changes to a right-pointing arrow, which, when clicked, selects the entire row.
	Placing the mouse pointer on a column header changes the pointer to a down-pointing arrow, which you can click to select the entire column.
	The I-beam appears when you are entering or editing text in the Formula Bar or within a cell.

Navigating in a Spreadsheet

If you are working with a large spreadsheet, it's convenient to know some techniques for moving around quickly. There are a number of mouse moves and keyboard techniques you can use. Some of them are the same as those used in Word.

Using the Scroll Bars to Navigate

When you navigate with scroll bars, the active cell does not move. After scrolling, you must click in the spreadsheet to reposition the active cell. You can see from the following figure that scrolling in Excel is similar to scrolling in Word.

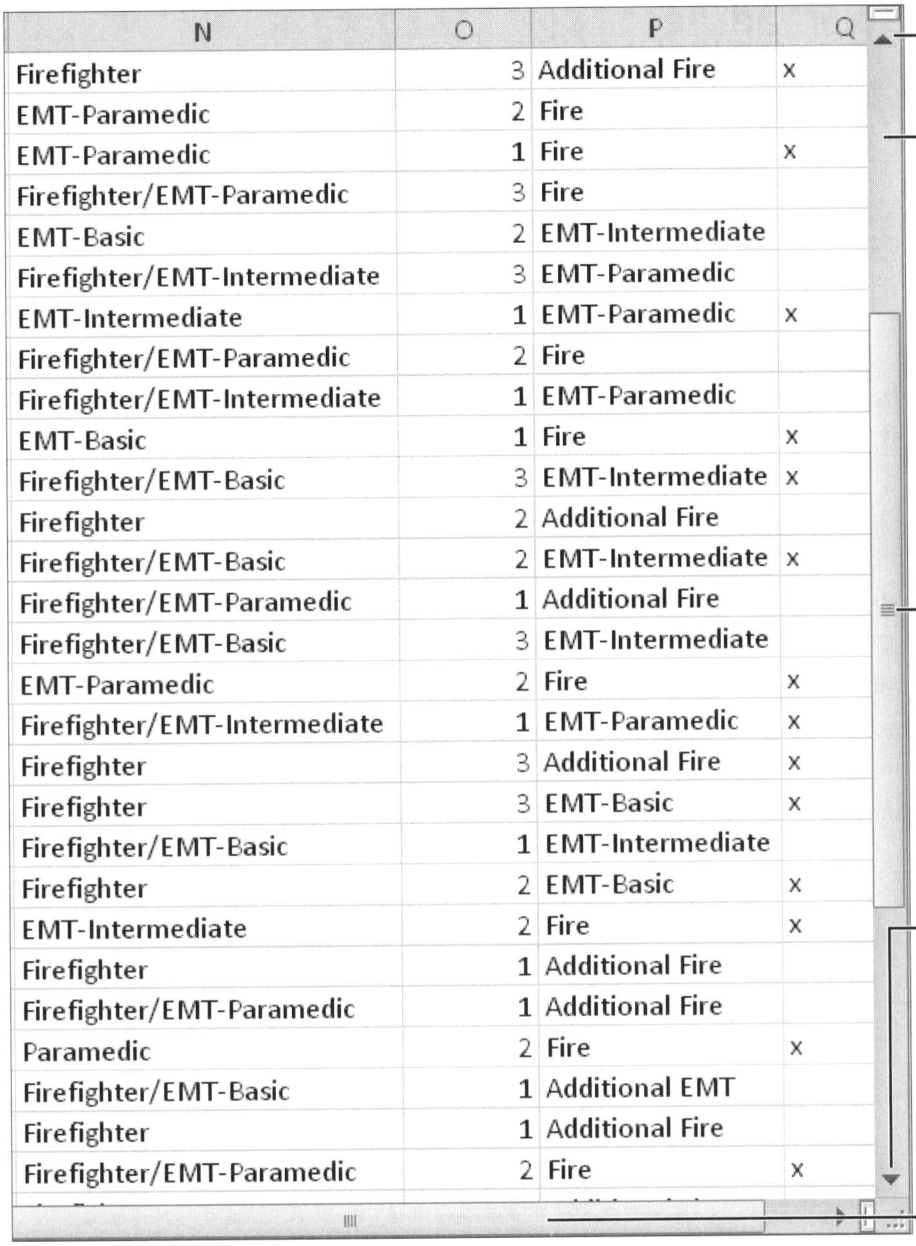

Clicking this button scrolls the spreadsheet up one row at a time.

Clicking the open part of the scroll bar, above or below the scroll box, moves the spreadsheet up or down one screen at a time.

Dragging the scroll box with the mouse pointer quickly moves you to a new location.

Clicking this button scrolls the spreadsheet down one row at a time.

Similar techniques apply to the horizontal scroll bar.

HANDS-ON 5.2 Scroll in a Spreadsheet

In this exercise, you will open a workbook and scroll around in a spreadsheet.

1. Click File and choose **Open** from the menu.
2. Navigate to the Lesson 05 folder and open Training Roster.
3. Follow these steps to use the scroll bar to navigate in a spreadsheet:

Ⓐ Click the **scroll down** button on the vertical scroll bar to move down one row. Press and hold down the **mouse button** while pointing at the scroll down button to rapidly scroll down the spreadsheet.

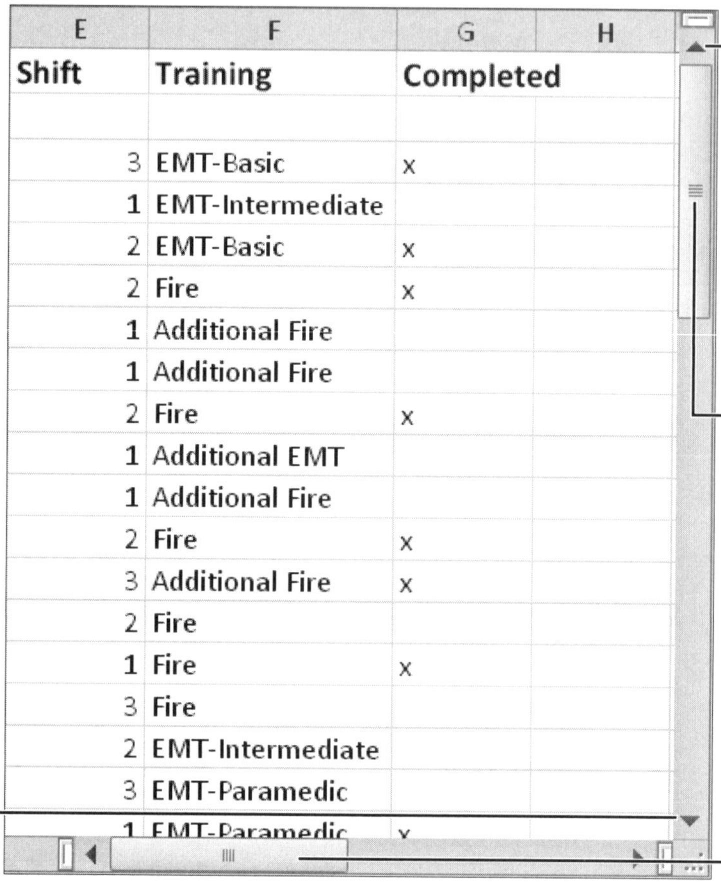

Ⓑ Click the **scroll up** button on the scroll bar once to move up one row. Press and hold down the **mouse button** while pointing at the **scroll up** button to rapidly scroll up to the top of the scroll bar.

Ⓒ Press and hold down the **mouse button** while pointing at the scroll box, then drag down to quickly move down the spreadsheet. (The change is not dramatic in this example since the spreadsheet is not very long.) Drag the scroll box to the top of the scroll bar.

Ⓓ Try these techniques using the horizontal scroll bar.

Notice that the active cell does not change position when you scroll through a spreadsheet.

Leave the file open. You will use it throughout the lesson.

Using the Keyboard to Navigate

If your hands are on the keyboard, it may be faster to use keyboard navigation. Excel has keyboard shortcuts for navigating, as shown in the following table. Unlike scrolling, when you navigate using the keyboard, the active cell moves with you.

QUICK REFERENCE: Navigating with the Keyboard in Excel

Command	Notes
Ctrl+Home	Moves to A1
Ctrl+End	Moves to the end of the data in the spreadsheet
Home	Moves to the beginning of the row
Page Down	Moves down one screen
Page Up	Moves up one screen
→ ← ↑ ↓	Moves one cell to the right, left, up, or down

HANDS-ON 5.3 Navigate with the Keyboard

In this exercise, you will use keyboard techniques to move around a spreadsheet.

1. **Tap** → ← ↑ ↓ on the keyboard a few times to move through the spreadsheet.
2. **Press and hold** ↓ to produce a repeat action effect.
   All four arrow keys have a repeat action if you hold them down.
3. **Hold down** Ctrl and **tap** Home to move to cell A1.
   Do you remember the same keystrokes in Word? You're getting twice the benefit from one learned task.
4. **Tap** Ctrl+End to move to the end of the data in the spreadsheet.
5. **Tap** Home to move to the beginning of the row.
6. **Press** Ctrl+Home to move back to A1.

Freezing Panes

You may have a spreadsheet so large that when you scroll down to see the last row of data, the headings at the tops of columns move off the screen. It can be difficult to understand the meaning of data if the column headings disappear. The same is true of a wide spreadsheet and row headings. Scrolling to the right could cause the headings to disappear, again making it difficult to understand what the data represents.

Freezing columns and rows allows you to keep the column and row headings visible while examining data in any part of the spreadsheet—even data that is not close to the headings. The Freeze Panes command options are described in the following table.

QUICK REFERENCE: Freezing Columns and Rows

Command	Notes
Freeze Top Row	As you scroll down the spreadsheet, the top row remains visible. The top row is whatever row appears at the top of the screen when you freeze panes. It may not be row 1 of the spreadsheet.
Freeze First Column	As you scroll to the right, the first column remains visible. The first column is whatever column appears at the left edge of the screen when you freeze panes. It may not be column A of the spreadsheet.
Freeze Panes	Select a cell and choose the Freeze Panes command to freeze everything above and to the left of the selected cell.
Unfreeze Panes	Unlocks the frozen columns and/or rows.

HANDS-ON 5.4 Freeze Panes

In this exercise, you will freeze rows and columns so they remain static when you scroll in the spreadsheet.

1. Scroll down the spreadsheet until the **column headings** disappear off the screen.

   Without the column headings, it's difficult to understand the meaning of the data.

2. **Press** [Ctrl]+[Home] to move to **cell A1**.

Freeze the First Row

3. Choose **View→Window→Freeze Panes** from the Ribbon.

4. Choose **Freeze Top Row** from the menu.

   Notice the dark line that appears below row 1, indicating that the freeze action is in effect.

NOTE! The *top row* is the row that happens to appear at the top of the screen at the time you choose Freeze Top Row from the menu, not necessarily row 1.

5. Follow these steps to see the effect of freezing the top row:

Ⓐ Scroll down the screen until **row 16** is just below row 1.

	A	B	C	D
1	**Last Nam**	**First Name**		**Rank**
16	Alexander	Martin		Firefighter/EMT-Paramedic
17	Mahal	Jasleen		EMT-Basic
18	Wright	Roger		Firefighter/EMT-Intermediate
19	Webster	Alan		EMT-Intermediate
20	Penbrook	Robert		Firefighter/EMT-Paramedic
21	Schultz	Edward		Firefighter/EMT-Intermediate
22	Waldek	John		EMT-Basic
23	Smith	Anthony		Firefighter/EMT-Basic
24	Swan	Edwin		Firefighter
25	Iverson	George		Firefighter/EMT-Basic

Ⓑ Notice that the column headings in row 1 are still visible, making the meaning of the data easy to understand.

6. Scroll back to the **top** of the spreadsheet.

Freeze the First Column

7. Choose **View→Window→Freeze Panes** from the Ribbon.

8. Choose **Freeze First Column** from the menu.

   This unfreezes the first row and freezes the first column. Notice that the dark line is no longer below row 1 and a dark line now appears to the right of column A.

   NOTE! The *first column* is the column that happens to appear at the left edge of the screen at the time you choose Freeze First Column, not necessarily column A.

9. Scroll to the **right** and notice that the first column remains in place.

Clear Freeze Panes

10. Choose **View→Window→Freeze Panes** from the Ribbon.

11. Choose **Unfreeze Panes** from the menu.

    The dark line to the right of column A disappears.

Freeze Columns and Rows at the Same Time

12. Select **cell D2** to make it the active cell.

13. Choose **View→Window→Freeze Panes** from the Ribbon.

14. Choose **Freeze Panes** from the menu.

    Notice the dark horizontal and vertical lines that indicate everything above and to the left of the active cell (D2) is frozen.

15. Follow these steps to scroll in both directions:

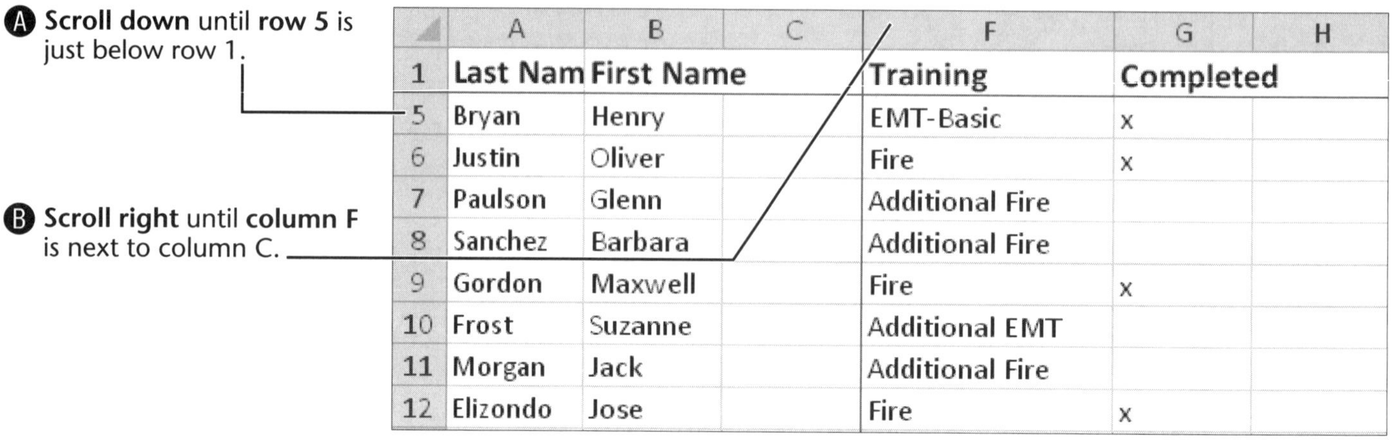

16. Choose **View→Window→Freeze Panes** from the Ribbon, and then choose **Unfreeze Panes** from the menu.

Entering Data in a Spreadsheet

Now that you're getting comfortable with spreadsheet terminology and navigation, it's time to learn to enter data so you can keep the training roster up to date with the latest information.

When you start to enter data in a spreadsheet, the Cancel and Enter buttons appear at the left side of the Formula Bar. This indicates that you are *in the process* of entering data.

Completing and Canceling Cell Entries

Once you type data in a cell, the next step is to complete the entry. Or, if you suddenly realize that you selected the wrong cell, you may want to cancel the entry. The following table describes the methods you can use to complete and cancel cell entries.

QUICK REFERENCE: Completing and Canceling Cell Entries

Method	Result
Tap [Enter]	Excel completes the entry; the active cell moves down one row.
Tap [Tab]	Excel completes the entry; the active cell moves to the right one column.
Tap an arrow key on the keyboard	Excel completes the entry; the active cell moves in the direction of the arrow.
Click the Enter ✓ button on the Formula Bar	Excel completes the entry; the active cell remains active.
Click the Cancel ✕ button on the Formula Bar	Excel removes any data typed in the cell; the active cell remains active.
Tap [Esc]	Excel removes any data typed in the cell; the active cell remains active.

HANDS-ON 5.5 Enter Data in a Spreadsheet

In this exercise, you will enter data in a spreadsheet using several data entry techniques as you add a new firefighter to the roster.

1. Follow these steps to enter data in the spreadsheet:

Ⓐ Select **cell A31** and type **`Montoya`**. Don't tap [Enter] yet.

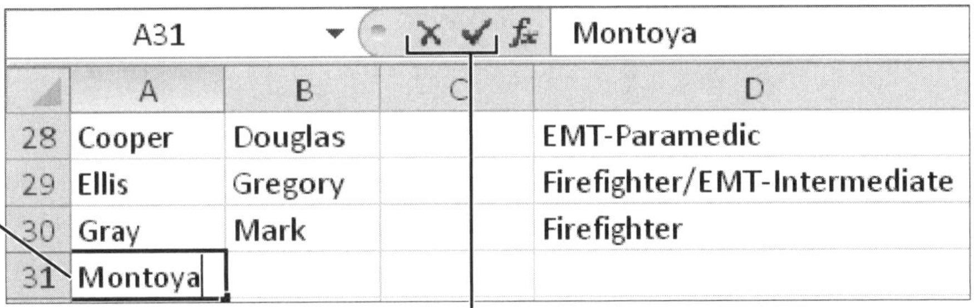

Ⓑ The Cancel and Enter buttons appear on the Formula Bar, which means you have not completed the entry.

Ⓒ **Tap** [Enter] to finish entering the data.

The Cancel and Enter buttons disappear from the Formula Bar and the active cell moves down one row.

2. Select **cell A31** again and look at the Formula Bar.

You see that the data you entered appears in the Formula Bar as well as in the cell. Later in this lesson, you will use the Formula Bar to make editing changes.

3. Follow these steps to enter data in cell B31:

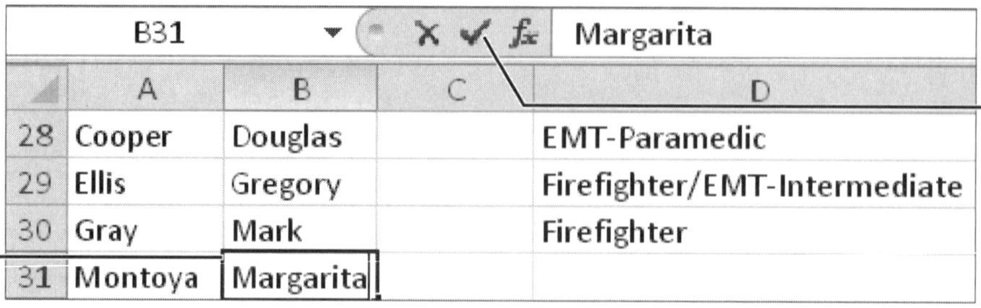

Cell B31 remains the active cell when you click the Enter button.

4. Select **cell D31** and type **Firefighter**, and this time **tap** [↓] to complete the entry.

   Tapping [↓] has the same effect as tapping [Enter]: the active cell moves down one row. Cell D32 is now the active cell.

5. Select **cell E31**, type **3**, and complete the entry by **tapping** [Tab].

   This moves the active cell one column to the right and cell F31 is now the active cell. You will enter the term *Fire* in cell F31. Because the word *Fire* already appears in column F, Excel will use AutoComplete (similar to Word) to enter the term for you.

6. Type **F** in cell F31 and watch as Excel autocompletes *Fire*.

7. **Tap** [Tab] to complete the entry.

   NOTE! If you want to type something other than what Excel proposes, just keep typing.

8. **Save** the file.

Editing in Excel

After entering data in a spreadsheet, you can modify it if there are errors or if the data changes. You can delete data, or you can replace data by simply typing over the current data. On the other hand, if it's a long or complex entry, you can edit the data (similar to editing in Word) in the Formula Bar or directly in the cell.

QUICK REFERENCE: Deleting, Replacing, and Editing Data

Task	Procedure
Delete an entry	Select the cell and tap [Delete].
Replace an entry	Select the cell, type the new data, and complete the entry.
Edit in the Formula Bar	Select the cell and its data appears in the Formula Bar. Click to place the insertion point in the Formula Bar, and then modify the data.
Use in-cell editing	Double-click the cell to place the insertion point in the cell. Modify the data in the cell.

HANDS-ON 5.6 Edit Data in a Spreadsheet

In this exercise, you will use several different editing techniques to modify your spreadsheet. You realize that Mark Gray (row 30) did not complete his Additional Fire training yet, so the first thing you will do is delete the "x" in cell G30.

1. Select **cell G30** and **tap** [Delete].

   Oliver Justin's (row 6) last name is incorrect. It should be *Jensen*.

2. Select **cell A6**, type **`Jensen`**, and **tap** [Enter].

   The correct name replaces the original entry. Next you will correct Oliver's title by adding the word *Firefighter* in front of *EMT-Intermediate*.

Edit in the Formula Bar

3. Follow these steps to make the correction.

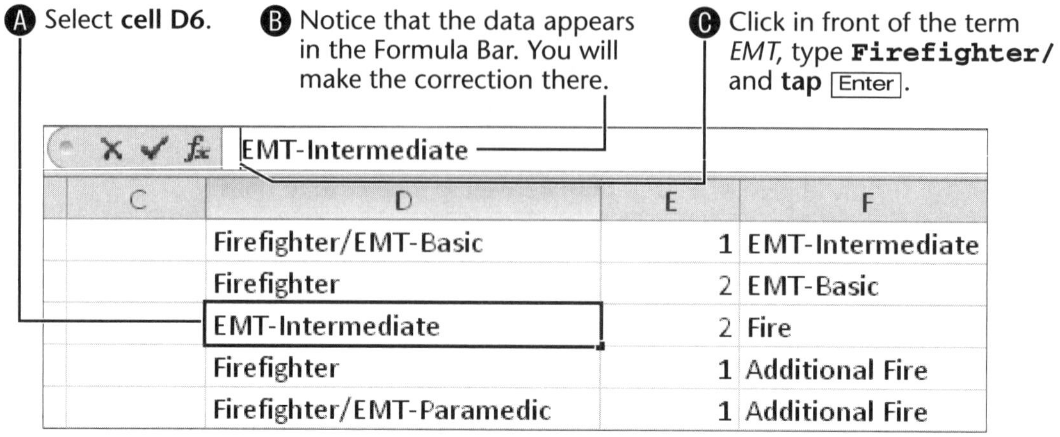

Because Oliver is already a firefighter, he doesn't need Fire training, he needs Additional Fire training. This time you will make the editing change directly in the cell.

Use In-cell Editing

4. **Double-click** cell F6.

   This places the insertion point in the cell and causes the mouse pointer to change to an I-beam.

5. If necessary, click in front of *Fire* and type **Additional**; then **tap** [Spacebar] and **tap** [Tab].

   The active cell is now cell G6. Oliver has not completed the Additional Fire training.

6. **Tap** [Delete] to remove the "x" from cell G6.

7. **Save** the file.

Aligning Cell Contents

By default, Excel aligns text to the left edge of cells and numbers to the right edge of cells. You can use the alignment buttons on the Ribbon to modify alignment within cells.

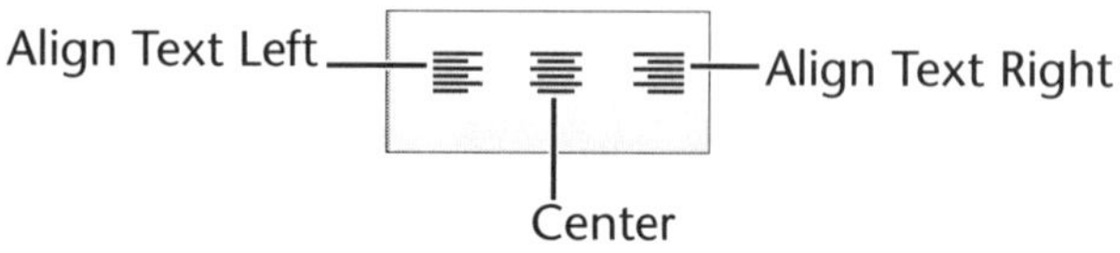

HANDS-ON 5.7 Align Data in Cells

In this exercise, you will use the alignment buttons to change the alignment of data in your spreadsheet.

1. Select **cell D1**.
2. Choose **Home→Alignment→Align Text Right** from the Ribbon.
3. Choose **Home→Alignment→Center** from the Ribbon.
4. Select **cell E1**.
5. Choose **Home→Alignment→Center** from the Ribbon.
6. Now **center** the text in **cell F1**.
7. **Save** your spreadsheet.

Working with Ranges of Cells

A range of cells is a group of adjacent cells. You select (or highlight) ranges of cells when you want to do something with them, such as formatting, moving, or copying them. You can also use cell ranges in formulas, which you will learn about in Lesson 6, Excel – Budgeting with Calculations and Charts.

You identify cell ranges by the cell addresses in the upper-left and lower-right corners of the range. A colon is placed between the two cell addresses, such as A1:C10. This is described as A1 *through* C10.

When you select a range of cells, a white cell appears in the upper-left corner of the range. This is the active cell. If you type data, it will appear in the white cell. The following Quick Reference table describes several techniques for selecting cells.

QUICK REFERENCE: Selecting Cell Ranges

Task	Procedure
Select a range	• Select the first cell in the range, press and hold the mouse button, and drag to the last cell. *or* • Select the first cell in the range, press and hold the [Shift] key, and click the last cell in the range. *or* • Click the first cell in the range, hold down the [Shift] key, and tap the arrow keys to select the range.
Select a column	• Click the column header. For example, to select column A, click directly on the A at the top of the column.
Select a row	• Click the row header. For example, to select row 1, click directly on the 1 at the beginning of the row.
Select the entire spreadsheet	• Click the Select All button in the upper-left corner of the spreadsheet. 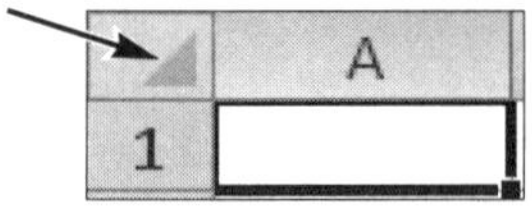

HANDS-ON 5.8 Select Ranges of Cells

In this exercise, you will use several techniques for selecting cell ranges.

1. Follow these steps to select the range A1:E9.

Ⓐ Position the mouse pointer in **cell A1**, press and hold the mouse button, and drag down and to the right to **cell E9**.

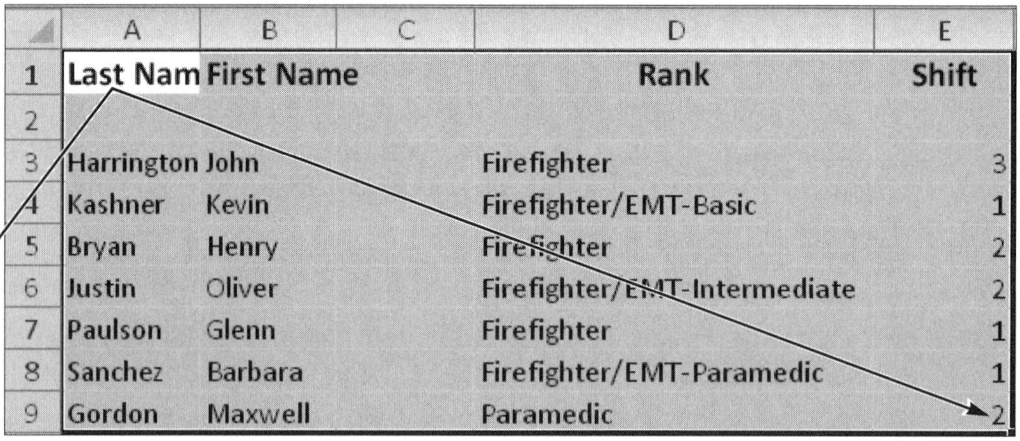

Ⓑ Release the mouse button and the range is selected. If you make a mistake, click anywhere in the spreadsheet to deselect the range and try again.

2. Click any cell to deselect the range.
3. Select **cell A1**.

4. **Hold down** Shift and click **cell E9** to select the range A1:E9.
5. Click any cell to deselect the range.

Select a Range with Arrow Keys

6. Click **cell A1**; then, **hold down** Shift and **tap** → four times to select through column E.
7. While **holding down** Shift, **tap** ↓ enough times to highlight through row 9.

   Notice that the highlighting of the row headers and column headers helps you see which rows and columns you selected.
8. Click any cell to deselect the range.

   Next you will select column D. When you select a column, the mouse pointer looks like a down-pointing black arrow.
9. Place the mouse pointer over the column header for **column D** and click.

   This selects the entire column—all the way down to row 1,048,576.

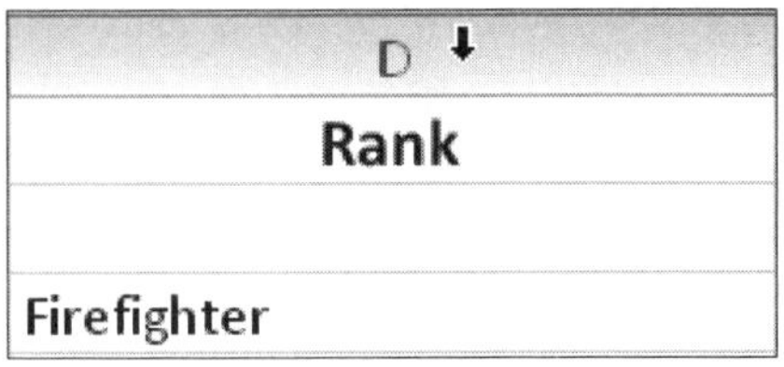

10. Place the mouse pointer over the row header for **row 1** and click.

This selects the entire row—all the way over to column 16,384.

11. Place the mouse pointer over the **Select All** button, as shown in the following figure, and click.

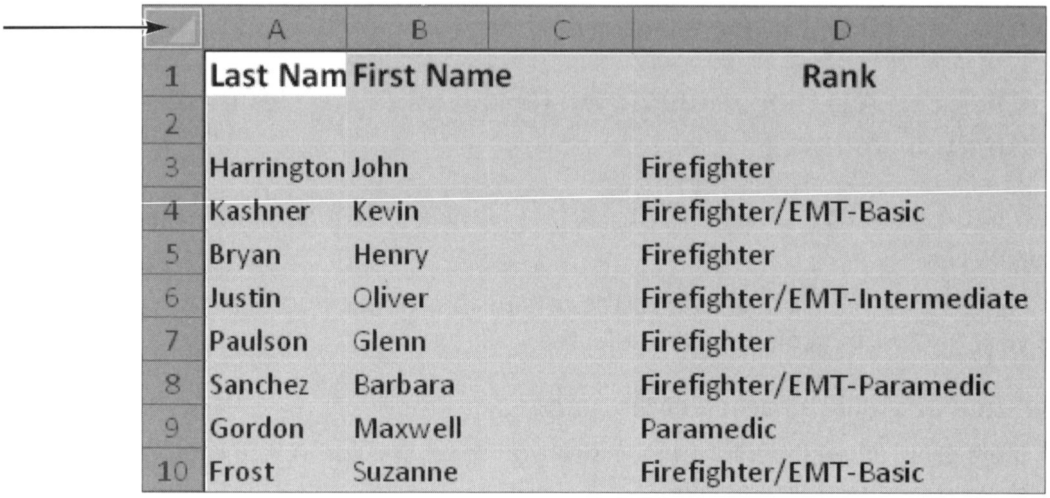

This selects the entire spreadsheet.

12. **Press** Ctrl+Home to deselect and make cell A1 the active cell.

Moving and Copying Data

Moving and copying data in a spreadsheet eliminates the need to retype it, thus saving time. When you move data, you remove it from its original position and place it in a new location. When you copy data, the original remains in place while a copy of the data is placed in a new location—so it's in both places.

The following Quick Reference table shows the sequence of steps for moving data.

QUICK REFERENCE: Moving Data with Cut and Paste

Task	Procedure
Move data	• Select the cell(s) you want to move. • Click the Cut button. • Click the destination cell. • Click the Paste button.

HANDS-ON 5.9 Move Data

In this exercise, you will use the Cut and Paste buttons to move data.

1. Follow these steps to move data from column F to column I:

A Select the **range F1:F10**.

B Choose **Home→Clipboard→Cut** from the Ribbon. (A flashing marquee surrounds the cut cells to indicate that you are in the process of moving cells.)

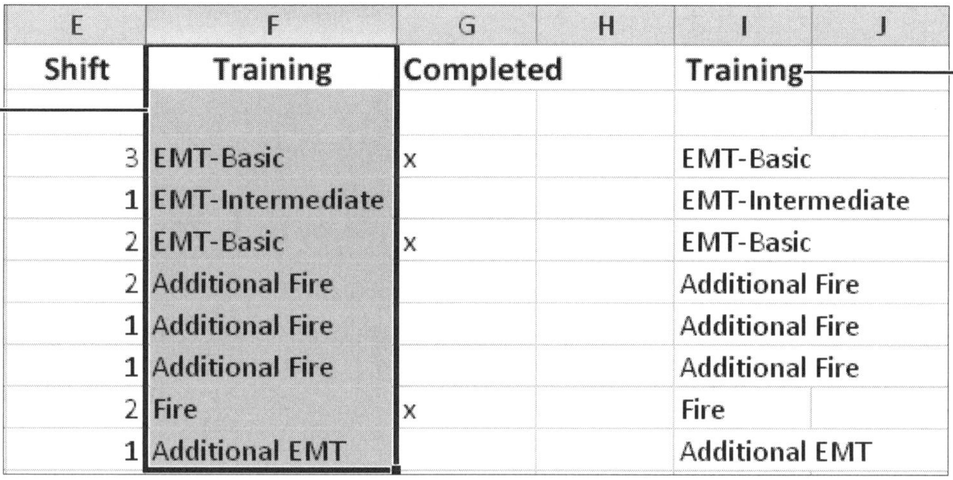

C Select **cell I1.**

D Choose **Home→Clipboard→Paste** from the Ribbon. The data moves from the original range to the new range. (At this point you should not have any data in F1:F10.)

2. **Save** the file.

Copying Data

You can use the Copy and Paste buttons on the Ribbon to copy data. The following Quick Reference table shows the sequence of steps for copying data.

QUICK REFERENCE: Copying Data with Copy and Paste

Task	Procedure
Copy and paste data	• Select the cell(s) you want to copy. • Click the button. • Click the destination cell. • Click the Paste button.

HANDS-ON 5.10 Copy Data

In this exercise, you will use the Copy and Paste buttons to make a copy of data in the spreadsheet.

1. Follow these steps to copy data from column I to column K:

Ⓐ Select the **range I1:I10**.

Ⓑ Choose **Home→Clipboard→Copy** from the Ribbon.

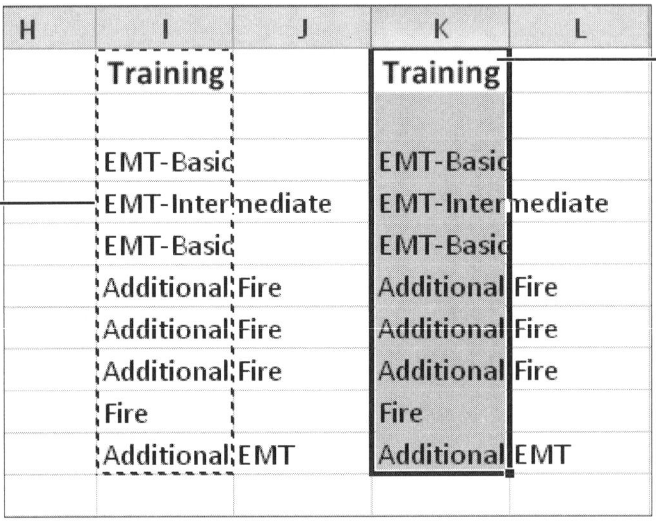

Ⓒ Select **cell K1**.

Ⓓ Choose **Home→Clipboard→Paste** from the Ribbon. A copy of the data appears in column K. Because you copied the data instead of moving it, the data is visible in both columns I and K.

The flashing marquee will disappear as you work in the spreadsheet; however, you can make it go away any time by tapping the Esc key.

2. If desired, **tap** Esc.

3. **Save** the file.

Sorting Data

Organizing data in a logical sequence often makes the data easier to understand and work with. Sorting information alphabetically or numerically is one of the primary capabilities of a spreadsheet program like Excel. This also means that you can create lists randomly, placing all new entries at the bottom of the list and then asking Excel to sort the list for you.

Kinds of Sorts

The kind of sort Excel offers to perform is based on the type of data in the column by which you want to sort. If you select a cell in an alphabetic column, Excel offers to sort from A to Z or from Z to A. If the column contains numbers, Excel proposes sorting from smallest to largest or from largest to smallest. If the column is populated with dates, Excel will sort from oldest to newest or from newest to oldest.

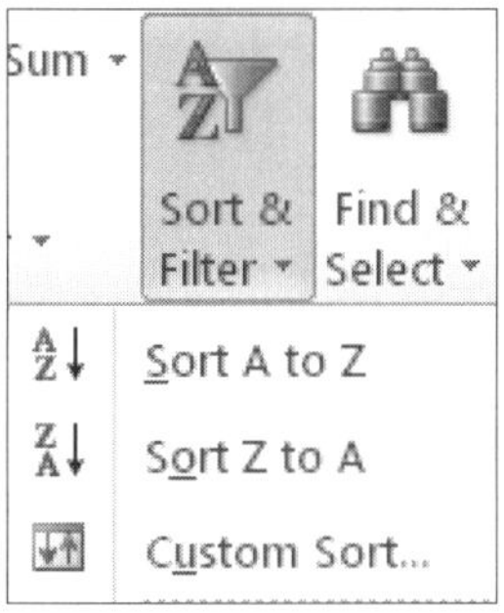

Alphabetic sort options

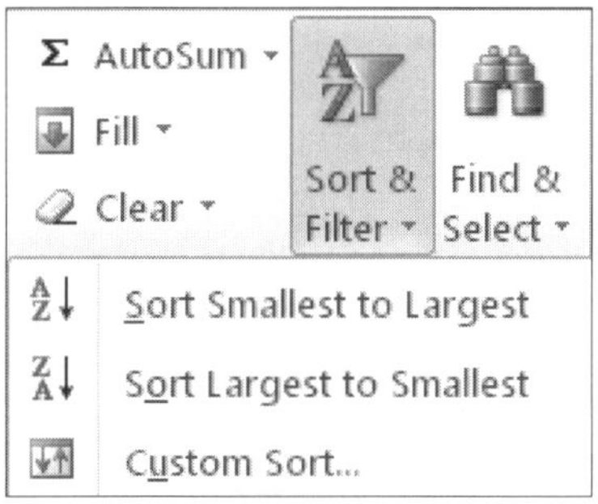

Numeric sort options

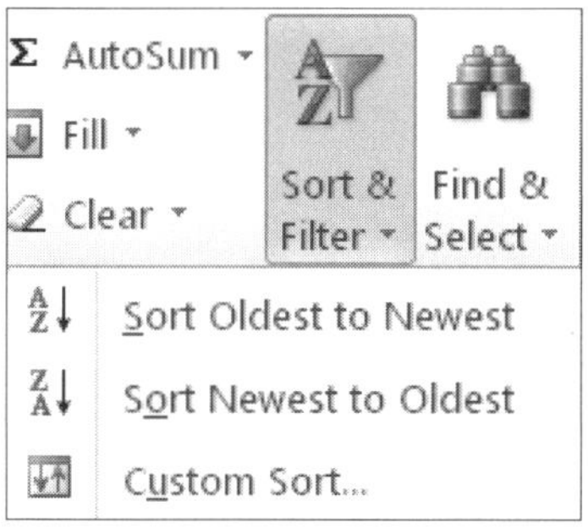

Date sort options

Structuring an Effective List

There are a few things you should keep in mind when creating a list that you can sort effectively.

- **No blanks:** There can be no blank columns or rows in a list. Blanks can cause serious problems when sorting a list. All data must be adjacent. (It's fine to have blank cells *within* a column/row, but the entire column or row cannot be blank.)
- **Consistent terminology:** This ensures that items that are meant to sort together stay together. For example, if you are a car dealer and you sell SUVs, you shouldn't refer to such vehicles as a *SUV* in one row and as a *sport utility* in another row. Excel does not consider these two terms to be the same.

HANDS-ON 5.11 Sort Data

In this exercise, you will execute an alphabetic sort, a numeric sort, and a date sort. You will begin by switching to the Sheet 2 page in your workbook.

1. Click the **Sheet 2** tab at the bottom of the workbook to switch to that spreadsheet.

   Notice that there are no blank columns or rows in this list. That's a prerequisite for a successful sort.

Perform an Alphabetic Sort

2. Select any cell in **column A** that is within the list.
3. Choose **Home→Editing→Sort & Filter** from the Ribbon.
4. Choose **Sort A to Z** from the menu.

   The list is now in alphabetic order by last name.

Perform a Date Sort

5. Select any cell in **column C** that is within the list.
6. Choose **Home→Editing→Sort & Filter** from the Ribbon.
7. Choose **Sort Oldest to Newest** from the menu.

   The oldest date appears at the top of the list.

Perform a Numeric Sort

8. Select any cell in **column E** that is within the list.
9. Choose **Home→Editing→Sort & Filter** from the Ribbon.
10. Choose **Sort Smallest to Largest** from the menu.

    The shifts are now in numeric order starting with the first shift.

11. **Save** the file.

Working with Columns and Rows

Excel provides the ability to widen and narrow columns and rows, meaning you can adjust columns to fit the data you enter in them. You also have the ability to add and delete columns and rows.

Resizing Columns and Rows

If data is too wide for a column, you can resize it so all of the text fits the column. If the data is narrow, you can narrow the column width.

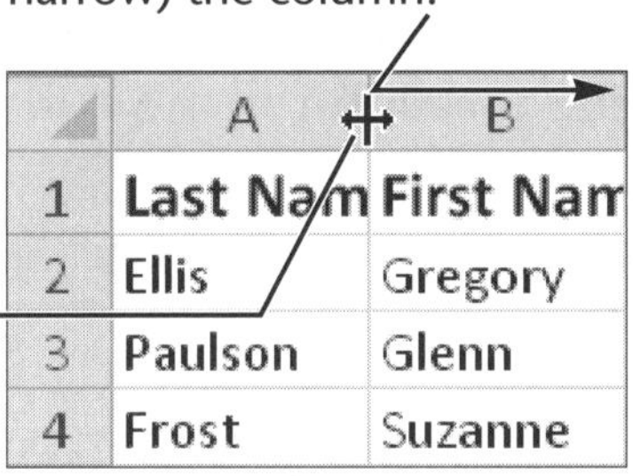

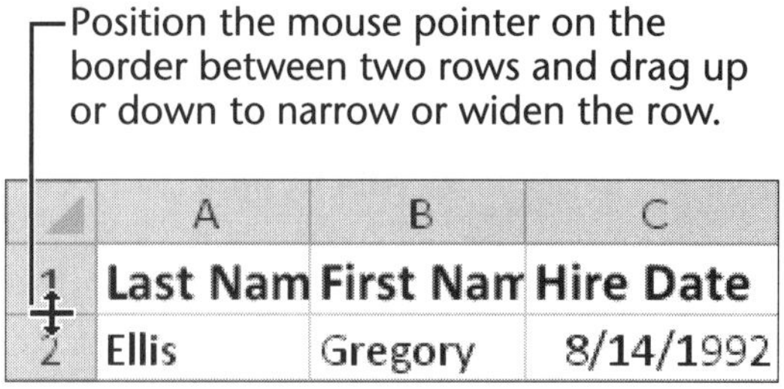

TIP! You can double-click the border between two column headers. This is known as *Best Fit,* and it makes the column wide enough to accommodate the widest entry in the column.

HANDS-ON 5.12 Resize Columns

In this exercise, you will resize columns A, B, and G to accommodate the width of the column headings.

Before You Begin: Make sure Sheet 2 is still active.

1. Position the mouse pointer on the border between **columns A and B,** as shown in the following figure.
   The mouse pointer changes to a double-headed arrow.

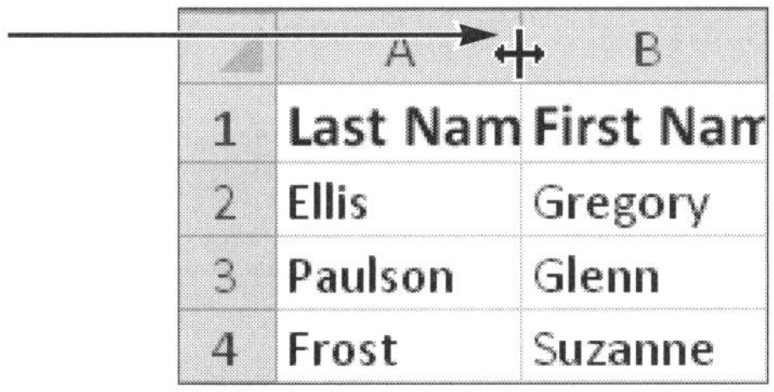

2. **Press and hold** down the **mouse button**, and then **drag** to the **right**.

3. **Release** the **mouse button** when you think *Last Name* is fully visible.
4. If you didn't make the column wide enough, repeat the process until you can see the entire column heading.
5. **Position** the mouse pointer on the border between **columns B and C**.

   The mouse pointer changes to a double-headed arrow.
6. **Press and hold down** the **mouse button**; then **drag** to the **right** to widen the column enough to see the complete column heading.

Double-click to Widen a Column

7. Position the mouse pointer between **columns G and H**.
8. When the pointer changes to a double-headed arrow, **double-click** and Excel makes the column wide enough for the column heading.
9. **Save** the file.

Inserting and Deleting Columns and Rows

Once you create a spreadsheet, you may discover that you need to add or remove entire columns or rows. For example, you may need to accommodate a change in the data. You can add or delete a single column or row, or you can add and delete multiple columns or rows at once.

QUICK REFERENCE: Inserting and Deleting Columns and Rows

Task	Procedure
Insert rows	• Select the row where you want the new row to appear. • Choose Home→Cells→Insert menu ▾ button from the Ribbon. • Choose Insert Sheet Rows from the menu.
Insert columns	• Select the column where you want the new column to appear. • Choose Home→Cells→Insert menu ▾ button from the Ribbon. • Choose Insert Sheet Columns from the menu.

Task	Procedure
Delete rows	• Select the row you want to delete. • Choose Home→Cells→Delete menu ▾ button from the Ribbon. • Choose Delete Sheet Rows from the menu.
Delete columns	• Select the Column you want to delete. • Choose Home→Cells→Delete menu ▾ button from the Ribbon. • Choose Delete Sheet Columns from the menu.

TIP! If you select multiple rows or columns before issuing the Insert or Delete command, the same number of rows or columns that you selected will be inserted or deleted.

HANDS-ON 5.13 Insert and Delete Columns and Rows

In this exercise, you will insert and delete columns and rows in your Training Roster file.

Before You Begin: Make sure Sheet 2 is still active.

Insert a Row

A firefighter just transferred from another station in your county. He was hired into the county in 1995. Rather than adding him at the bottom of the list and resorting the data, you'll just add him above row 4.

1. **Position** the **mouse pointer** on the row header for **row 4**, as shown in the following illustration, and then **click** to select the row.

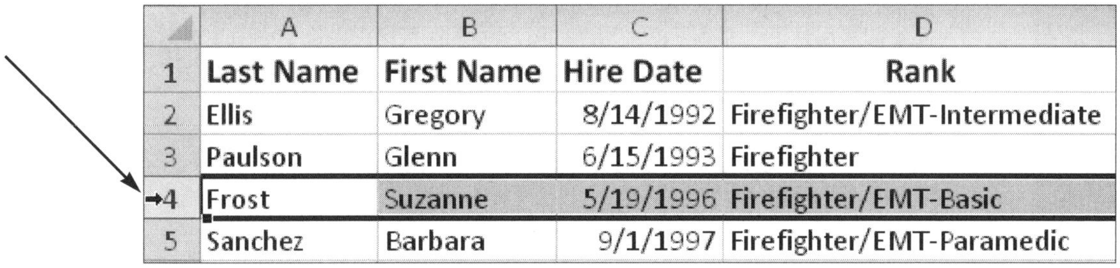

	A	B	C	D
1	Last Name	First Name	Hire Date	Rank
2	Ellis	Gregory	8/14/1992	Firefighter/EMT-Intermediate
3	Paulson	Glenn	6/15/1993	Firefighter
4	Frost	Suzanne	5/19/1996	Firefighter/EMT-Basic
5	Sanchez	Barbara	9/1/1997	Firefighter/EMT-Paramedic

2. Choose **Home→Cells→Insert** menu ▾ button from the Ribbon.

3. Choose **Insert Sheet Rows** from the menu.

   Row 4 is now a blank row.

4. Type the following information shown in row 4:

	A	B	C	D	E	F	G
1	**Last Name**	**First Name**	**Hire Date**	**Rank**	**Shift**	**Training**	**Completed**
2	Ellis	Gregory	8/14/1992	Firefighter/EMT-Intermediate	1	EMT-Paramedic	x
3	Paulson	Glenn	6/15/1993	Firefighter	1	Additional Fire	
4	Malik	Hasan	12/4/1995	Firefighter/EMT-Basic	1	EMT-Paramedic	

Insert a Column

Some of the firefighters are involved in community outreach programs. As part of the database, the chief wants to track which firefighters are involved in which programs. Next you will add a column for outreach tracking. You want to insert the new column between columns D and E.

5. Position the mouse pointer at the top of **column E.**

6. When the mouse pointer changes to a **down-pointing arrow**, click to select the column.

D	E	F
Rank	**Shift**	**Training**
Firefighter/EMT-Intermediate	1	EMT-Paramedic
Firefighter	1	Additional Fire

7. Choose **Home→Cells→Insert** menu ▾ button from the Ribbon.

8. Choose **Insert Sheet Columns** from the menu.

After showing the database to the chief, he said he would rather have the Community Outreach column as the last column. Next you will delete the column you just added.

Delete a Column

9. If necessary, position the mouse pointer on the column header for **column E** and click to select the column.
10. Choose **Home→Cells→Delete** menu ▾ button from the Ribbon.
11. Choose **Delete Sheet Columns** from the menu.
    Next you will type the new column heading in H1.
12. Click **cell H1**, type **`Community Outreach`**, and **tap** [Enter].
    Now you need to widen the column to accommodate the long heading.
13. Position the mouse pointer on the border between **columns H and I**.
14. When the mouse pointer changes to a double-headed arrow, **double-click** to widen column H.
15. **Save** and then **close** the spreadsheet.

Concepts Review

To check your knowledge of the key concepts introduced in this lesson, complete the Concepts Review quiz on this and the next page. Or, you can take the quiz online by going to the URL **labyrinthelab.com/wtmo10**.

True/False Questions

			Page number
1. When you navigate with scroll bars, the active cell does not move.	**true**	**false**	______
2. When you are in the process of entering data in a spreadsheet, the Cancel and Enter buttons appear on the Formula Bar.	**true**	**false**	______
3. Only the cells in columns A through Z have addresses.	**true**	**false**	______
4. Excel's Sort feature allows you to sort numbers but not dates.	**true**	**false**	______
5. If you want to sort a list, you should not have any blank columns or rows in the list.	**true**	**false**	______
6. By default, Excel aligns numbers to the left edge of the cell.	**true**	**false**	______

Multiple Choice Questions

7. What are the three kinds of entries in spreadsheets?

   Page number: ______

   a. Formulas, text, and numbers

   b. Formulas, numbers, and the Ribbon

   c. Numbers, text, and cells

   d. Numbers, formulas, and columns

8. Use the Freeze Panes feature when _____.

   Page number: ______

   a. you do not want the data to be modified in a spreadsheet

   b. you want to keep column titles visible while scrolling down in a spreadsheet

   c. you want to select a range of cells

   d. you want to copy data

9. You may want to add columns or rows to a spreadsheet because _____.

   Page number: ______

   a. typically there are not enough cells in an Excel spreadsheet

   b. you have to add new columns and rows before you can sort data

   c. you must add new columns and rows before you can freeze panes

   d. you need to accommodate a change in the data

10. Which of the following is *not* true about cell ranges?

    Page number: ______

    a. A range of cells is a group of adjacent cells.

    b. You must select a range of cells before moving or copying them.

    c. When you select a range of cells, the active cell appears in the center of the range.

    d. Cell ranges are identified by the cell addresses in the upper-left and lower-right corners of the range.

Skill Builders

SKILL BUILDER 5.1 Enter Data and Work with Columns and Rows

In this exercise, you will review techniques for entering data in a spreadsheet. You are keeping a list of places your friends might like to see when they visit you. Now you are going to add some more places of interest to your list. Remember, entering data is a two-step process. You will also use this opportunity to change the width of a column and to delete a column and a row.

1. Open sb-Tourist Attractions from your Lesson 05 folder.
2. Select **cell A17** and type **`Blues Festival`**, then **tap** [→] twice to finish entering the data and move to column C.
   Cell C17 is now the active cell.
3. Type **`Fort Mason`** and **tap** [→] to finish entering the data.
   Cell D17 is now the active cell.
4. Type **`September`** and **tap** [Enter] to finish entering the data.
5. **Tap** [Home] to move the active cell to A18.
6. Type **`Grand National Rodeo`** and **tap** [→] twice to move to cell C18.
7. Type **`Cow Palace`** and then **tap** [Tab] to enter the data and move to cell D18.
8. Type **`October-November`** in cell D18 and **tap** [Enter] to complete the entry.

Adjust a Column Width

The data in column A is flowing into column B. You will adjust column A to accommodate the data.

9. Position the mouse pointer between **columns A and B**.
10. When the mouse pointer changes to a **double-headed arrow**, drag to the right until the dotted vertical line is to the right of the longest entry; then, release the mouse button.

Delete a Column and Row

You no longer need column B, and you would also like to delete the blank row 2.

11. Position the mouse pointer on the column header for **column B.**
12. When the mouse pointer changes to a **down-pointing arrow**, click to select the column.
13. Choose **Home→Cells→Delete** menu ▾ button from the Ribbon.
14. Choose **Delete Sheet Columns** from the menu.
15. Position the mouse pointer on the row header for **row 2.**
16. When the mouse pointer changes to a **right-pointing arrow**, click to select the row.
17. Choose **Home→Cells→Delete** menu ▾ button from the Ribbon.
18. Choose **Delete Sheet Rows** from the menu.
19. **Save** and then **close** the spreadsheet.

SKILL BUILDER 5.2 Navigate, Freeze Panes, and Sort Data

In this exercise, you will move around a spreadsheet, freeze panes, and sort data. Your boss asked to see the data represented in a few different ways, and Excel's Freeze Panes and Sort features make preparing data for your boss's review a simple matter.

1. Open sb-Employee Roster from your Lesson 05 folder.
2. Click the **scroll down** button at the bottom of the scroll bar three times to place row 4 at the top of the spreadsheet.
3. Click the **scroll up** button at the top of the scroll bar three times to place row 1 at the top of the window.
4. Click the open part of the **scroll bar** below the scroll box to move down one screen.
5. **Press** [Ctrl]+[Home] to move to cell A1.
6. **Press** [Ctrl]+[End] to move to the end of the data in the spreadsheet.
7. **Tap** [Home] to move to the beginning of the row.
8. **Tap** [Page Up] to move up one screen.

Freeze Columns and Rows at the Same Time

9. Click **cell C2**.
10. Choose **View→Window→Freeze Panes** from the Ribbon.
11. Choose **Freeze Panes** from the menu.
12. Scroll down until **row 44** is visible.
    Notice that you can still see the column titles.
13. Scroll to the right until **column F** is next to **column B**.

Unfreeze Panes

14. Choose **View→Window→Freeze Panes** from the Ribbon.
15. Choose **Unfreeze Panes** from the menu.

Sort Data

16. Click anywhere in **column I** within the list.
17. Choose **Home→Editing→Sort & Filter** from the Ribbon.
18. Choose **Sort A to Z** from the menu.
    The list is now in alphabetic order by department. Next you will sort by zip code.
19. Click anywhere in **column G** within the list.
20. Choose **Home→Editing→Sort & Filter** from the Ribbon.
21. Choose **Sort Smallest to Largest** from the menu.
    Finally, you will sort by last name.
22. Select **cell A2**.
23. Choose **Home→Editing→Sort & Filter** from the Ribbon.
24. Choose **Sort A to Z** from the menu.
25. **Save** and then **close** the spreadsheet.

SKILL BUILDER 5.3 Select Ranges, Edit, and Copy Data

In this exercise, you will make editing changes and copy data from one spreadsheet to three other spreadsheets. Your manager asked you to set up an Expenses and Revenues report she can use to track all four regions she is responsible for. The ability to copy data makes this an easy task.

Make Editing Changes

1. Open sb-Expenses and Revenues by Region from your Lesson 05 folder.

   Under Expenses, the Rent category should really be Rent/Utilities, so you will make that change first. Then you will add an Advertising category to Expenses.

2. Select **cell B5** and notice the contents of cell B5 in the Formula Bar.
3. Click in the **Formula Bar** following the word *Rent,* type **`/Utilities`**, and **tap** [Enter].

   Now you'll insert a blank row above row 6 for the Advertising expense category.

4. Position the mouse pointer on the row header for **row 6.**
5. When the mouse pointer changes to a **right-pointing arrow**, click to select the row.
6. Choose **Home→Cells→Insert** menu ▾ button from the Ribbon.
7. Choose **Insert Sheet Rows** from the menu.
8. Select **cell B6** and type **`Advertising`** then **tap** [Enter].

Copy Data from One Spreadsheet to Another

You've already set up spreadsheet tabs for the South, East, and West regions. Since all four regions have the same expense and revenue items, you can just copy the data from the North Region into the other spreadsheets.

9. Select **cell B2** and then **hold down** [Shift] and click **cell D16** to select a range of cells.
10. Choose **Home→Clipboard→Copy** from the Ribbon.
11. Click the **South Region tab** to switch to that spreadsheet and then select **cell B2.**
12. Choose **Home→Clipboard→Paste** from the Ribbon.

    The data was copied, but notice that the column widths are different from the original. Next you will use an Excel SmartTag to keep the column widths the same as the North Region.

13. Follow these steps to keep the original column widths:

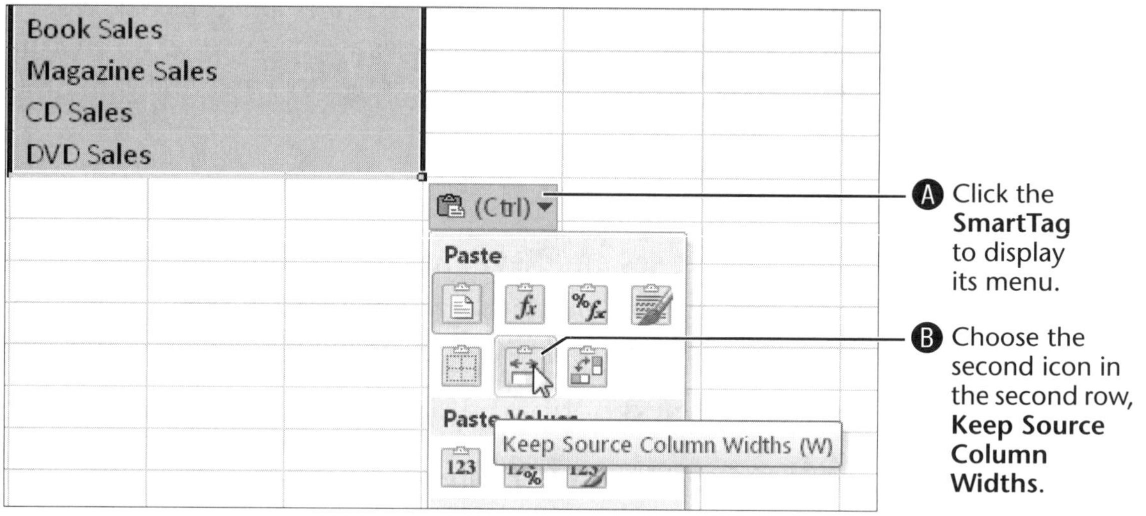

The column widths now match those in the North Region.

14. Click the **North Region** tab and notice that the flashing marquee is still active, indicating that the copied material is still in the Clipboard, so you don't have to copy it again.

Copy the Data to the East and West Regions

15. Click the **East Region** tab to switch to that spreadsheet and then select **cell B2**.

16. Choose **Home→Clipboard→Paste** from the Ribbon.

17. Click the **SmartTag** at the bottom-right corner of the pasted data and choose the second icon in the second row, **Keep Source Column Widths**.

    You can now go straight to the West Region tab since the copied information is still in the Clipboard.

18. Click the **West Region** tab and select **cell B2**.

19. Choose **Home→Clipboard→Paste** from the Ribbon.

20. Use the **SmartTag** to maintain the column widths from the original data.

21. Switch back to the **South Region** tab and correct the region name in **cell D2**.

22. Now correct the **East and West Region** names.

23. **Save** and then **close** the document.

LESSON 6

Excel – Budgeting with Calculations and Charts

In this lesson, you will perform calculations and create charts in Excel, construct your own formulas, use some of Excel's most popular built-in functions, and build eye-catching column and pie charts that summarize data and reveal numeric trends. *Picturing* your data in charts makes it easy to understand the data at a glance.

LESSON OBJECTIVES

After studying this lesson, you will be able to:

- Work with Excel's mathematical operators
- Build formulas
- Perform calculations using Excel's built-in functions
- Copy formulas and functions
- Create charts to visualize your data

Student resources **labyrinthelab.com/wtmo10**

Case Study: Tracking Inventory Expenses

Ken Turner owns a marine supply store on San Francisco Bay. He carefully tracks his inventory budget against actual costs to make sure he keeps his expenses in line.

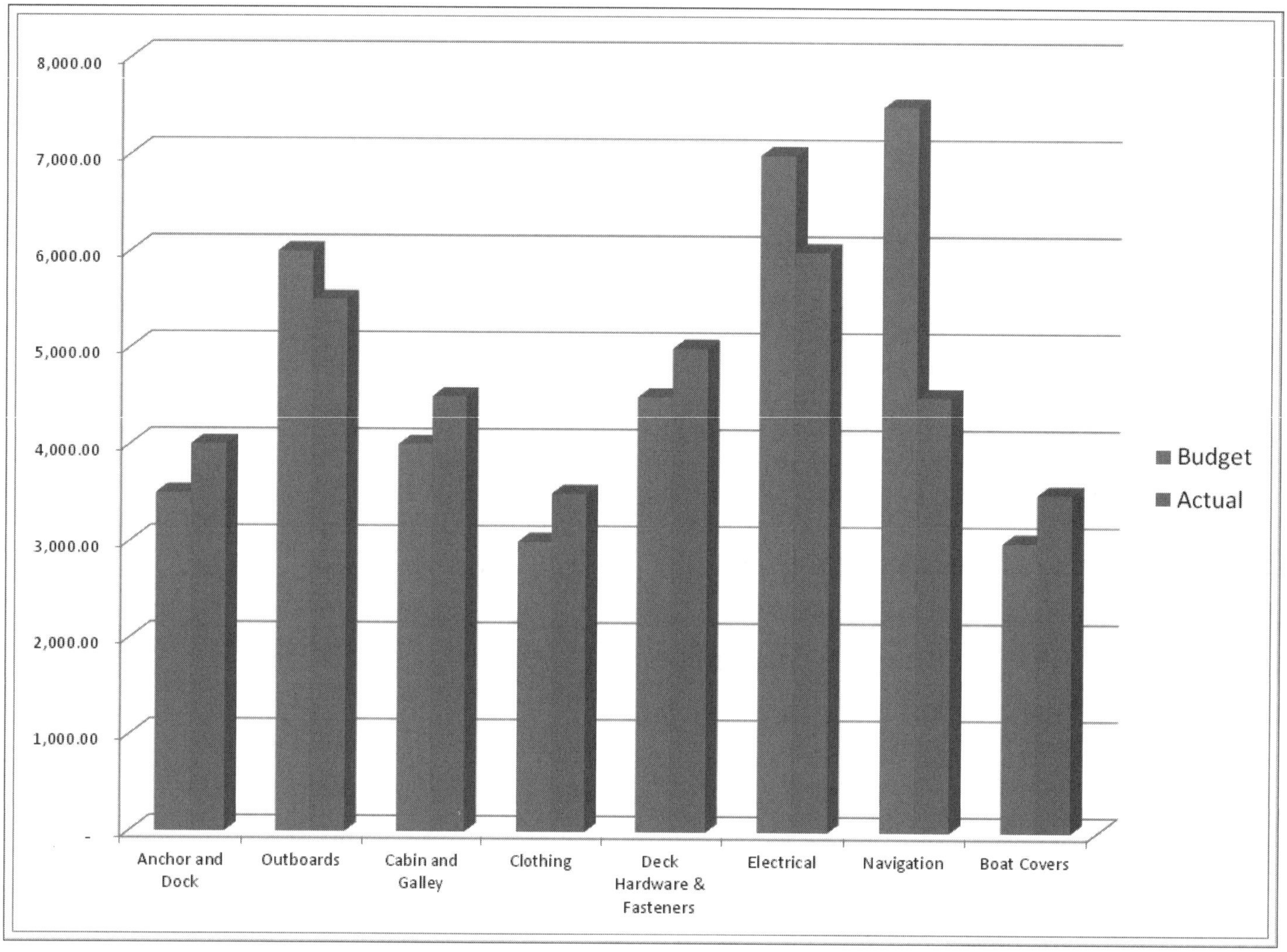

Defining Formulas

Does the word *formula* make you hyperventilate? If the answer is yes, you may be one of those unfortunate people who had an unpleasant introduction to math. Did you know that 2+2 is a formula? Okay, now you can relax.

Just because you use a spreadsheet to perform calculations, it does not mean that you will suddenly use some strange branch of mathematics. You are going to use the kind of math you have always used; you are just going to do it electronically.

Excel's Mathematical Operators

Mind you, there are a few slight differences in performing calculations electronically versus on paper, but they are not difficult to understand.

You are familiar with the signs used for addition, subtraction, multiplication, and division. If you look around on your keyboard for the division sign you normally use, you won't find it. In Excel, you use the forward slash (/) for the division sign. You use the asterisk (*) for the multiplication sign.

QUICK REFERENCE: Reviewing Excel's Mathematical Operators

Operation	Symbol
Add	+
Subtract	-
Multiply	*
Divide	/

An easy way to remember the operators is to look at the number pad (if your computer has one) on the right side of the keyboard. You can use the keys shown in the following illustration when you create formulas. There are duplicates of these keys on the main part of the keyboard. You can use whichever keys you prefer—or even a combination of them. They all work the same way.

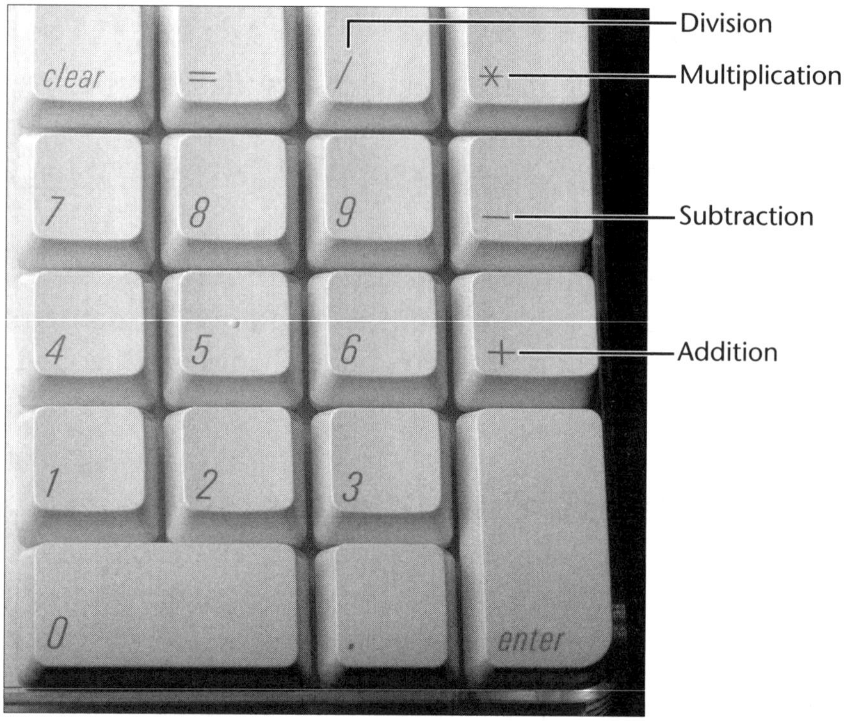

How to Type a Formula

You take a slightly different approach when creating electronic formulas than you do if you are jotting down a formula on a notepad. For example, the placement of the equals (=) sign is different from what you might expect, and in addition to using numbers in formulas, you can also use cell addresses, which is typically the preferred method. Both issues will be discussed in more detail in a moment.

Where's the Equals Sign? In Excel, you use the same equals (=) sign you've always used, it's just that you place it at the beginning of the formula rather than at the end.

Instead of typing

2+2=

You type

=2+2

Why? When you enter data in a spreadsheet, your computer is watching to see what kind of data it is. If the first thing it sees is a number or an alphabetic character, it assumes that plain old data is coming down the line and it doesn't have to do anything special. If your computer sees an equals (=) sign it figures, "Hey, this is a formula. I'd better pay attention, because I have some work to do. I have to figure out the answer to this formula."

Numbers or Cell Addresses? You can create formulas using numbers as in the preceding =2+2 example; however, most of the time you should use cell addresses, such as =A1+A2. The reason for this is that if you use numbers in a formula and later decide to change one of those numbers in the spreadsheet, the formula *will not* recalculate. If you use cell addresses, the formula *will* recalculate.

HANDS-ON 6.1 Enter Formulas in a Spreadsheet

In this exercise, you will create formulas in a budget spreadsheet using two different techniques. You will begin by calculating the Qtr 1 Budget Total for Other Expenses. Later you will total the entire column, but for now you will just use the four numbers in Other Expenses to keep it simple.

1. If necessary, start **Excel.**
2. Open Pacific Marine Expense Budget from your Lesson 06 folder.
3. Take a moment to look over the spreadsheet.

Enter a Formula

4. Select **cell B17**.

   You always start a formula by selecting the cell that will contain the answer.

   TIP! When you type cell addresses in a formula, you can use either upper- or lowercase letters. Excel will automatically convert lowercase addresses to uppercase.

5. **Type** the formula **=B13+B14+B15+B16** and **tap** [Enter].

   The answer 6,200.00 appears in B17.

6. Select **cell B17** and look at the Formula Bar.

   While the answer appears in cell B17, the formula behind the answer appears in the Formula Bar. This makes it easy to double-check your formulas for accuracy.

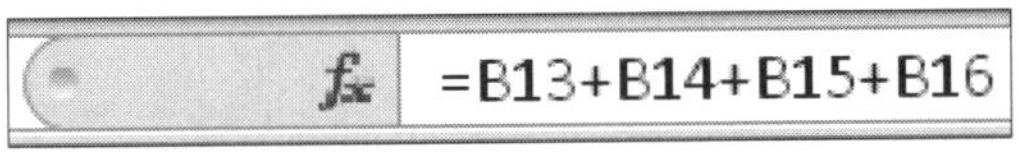

Getting the Mouse to Help Type a Formula

Now you'll try another formula, but this time you'll get the mouse to help you. You will calculate the Qtr 1 Actual Total for Other Expenses. Again, you are just using four numbers for now to keep it simple.

7. Follow these steps to create a formula using the mouse:

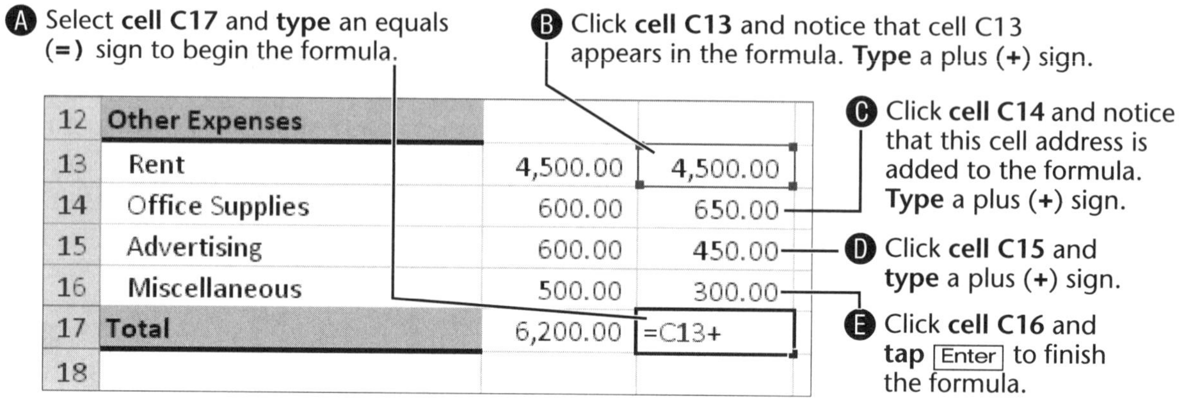

TIP! Using the mouse to help you create formulas is easy and reduces the likelihood that you will make a typo.

8. Select **cell C17** and look at the Formula Bar.

   The answer appears in cell C17 and the formula appears in the Formula Bar.

Edit a Number That Appears in a Formula

You just discovered that the Actual figure for Miscellaneous expenses should be 400.00 instead of 300.00. Bear in mind that the current answer in cell C17 is 5,900.00.

9. Select **cell C16**, type **400**, and **tap** [Enter].

   Look at the answer in cell C17 (6,000.00). The formula automatically recalculates. Remember, if you use cell addresses in formulas instead of numbers, the formulas recalculate automatically.

   In the next topic, you'll learn a slicker way to add a column of numbers, so you can delete the formulas you created in this exercise.

10. Click and drag to select **cells B17 and C17.**

11. **Tap** [Delete].

12. **Save** the spreadsheet.

    Leave the file open. You will use it throughout the lesson.

Using Built-in Functions

There is another approach you can use to perform calculations. The Excel program has built-in functions that contain formulas that you don't have to write from scratch. This is a real time-saver! The following table shows some of Excel's most popular functions.

QUICK REFERENCE: Outlining Common Excel Functions

Function	Purpose
=SUM(A1:A100)	This function adds the range A1 through A100.
=MAX(A1:A100)	This function finds the largest number in the range A1 through A100.
=MIN(A1:A100)	This function finds the smallest number in the range A1 through A100.
=AVERAGE(A1:A100)	This function finds the average for the range A1 through A100.

How Functions Are Constructed

Functions are built in a specific manner.

- Like all formulas, functions begin with an equals (=) sign.
- Next is the name of the function, such as SUM or AVERAGE.
- After that is a set of parentheses that usually contains one or more arguments. An *argument* is information necessary for the calculation. The range A1:A100 is the argument in each of the examples in the preceding table.

The AutoSum Button

Σ Probably the most frequently used function is SUM; therefore, Excel provides the convenient AutoSum button on the Ribbon to automatically calculate sums for you.

HANDS-ON 6.2 Use the Sum Function

In this exercise, you will use the SUM function to add a series of numbers in the Budget and Actual columns for the first quarter. First, you will *manually* type the function, and then you will use the AutoSum button on the Ribbon to *automatically* enter the function.

1. Select **cell B17**, type the function **`=SUM(B4:B16)`**, and **tap** [Enter] to complete the function. Don't be concerned about the Excel prompts that pop up when you type functions. You will not use them in this lesson, so you can ignore them.

   Remember, in the last exercise you only added the four numbers in rows 13 through 16 to avoid typing lots of cell addresses. Now that you have the convenient SUM function, you can easily indicate a *range* of cell addresses rather than typing each cell address. This method is certainly a lot more convenient when adding a long row or column of numbers.

   Next, you will use the AutoSum button to automatically create a formula.

2. Select **cell C17**.

3. Choose **Home→Editing→AutoSum** [Σ] from the Ribbon.

   The AutoSum feature places a flashing marquee around cells C13 through C16. AutoSum only went up to C13 because of the blank cell in C12. This is not correct; you want to add the entire column, C4:C16. No problem; you can easily override AutoSum's decision.

Override AutoSum

4. Follow these steps to total the entire column:

Ⓐ Place the **mouse pointer** on the tiny square in the upper-right corner of the box surrounding the **range C13:C16**. The pointer changes to a double-headed arrow.

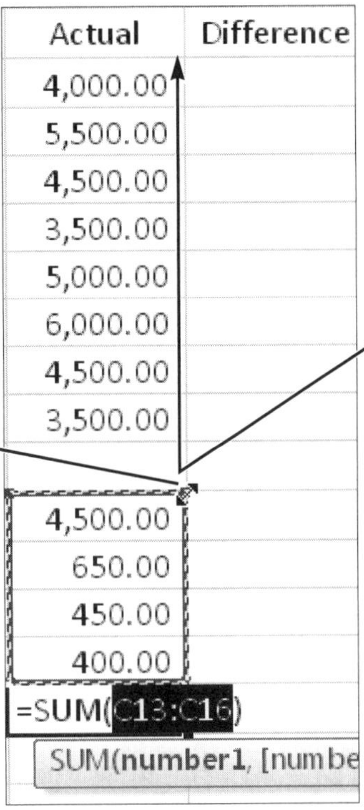

Ⓑ Click and drag up to the top of **cell C4** to place the box around the entire column of numbers; release the mouse button.

The formula is now =SUM(C4:C16).

5. **Tap** [Enter] to complete the formula.

Make AutoSum Do It Your Way

Here's another technique to make sure AutoSum adds the numbers you want it to.

6. Click and drag to select the **range E4:E17**.

   You're selecting the column of numbers you want to add plus a blank cell at the bottom of the column. This is telling Excel to place the answer in the blank cell.

7. Choose **Home→Editing→AutoSum** [Σ] from the Ribbon.

   Excel places the answer in cell E17.

8. Click **cell E17** and check out the formula in the Formula Bar.

9. Use the same technique to add the numbers in **column F**.

   You can also use that technique with multiple columns at the same time.

Use AutoSum with Multiple Columns

10. Select the **range H4:I17**.
11. Choose **Home→Editing→AutoSum** [Σ] from the Ribbon.
    Excel placed answers in cells H17 and I17.
12. Check out the formulas in the Formula Bar.
13. Use the same technique to add the numbers in **columns K and L** at the same time.

Enter a Subtraction Formula to Calculate the Difference between the Budgeted and Actual Figures

There is no built-in function for a simple subtraction problem, so you need to create this formula yourself—but you can get the mouse to give you a hand (paw).

14. Select **cell D4** and **type** an equals (=) sign.
15. Click **cell B4** and **type** a minus (-) sign.
16. Click **cell C4** and then **tap** [Enter] to finish the formula.
17. Click **cell D4** and check the Formula Bar.
    The Actual Anchor and Dock inventory expense was 500.00 over budget; therefore, the answer is in parentheses to indicate a negative number.
    You don't have to retype this formula for all the numbers in columns B and C. Later you will learn to copy formulas—another big time-saver in Excel.
18. Select **cell G4** and **type** an equals (=) sign.
19. Click **cell E4** and **type** a minus (-) sign.
20. Click **cell F4** and then **tap** [Enter] to finish the formula.
21. Use the same technique to enter subtraction formulas in **cells J4 and M4**.
    The parentheses in the answers indicate that you were over budget for Anchor and Dock supplies for the first three quarters and under budget for the fourth quarter.
22. **Save** the spreadsheet.

Calculating with AVERAGE, MAX, and MIN

The AVERAGE function calculates the average of a range of cells, while the MAX function finds the largest number in a range. The MIN function determines the smallest number in a range.

HANDS-ON 6.3 Use the AVERAGE, MAX, and MIN Functions

In this exercise, you will use the AVERAGE, MAX, and MIN functions to quickly analyze the Inventory data in the second page of your workbook.

1. Click the **Inventory Analysis** tab at the bottom of the workbook to switch to that spreadsheet.

   First you will calculate the average of the four quarters. Again, you will get the mouse to help you.

2. Select **cell F2** and type **=AVERAGE(** but don't type the cell addresses.
3. Click and drag to select the **range B2:E2.**

   Notice that the range addresses automatically appear in the formula. You don't have to type the right parenthesis; Excel will do that for you.

4. **Tap** [Enter].
5. Select **cell F2** and check out the Formula Bar.

   You can see that Excel put the right parenthesis in the formula for you.

Calculate the Highest and Lowest Quarters

6. Select **cell G2** and type **=MAX(** but don't type the cell addresses.
7. Click and drag to select the **range B2:E2** and **tap** [Tab] to finish the function and make cell H2 active.
8. Type **=MIN(** in cell H2.
9. Click and drag to select the **range B2:E2** and tap [Enter].

   Remember, you're going to learn to copy formulas soon, so you don't have to create these formulas for every row.

Copying Formulas and Functions

You can copy formulas and functions because Excel automatically changes cell addresses in a copied formula *relative to* where it is copied. For example, if the =SUM(A1:A100) function is copied one column to the right (column B), the function changes to =SUM(B1:B100).

Here's another example: If you copy the function =SUM(B9:H9) down one row (row 10), the function changes to =SUM(B10:H10). This is known as *relative referencing* and it is one of the great powers of electronic spreadsheets. Without relative referencing, you would have to create formulas and functions one at a time.

You can use the same Copy button to copy formulas that you use to copy other types of data.

HANDS-ON 6.4 Copy Functions and Formulas

In this exercise, you will copy functions and formulas in both spreadsheets in your workbook. You will start with the =AVERAGE function in F2.

1. Select **cell F2**.
2. Choose **Home→Clipboard→Copy** from the Ribbon.
   Excel places a flashing marquee around the cell you are copying.
3. Select the **range F3:F9**.
4. Choose **Home→Clipboard→Paste** from the Ribbon.
5. **Tap** [Esc] to turn off the marquee.
6. Click **cell F2** and examine the formula; click **cell F3** and examine the formula.
   Notice that the range of cells inside the parentheses changed from B2:E2 to B3:E3. Excel changed the cell addresses *relative to* where the formula was copied.

Copy the MAX and MIN Functions

7. Select **cell G2**.
8. Choose **Home→Clipboard→Copy** from the Ribbon.
9. Select the **range G3:G9**.
10. Choose **Home→Clipboard→Paste** from the Ribbon.
11. Select **cell H2** and copy the function from cell H2 into **H3:H9**.

Calculate the Inventory Totals for All Four Quarters

12. Select the **range B2:E10**.
13. Choose **Home→Editing→AutoSum** Σ from the Ribbon.

    Excel places the total for each column in row 10.

Copy the Formulas That Calculate the Difference between Budget and Actual Numbers

14. Click the **Expense Budget** tab at the bottom of the workbook to switch to that spreadsheet.
15. Select **cell D4**.
16. Choose **Home→Clipboard→Copy** from the Ribbon.
17. Select the **range D5:D16**.

    Note that you won't copy the formula to D17 since row 17 is labeled as a Total row. You are not totaling the Difference column; you are copying the subtraction formula.
18. Choose **Home→Clipboard→Paste** from the Ribbon.

    Take a moment to examine a couple of copied formulas and notice that the cell addresses changed in a relative fashion.

    Row 12 should be blank, so now you will delete the formula in D12.
19. Select **cell D12** and **tap** [Delete].
20. Use the same technique to copy the Difference formulas in **columns G, J, and M**; then, delete **cells G12, J12, and M12**.
21. **Save** the spreadsheet.

Using Charts to Visualize Data

Excel's charting features make charting data easy, and the results are stunning. Depicting your data with charts allows you to easily see trends and make comparisons in your data.

Excel offers a wide variety of chart types. Two of the most common are column and pie charts. Column charts compare categories of data using vertical columns. Each column represents values from a data series in the spreadsheet. Pie charts are round (like pies) and are used for comparing parts (slices) of the whole (pie).

How Do I Know Which Cells to Select?

To create a chart, you start by selecting the data you want to represent. Knowing which cells to select prior to creating the chart is important.

Column Charts Column charts compare values across categories. For a column chart, you select the data but not the total row or total column. The following data selection allows you to compare the various Inventory categories to each other by quarter, but it does not include the totals from row 10.

	A	B	C	D	E	F
1	Actual Inventory Expense	Qtr 1	Qtr 2	Qtr 3	Qtr 4	Avg of Qtrs
2	Anchor and Dock	4,000.00	3,500.00	3,000.00	2,500.00	3,250.00
3	Outboards	5,500.00	3,000.00	5,000.00	7,000.00	5,125.00
4	Cabin and Galley	4,500.00	4,500.00	4,000.00	4,500.00	4,375.00
5	Clothing	3,500.00	1,500.00	3,500.00	3,000.00	2,875.00
6	Deck Hardware & Fasteners	5,000.00	4,000.00	6,000.00	3,750.00	4,687.50
7	Electrical	6,000.00	6,750.00	4,500.00	6,500.00	5,937.50
8	Navigation	4,500.00	4,500.00	5,500.00	4,000.00	4,625.00
9	Boat Covers	3,500.00	4,000.00	3,000.00	4,500.00	3,750.00
10	Total	36,500.00	31,750.00	34,500.00	35,750.00	

The following chart was created from the data selected in the previous illustration. It compares the Inventory categories across four quarters. For example, you can see that Qtr 1 was the highest inventory cost for Anchor and Dock supplies, while Qtr 4 was the highest inventory cost for Outboards.

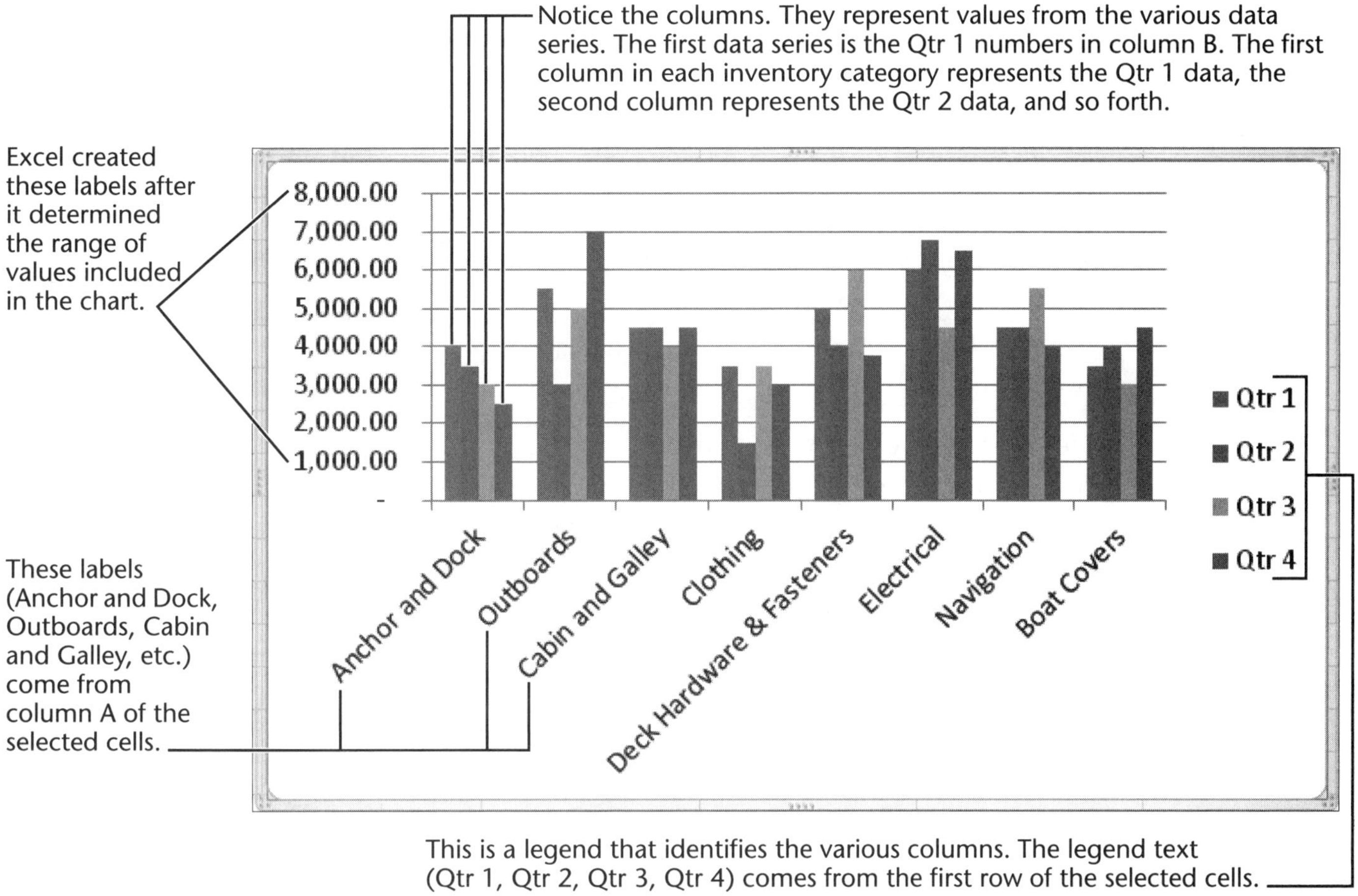

Pie Charts Pie charts compare pieces of the whole. You typically select two sets of data: the values to be represented by the slices of the pie (totals in row 10 in the following example) and the legend data to identify the slices (row 1 in the following example).

TIP! To select nonadjacent ranges of cells, select the first range, and then press and hold [Ctrl] while dragging over additional ranges.

Legend labels

	A	B	C	D	E
1	Actual Inventory Expense	Qtr 1	Qtr 2	Qtr 3	Qtr 4
2	Anchor and Dock	4,000.00	3,500.00	3,000.00	2,500.00
3	Outboards	5,500.00	3,000.00	5,000.00	7,000.00
4	Cabin and Galley	4,500.00	4,500.00	4,000.00	4,500.00
5	Clothing	3,500.00	1,500.00	3,500.00	3,000.00
6	Deck Hardware & Fasteners	5,000.00	4,000.00	6,000.00	3,750.00
7	Electrical	6,000.00	6,750.00	4,500.00	6,500.00
8	Navigation	4,500.00	4,500.00	5,500.00	4,000.00
9	Boat Covers	3,500.00	4,000.00	3,000.00	4,500.00
10	Total	36,500.00	31,750.00	34,500.00	35,750.00
11					

Values represented by the slices of the pie

The following chart was created from the data selected in the previous spreadsheet illustration. The slices compare the total Inventory expense for each of the four quarters to each other. In the following example, the Inventory expenses for each quarter are almost equal.

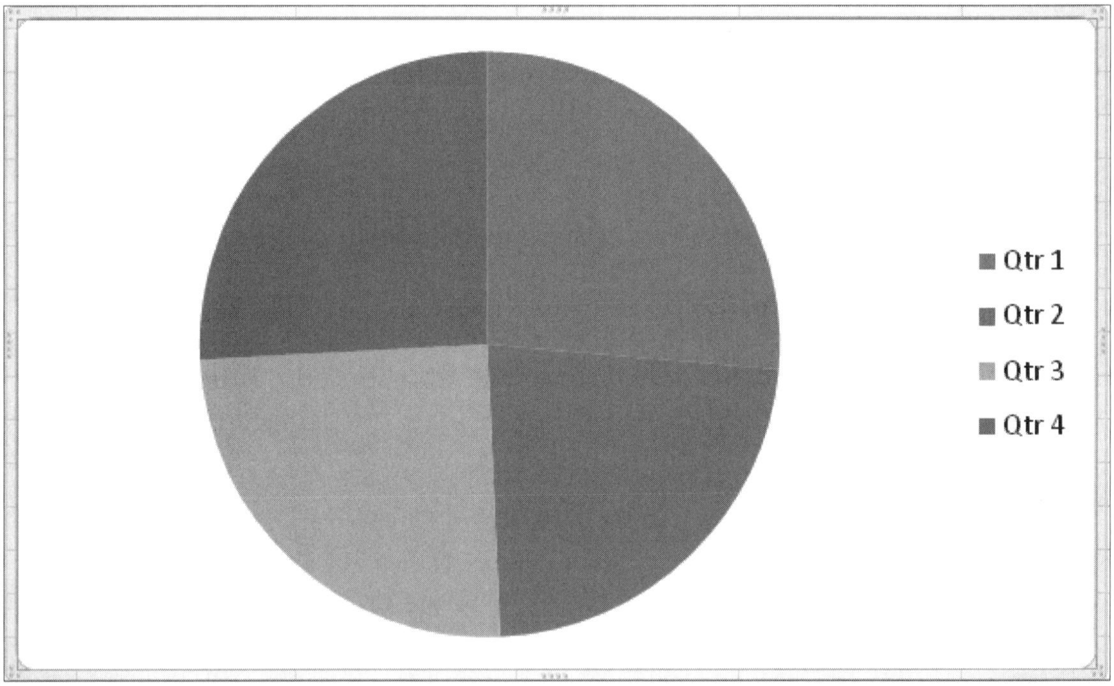

Embedded Charts Compared to Chart Sheets

A chart can either be embedded with the data in the spreadsheet or it can appear on a separate sheet in the workbook. An embedded chart provides the benefit of making it easy to compare the data in the spreadsheet with the columns or slices in the chart.

On the other hand, you may prefer to examine trends and comparisons without focusing on numeric detail. A chart sheet works well for that situation. A chart sheet also makes it easy to print only the chart without the surrounding data.

HANDS-ON 6.5 Visualize Your Data with Charts

In this exercise, you will create two charts, a column chart and a pie chart, and you will create both embedded charts and a chart sheet.

Create a Column Chart

1. Click the **Inventory Analysis** tab to switch to that spreadsheet.
2. Select the **range A1:E9**.
3. Choose **Insert→Charts→Column**  from the Ribbon.
   The column chart gallery appears, from which you can choose various types of column charts.
4. Choose the **first chart type** in the **2-D Column category**, as shown in the following figure.

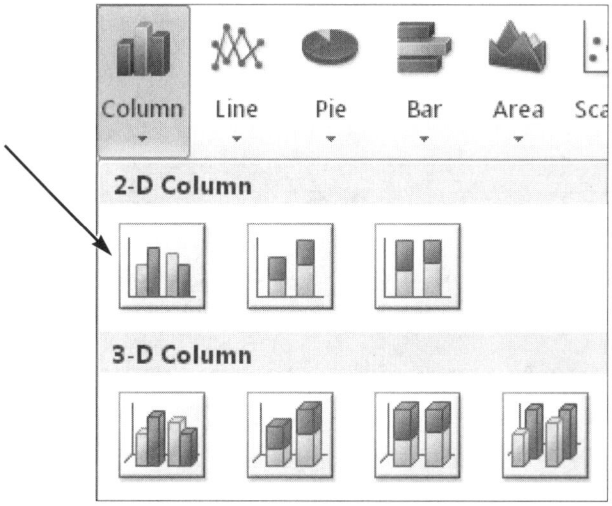

The chart appears in the spreadsheet. It is covering some of the data. (You will learn to move the chart to a new location within the spreadsheet in the next exercise.) The border surrounding the chart indicates that it is selected. The chart must be selected if you want to make changes to it. Notice the contextual Chart Tools tabs that appear on the Ribbon when the chart is selected: Design, Layout, and Format.

Deselect and Select the Chart

5. Click in the **spreadsheet** to deselect the chart.

   The chart's surrounding border disappears.

6. Click the **outer edge of the chart** and the border reappears.

Create a Chart Sheet

Now you will move the embedded chart to its own chart sheet.

7. Choose **Design→Location→Move Chart** from the Ribbon.

   The Move Chart dialog box appears. Here you can specify to move the chart to a New Sheet. The Object In option refers to embedding a chart as an object in the spreadsheet, which is the option currently in effect.

8. Choose **New Sheet**, as shown in the following figure, and click **OK**.

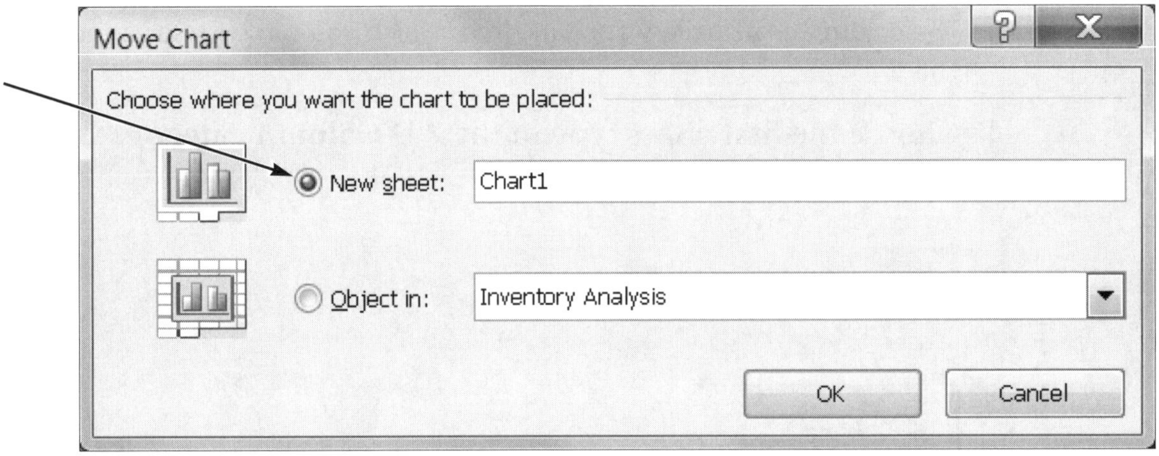

   The chart now has its own sheet in the workbook. Notice the Chart 1 tab at the bottom of the workbook.

9. Click the **Inventory Analysis** tab to return to the inventory data.

   Notice that the embedded chart no longer appears in the spreadsheet.

Create a Pie Chart

Because a pie chart represents the pieces of the whole, you will select data from the Total row to be represented by the slices of the pie. You will also select the column headings, which will appear in the legend.

Remember: You can select multiple nonadjacent ranges by holding down the [Ctrl] key when selecting the second and subsequent ranges.

10. Select the **range B1:E1**.

11. **Hold down** Ctrl and select the **range B10:E10;** then release the Ctrl key.

The numbers in B10:E10 will determine the size of the slices. The entries in B1:E1 will become the entries in the legend, describing the meanings of the slices.

12. Choose **Insert→Charts→Pie** from the Ribbon.

The pie chart gallery appears.

13. Choose the **first chart type** in the **3-D Pie category**, as shown in the following figure.

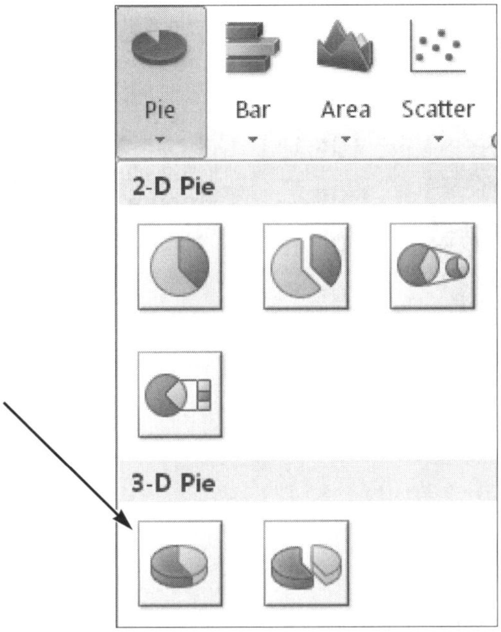

The pie chart now appears, embedded in the spreadsheet.

14. **Save** the file.

Moving and Resizing an Embedded Chart You can move an embedded chart within a spreadsheet by dragging it with the mouse pointer when the pointer looks like a four-headed arrow. You can resize the chart when the mouse pointer looks like a double-headed arrow.

The chart must be selected before you can move it. The appearance of this border indicates that the chart is selected.

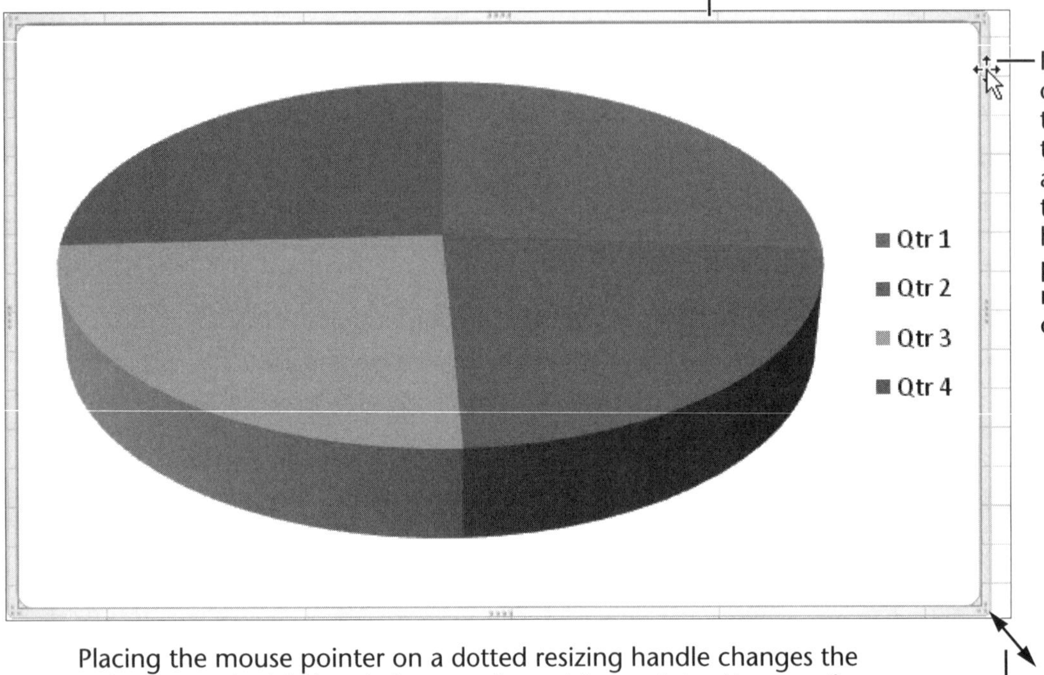

Position the mouse pointer on the border (but not on the dotted resizing handles that appear in the border) and the mouse changes to the move pointer, a four-headed arrow. You can then press and hold down the mouse button and drag the chart to a new location.

Placing the mouse pointer on a dotted resizing handle changes the pointer to a double-headed arrow, the resizing pointer. You can then press and hold down the mouse button and drag to change the size of the object. This is similar to resizing graphic objects in Word.

HANDS-ON 6.6 Move and Resize an Embedded Chart

In this exercise, you will move the embedded pie chart below the spreadsheet data. Then you will resize it.

1. If necessary, click the **outer edge** of the chart to select it.

2. Follow these steps to move the chart:

A Place the **mouse pointer** on the border of the chart (but not on a dotted resizing handle in the border). Notice that the mouse pointer looks like a four-headed arrow now.

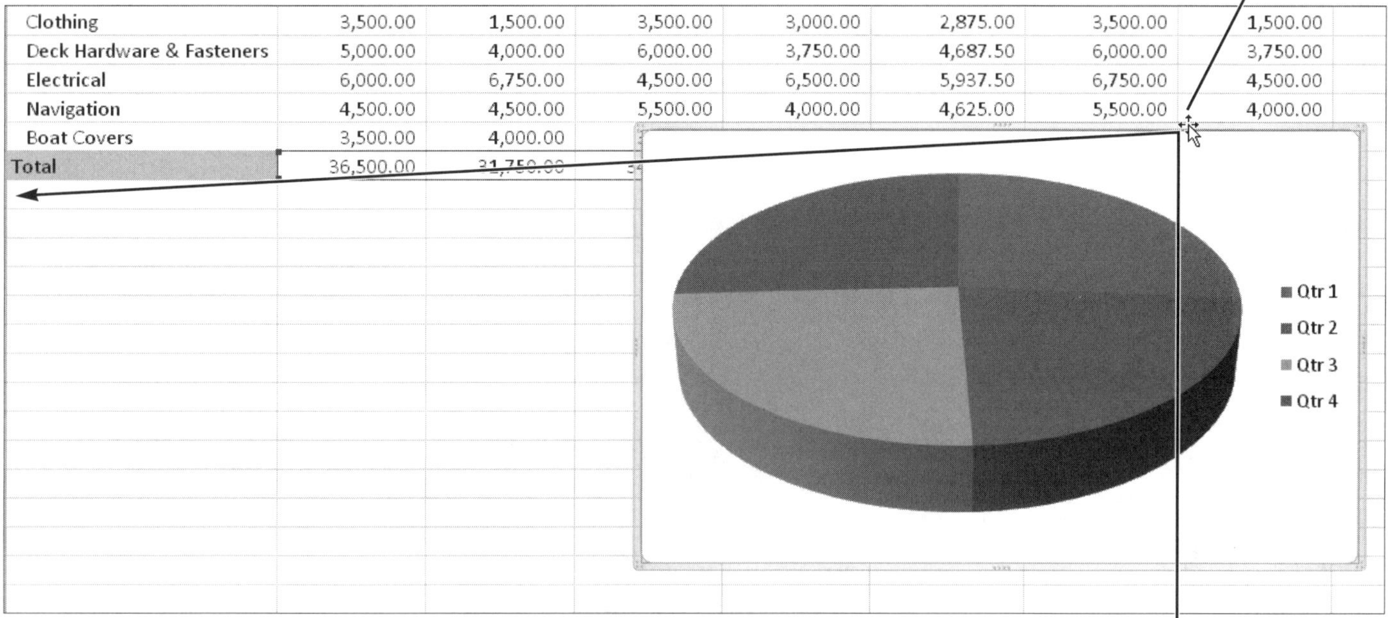

B Press and hold down the **mouse button**, and then drag the chart to position the **upper-left corner** of the chart as shown here—in column A and below the Total row. Release the mouse button.

Resize the Chart

3. If necessary, **scroll down** until the bottom-right corner of the chart border is visible.

4. Place the mouse pointer on the **bottom-right resizing handle.** The pointer changes to a two-headed arrow, as shown in the following illustration.

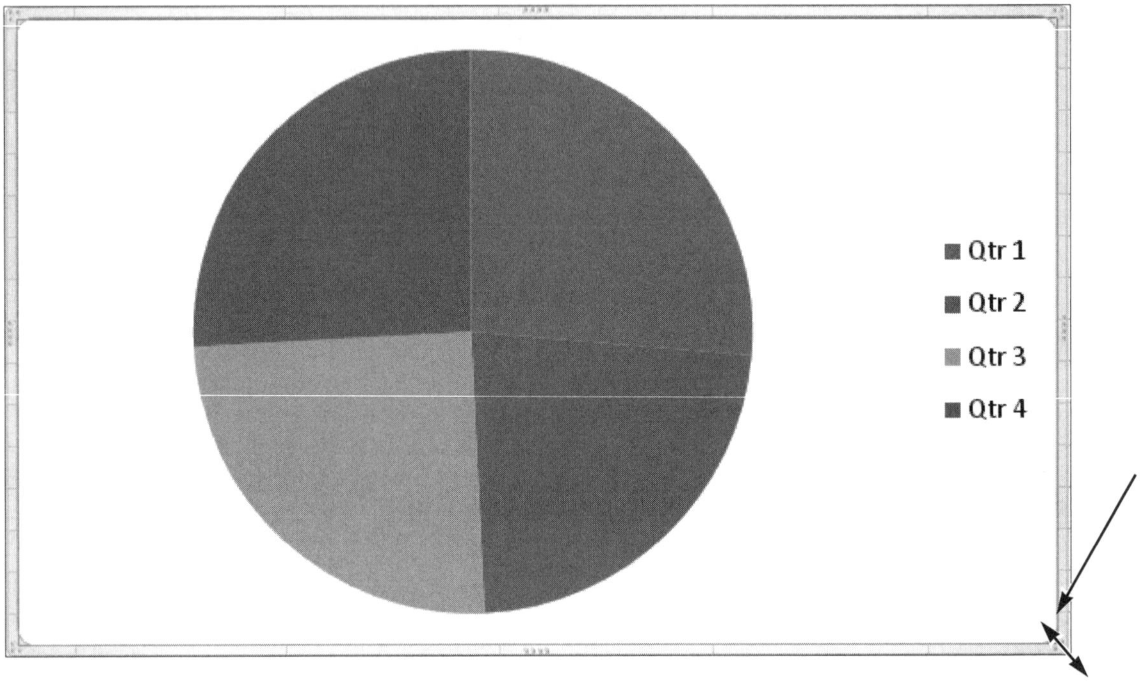

5. Drag up and to the left about a **half inch** to make the chart smaller.

6. Click in the **spreadsheet** to deselect the chart.

7. **Save** the file.

Using Design Tools

When you select a chart, three new Chart Tools tabs appear on the Ribbon: Design, Layout, and Format. In this lesson, you will spend some time working with the Design tab. It contains some appealing features for modifying your chart.

Switch Row/Column Data Switching the row and column data in a column chart provides an interesting change of perspective in analyzing your data. The following illustration displays the quarters as the legend and the inventory categories as the labels for the columns in the chart.

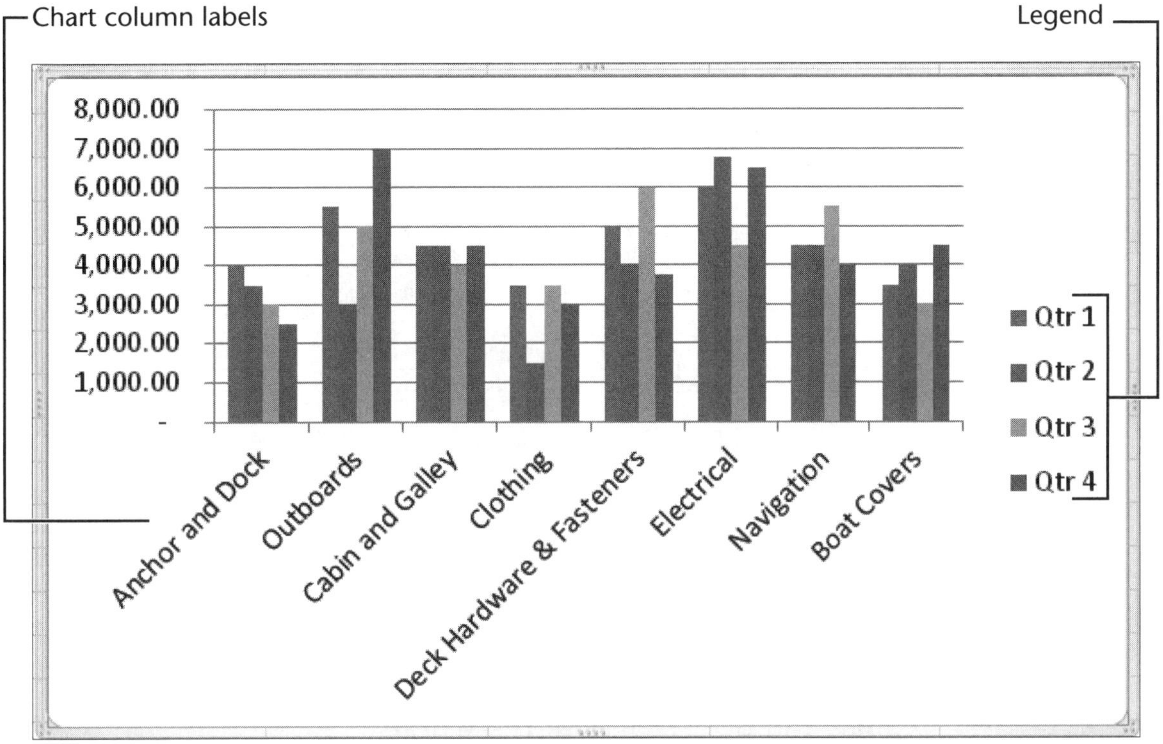

Switching the row and column data provides the following new perspective. Notice that the quarters now appear at the bottom of the chart as column labels and the categories make up the legend.

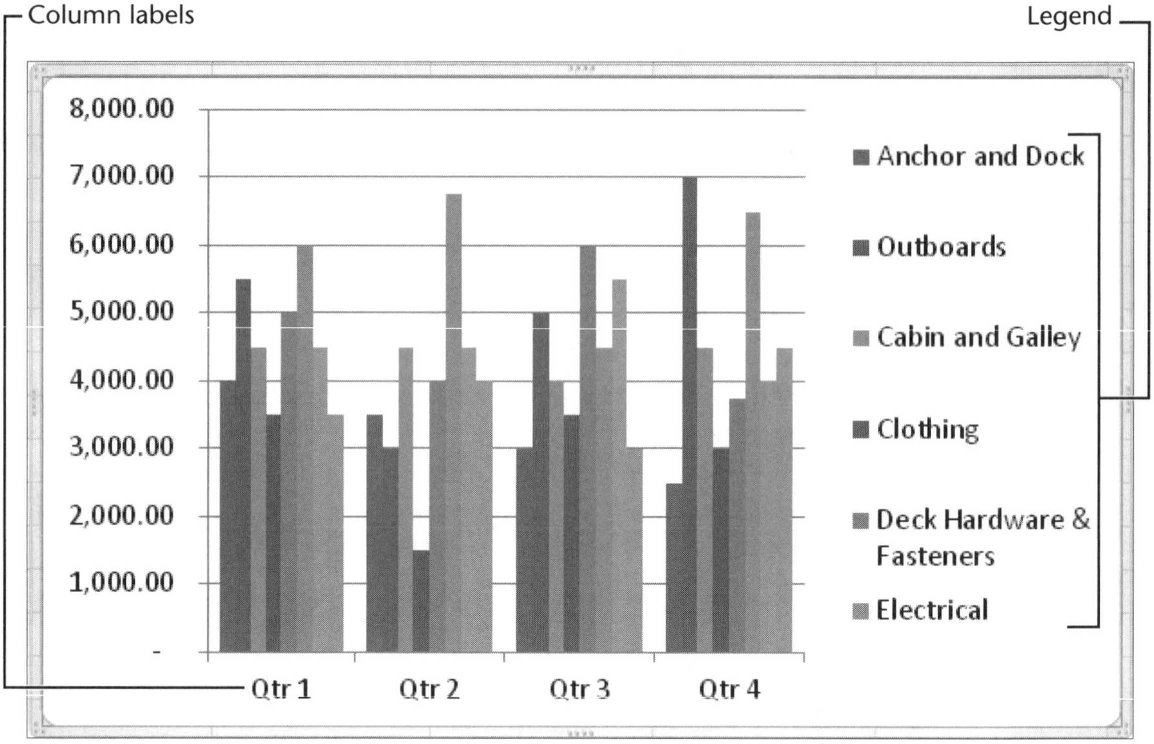

Chart Layouts The Chart Layouts group on the Design tab provides various methods for labeling pieces of a chart, including numeric values and percentages of the whole.

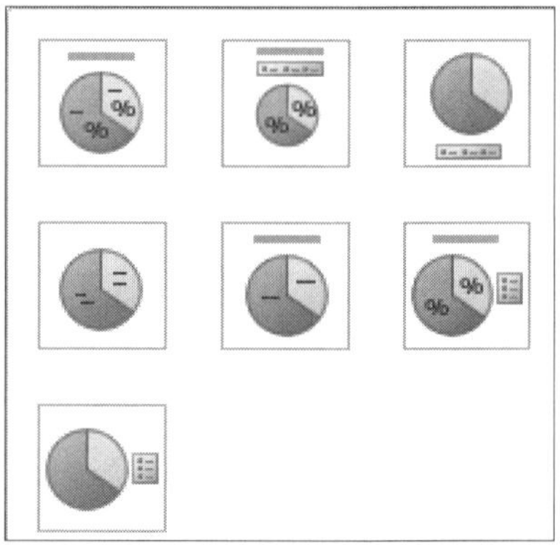

In the following example, the chosen layout displays the slices of the pie as percentages of the whole. Excel added a Chart Title object, which you can modify with your own words.

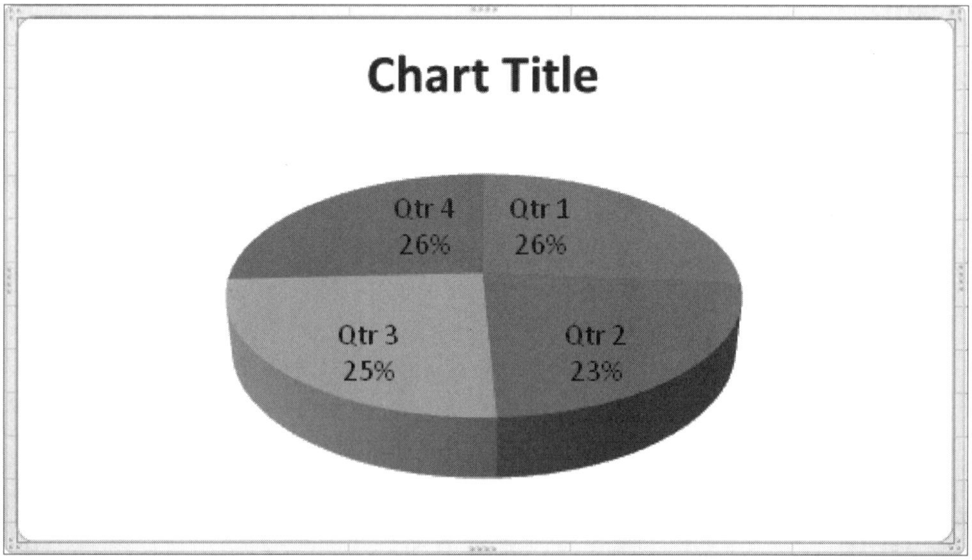

Chart Styles The Chart Styles gallery offers a variety of exciting design and color combinations you can apply to your charts.

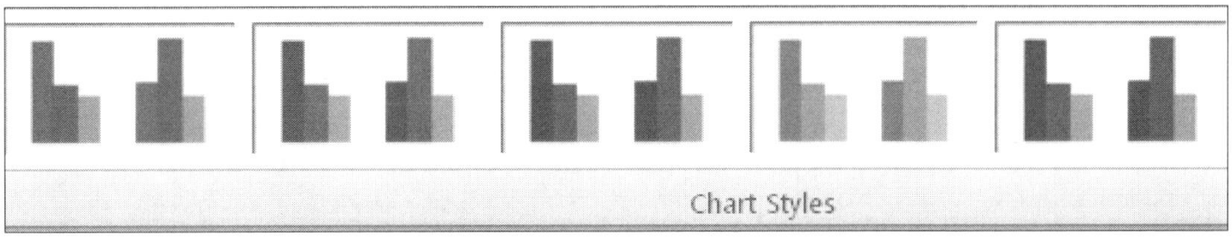

This dramatic change to the chart style was accomplished with a simple click of the mouse.

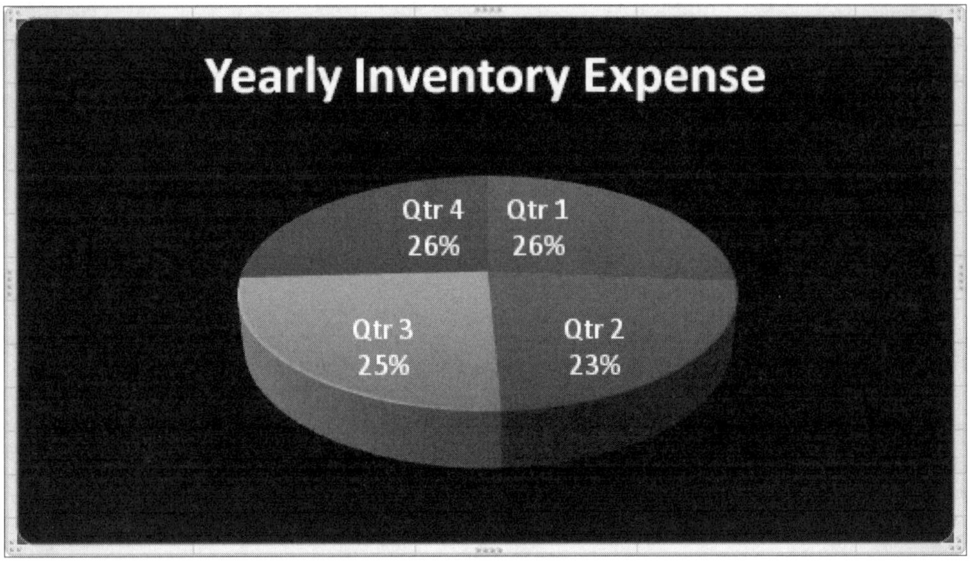

HANDS-ON 6.7 Modify the Chart Design

In this exercise, you will modify the design of charts by switching row and column data, applying a new layout, and applying a new chart style.

Switch Row/Column Data

1. Click the **Chart 1** tab at the bottom of the workbook to display the column chart.

   Observe the labels at the bottom of the chart and the legend on the right side of the chart. These will switch places when you switch the row and column data.

2. Choose **Design→Data→Switch Row/Column** from the Ribbon.

   Observe the changes to the chart. The quarters now appear at the bottom of the chart and the legend contains the inventory categories.

Change the Chart Layout

3. Click the **Inventory Analysis** tab at the bottom of the workbook to return to the pie chart.

4. If necessary, click the **outer edge** of the chart to select it.

5. If necessary, click the **Design** tab in Chart Tools.

6. Click the **More** button to display the Chart Layouts group, as shown in the following figure.

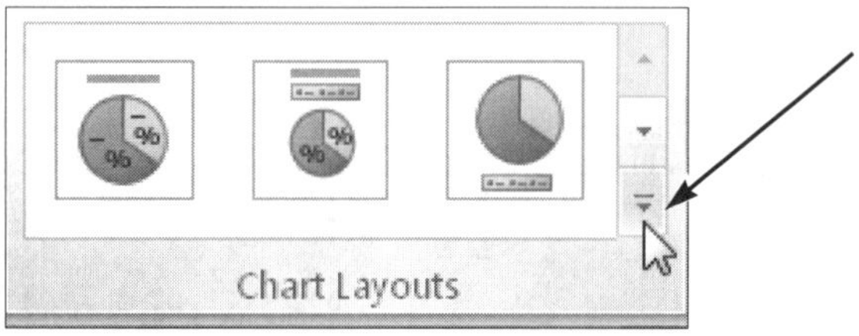

7. Choose **Layout 6**, as shown in the following illustration.

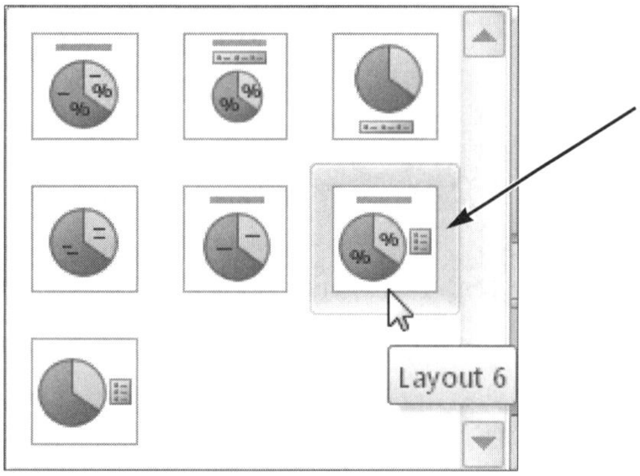

8. Follow these steps to observe the changes to the chart:

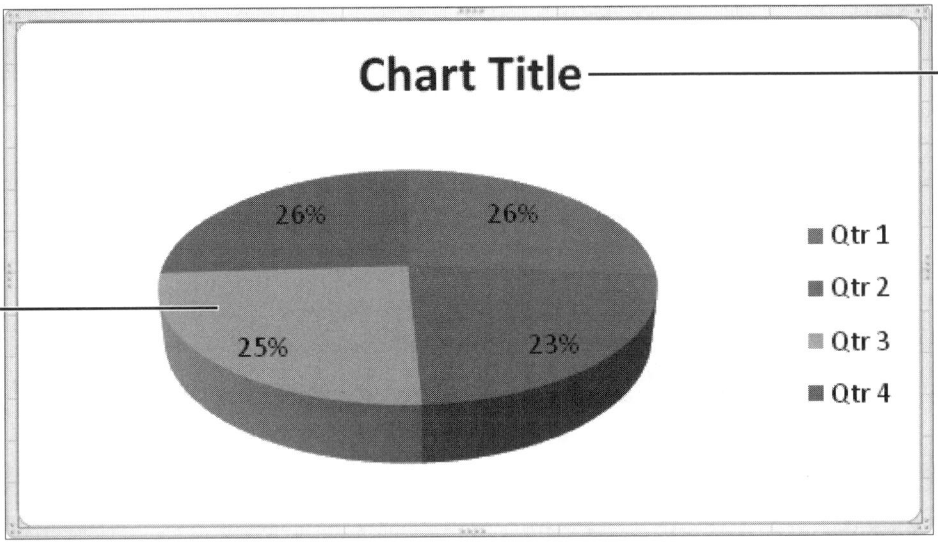

Ⓐ Notice that Excel displays the percent of total for each slice of the pie.

Ⓑ Notice that a Chart Title object is added to the chart.

Add a Chart Title

9. Click the **Chart Title** object to select it; then, click and drag across the text in the **title object** to select the text.

10. Type **`Yearly Inventory Expense`** as the new chart title.

11. Click the **border** of the chart object to deselect the Chart Title object.

Change the Chart Style

12. Click the **More** button at the right edge of the Chart Styles gallery to display the entire gallery.

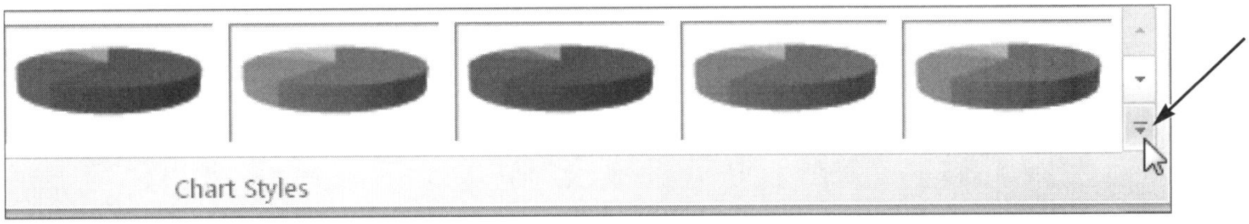

13. Choose **Style 42** toward the bottom-left corner of the gallery. Use **ToolTips** to assist you if necessary.

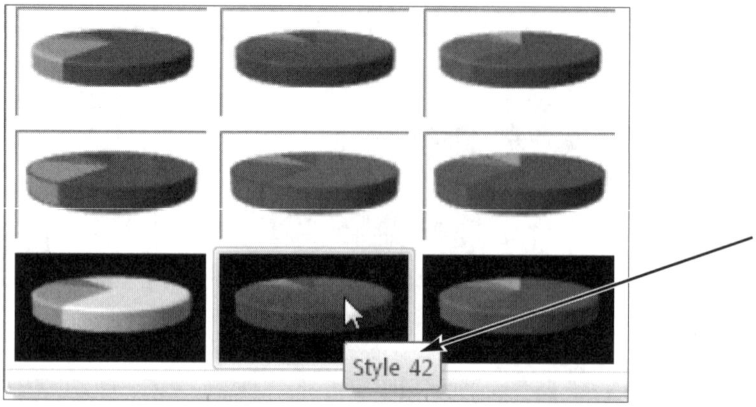

The chart now has a dramatic new look.

14. **Save**  and then **close** the file.

Concepts Review

To check your knowledge of the key concepts introduced in this lesson, complete the Concepts Review quiz on this and the next page. Or, you can take the quiz online by going to the URL **labyrinthelab.com/wtmo10**.

True/False Questions

			Page number
1. Using charts allows you to easily see trends and make comparisons about your data.	**true**	**false**	______
2. All formulas and functions begin with an equals (=) sign.	**true**	**false**	______
3. The multiplication symbol in Excel is "x."	**true**	**false**	______
4. Excel automatically changes the cell addresses in a copied formula relative to where it is copied.	**true**	**false**	______
5. If you want your formulas to recalculate when a number changes, you should use numbers in your formulas instead of cell addresses.	**true**	**false**	______
6. An Excel chart can be embedded in a spreadsheet or it can appear on a separate chart sheet.	**true**	**false**	______

Multiple Choice Questions

7. Which of the following is *not* one of Excel's built-in functions?

   Page number: ______

   a. MAX
   b. SUBTRACT
   c. AVERAGE
   d. SUM

8. Which of the following is a mathematical operator in Excel?

   Page number: ______

   a. ?
   b. /
   c. &
   d. #

9. Which of the following is *not* an Excel chart type?

   Page number: ______

   a. Pie
   b. Line
   c. Column
   d. Medical

10. Why do Excel formulas begin with an equals sign?

    Page number: ______

    a. It's easier to type the equals sign at the beginning of the formula than at the end.
    b. Excel uses a different branch of mathematics than you learned in school.
    c. It indicates to Excel that the data is a formula rather than regular text or numbers.
    d. It's the only key on the keyboard that is not reserved for other purposes.

Skill Builders

SKILL BUILDER 6.1 Track the Seniors Club Annual Golf Tournament

In this exercise, you will use some of Excel's built-in functions. You are in charge of keeping track of the golf scores for the Seniors Club annual golf tournament. It's the perfect opportunity for you to get more experience with entering and copying functions.

1. Open sb-Golf Scores from your Lesson 06 folder.
2. Enter the data for **rows 6 through 11** as shown in the following illustration.

	A	B	C	D	E	F	G	H	I
1	Seniors Club Annual Golf Tournament								
2									
3									
4									
5	Name	Day 1	Day 2	Day 3	Day 4	Tournament Total	Tournament Avg	Tournament Max	Tournament Min
6	Mukesh Patel	70	66	67	68				
7	Susan Kashner	72	68	69	71				
8	Moses LeVan	71	70	73	73				
9	Rosa Menendez	70	69	76	75				
10	Margaret Schultz	73	71	71	76				
11	Maria Alvarez	69	75	75	72				

Use the Sum Function

3. Select **cell F6**.
4. Choose **Home→Editing→AutoSum** [Σ] from the Ribbon.
   Excel places a marquee around Mukesh Patel's scores for the four days of the tournament.
5. Click the **Enter** [✓] button on the Formula Bar to finish entering the function.
   Now you will copy the function for the rest of the players. Cell F6 should still be the active cell.
6. Choose **Home→Clipboard→Copy** from the Ribbon.
7. Select the **range F7:F11**.
8. Choose **Home→Clipboard→Paste** from the Ribbon.
9. **Tap** [Esc] to remove the flashing marquee.

Mukesh Patel is our winner! He has the lowest score for the four-day tournament. Next you will calculate Mukesh's average score.

Use the AVERAGE, MAX, and MIN Functions

10. Select **cell G6** and type **=AVERAGE(** .

    Now you will calculate Mukesh's maximum and minimum scores.

11. Select the **range B6:E6** and then **tap** [Tab] to complete the formula.
12. Make sure **cell H6** is the active cell and then type **=MAX(** .
13. Select the **range B6:E6** and **tap** [Tab] to finish entering the formula.
14. Make sure **cell I6** is the active cell and then type =**MIN(** .
15. Select the **range B6:E6** and **tap** [Enter].

Copy Three Functions at Once

Now you will copy all three functions for the rest of the players.

16. Select the **range G6:I6**.
17. Choose **Home→Clipboard→Copy** from the Ribbon.
18. Select the **range G7:I11**.
19. Choose **Home→Clipboard→Paste** from the Ribbon.

    Now you see the average, maximum, and minimum scores for all of the players.

20. **Tap** [Esc] to turn off the marquee.
21. **Save** and then **close** the file.

SKILL BUILDER 6.2 Calculate Nutrients and Chart the Data

In this exercise, you will use Excel to examine the nutritional value of various foods. You will also use the chart feature to depict those values.

Your doctor has been complaining about your fondness for junk food. She would like you to get more calcium, protein, and fiber and less cholesterol and saturated fats in your diet.

1. Open sb-Counting Nutrients from the Lesson 06 folder.

Use the MAX and MIN Functions

Now you will use the MAX and MIN functions to determine which foods are the highest and lowest in various nutrient categories.

2. Select **cell C12** and type **`=MAX(`** .
3. Select the **range C5:C10** and **tap** [Enter].
   Broccoli wins in the Calcium category.
4. Type **`=MIN(`** in **cell C13**.
5. Select the **range C5:C10** and **tap** [Enter].

Copy the Formulas

6. Select the **range C12:C13**.
7. Choose **Home→Clipboard→Copy** from the Ribbon.
8. Select the **range D12:G13**.
9. Choose **Home→Clipboard→Paste** from the Ribbon.
10. **Tap** [Esc] to turn off the marquee.
    Now you see the maximum and minimum values for each nutrient category.

Chart the Nutrients

11. Select the **range B4:G10**.
12. Choose **Insert→Chart→Column** from the Ribbon.

13. Choose the **first chart type** in the **3-D category**, as shown in the following figure.

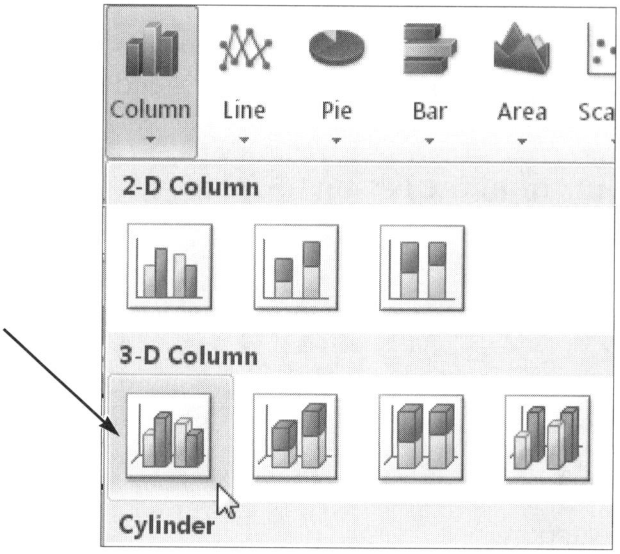

Notice which of the foods are high and low in the various nutrient categories.

14. Drag the chart **below** the data and position it as you deem appropriate.
15. Click in the spreadsheet to deselect the chart.
16. **Save** and then **close** the file.

SKILL BUILDER 6.3

Create a Household Budget

In this exercise, you will use your Excel skills to add formulas to your household budget. First you will compute the total monthly income and then you will find the total for all expense categories. Finally, you will subtract total expenses from total income to determine if you are over or under budget for the month.

Use the SUM Function

1. Open sb-Household Budget from the Lesson 06 folder.
2. Select **cell C8**.
3. Choose **Home→Editing→AutoSum** Σ from the Ribbon.
4. **Tap** Enter to complete the formula.
   There's your total monthly income. Let's hope it's enough to cover the expenses.
5. Select **cell C14**.

6. Choose **Home→Editing→AutoSum** [Σ] from the Ribbon.

7. **Tap** [Enter] to complete the formula.

8. Use [Σ] to enter the totals for the remaining expense categories in **cells C22, C30, and C35.**

   Next you will compute Total Expenses for January.

Create Formulas from Scratch

9. Select **cell C38** and use the mouse to help you create this formula:

10. **=C14+C22+C30+C35**.

11. **Tap** [Enter] to complete the formula.

    Next you will determine whether you are under or over budget by subtracting your Total Expenses from your Total Monthly Income.

12. Make sure **cell C39** is the active cell.

13. **Enter** the formula **=C8-C38** and **tap** [Enter].

    Congratulations! You are well under budget for the month.

14. **Save** [save icon] and then **close** the file.

SKILL BUILDER 6.4 Track Your Stocks

In this exercise, you will track a stock you are thinking about investing in. You want to examine its performance over time to see how it's doing.

Calculate the Stock Value

1. Open sb-Stock Tracker from your Lesson 06 folder.

   Seven weeks ago the XYZ stock closed at 36. You want to see how you would have fared if you had purchased 100 shares of the stock. First you will calculate what the total purchase price would have been by multiplying the original price per share by the number of shares owned.

2. Select **cell E4** and **type** the formula **=C4*D4**.

3. Click the **Enter** [✓] button on the Formula Bar.

4. Copy the formula in cell **E4 down through cell E9.**

5. Use the following information to enter Week End Prices in the range B4:B9:

Week 1	38
Week 2	39
Week 3	42
Week 4	35
Week 5	37
Week 6	39

Calculate the Current Value

Now you will calculate the current value for each week-ending period by multiplying the week-end price by the number of shares owned.

6. Select **cell F4** and **type** the formula **`=B4*D4`**.
7. Click the **Enter** button to complete the formula.
8. Copy the formula in **cell F4 down through cell F9**.

Calculate Total Earnings

Next you will compute the total earnings for each week-ending period by subtracting the total purchase price from the current value.

9. Click **cell G4**, type the formula **`=F4-E4`**, and click the **Enter** button.
10. Copy the formula in **cell G4** down through **cell G9**.
11. **Tap** [Esc] to turn off the marquee.

Chart Your Data

12. Select the **range F3:G9**.
13. Choose **Insert→Charts→Column** from the Ribbon.

14. Choose the **first chart** type in the **Cylinder category**, as shown in the following figure.

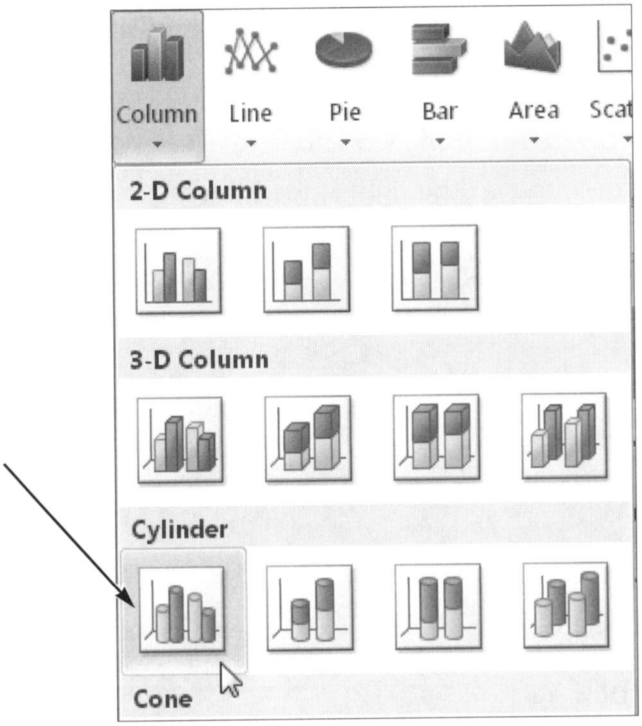

15. Drag the chart **below** the data.

16. Click in the spreadsheet to deselect the chart.

17. **Save** and then **close** the file.

SKILL BUILDER 6.5 Graph a Giraffe

In this exercise, you will create a giraffe graph. You and your granddaughter, Leona, went to the zoo and she was fascinated with the giraffes. The zookeeper told Leona the height of each giraffe. Now Leona wants to use Excel to graph the giraffes.

1. Open sb-Giraffe Heights from the Lesson 06 folder.

   You and Leona saw several giraffes: two adult males, three adult females, two yearlings, and two babies.

2. Select the **range A3:D6**.

3. Choose **Insert→Charts→Columns** from the Ribbon.

4. Choose the **first chart** type in the **3-D Column category**.

Move the Chart to Its Own Sheet

5. Make sure the **chart** is selected.
6. Choose **Design→Location→Move Chart** from the Ribbon.
7. Choose the **New Sheet** option in the Move Chart dialog box and click **OK**.

   The chart now appears on its own page in the workbook.

   Your chart looks great, but the legend on the right side of the graph doesn't really serve a purpose here. Let's delete it.
8. Click the **legend** once to select it.

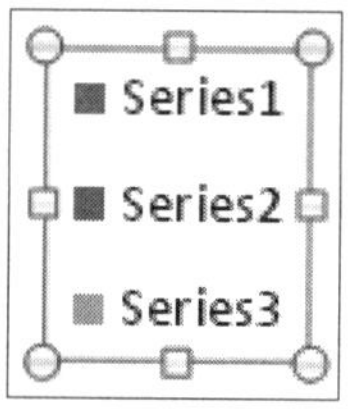

9. **Tap** [Delete] to remove the legend.
10. **Save** and then **close** the file.
11. Click File and choose **Exit** from the menu to close Excel.

LESSON 7

PowerPoint – Creating Powerful Presentations

In this lesson, you will learn the basics of PowerPoint 2010. You will create a PowerPoint presentation, apply a variety of layouts and design themes to your slides, explore several ways to view your slides, and add interest to your presentation with clip art, animations, and transitions.

LESSON OBJECTIVES

After studying this lesson, you will be able to:

- Identify key parts of the PowerPoint window
- Navigate through a presentation
- Work with design themes and slide layouts
- Explore the different PowerPoint views
- Add clip art, animations, and transitions

Student resources ***labyrinthelab.com/wtmo10***

Case Study: Creating an Email Presentation

Alec Harkins is a time management expert. He has been invited to give a presentation on efficient use of email at Central College Career Day next month. Knowing the impact of email in the world today, he wants to create a presentation that will give his audience the tools they need to get their email under control. Alec's dynamic speaking abilities, coupled with PowerPoint's robust presentation features, are sure to win over the audience.

Alec adds interest to his presentation with clip art.

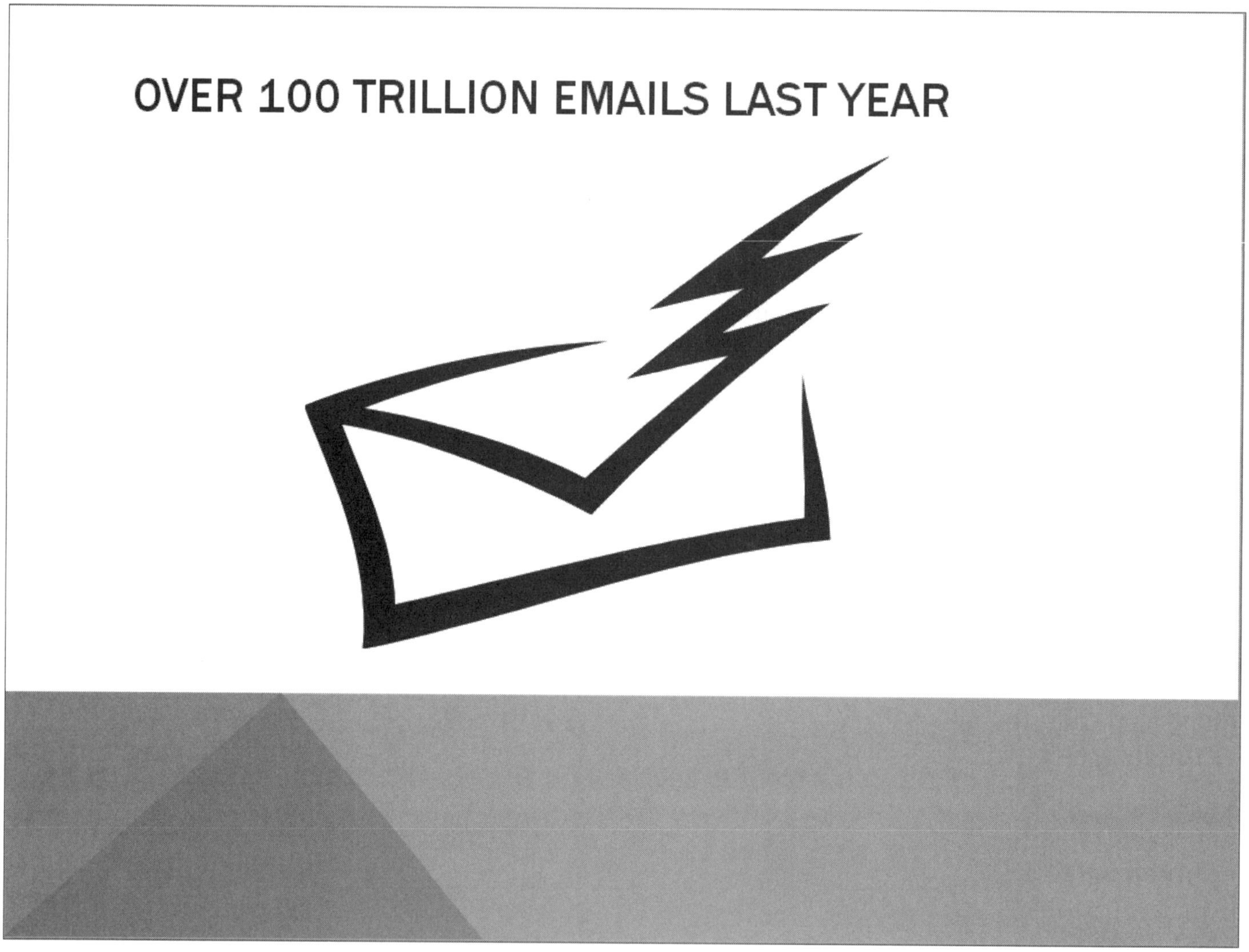

Presenting PowerPoint

PowerPoint 2010 is an intuitive, powerful presentation graphics program that enables you to create dynamic, multimedia presentations. You can deliver your presentation directly from your computer or by using an overhead video projection system.

PowerPoint provides powerful tools that let you concentrate on the content of your presentation instead of focusing on design details. Using PowerPoint's built-in design themes, animations, and transitions, you can rapidly create highly effective, professional presentations. PowerPoint tools help you organize, develop, and deliver your presentation with precision, control, and creativity.

Starting PowerPoint

You start PowerPoint just like other Microsoft Office 2010 programs. You use the Start button on the bottom-left corner of your Windows Desktop. The Start button has a different look depending on whether your computer uses Win 7, Win Vista, or Win XP.

Win 7/Vista

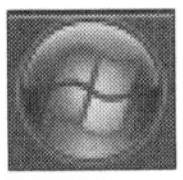

Win XP

The program icon that opens the PowerPoint program window is in the Microsoft Office folder, which appears when you click the All Programs menu after clicking the Start button.

HANDS-ON 7.1 Start PowerPoint

In this exercise, you will start PowerPoint using the Start button on the taskbar and the All Programs menu.

1. Click the **Start** / button, and then click the **All Programs** menu.
2. Click the **Microsoft Office** folder that appears in the menu, and then click **Microsoft PowerPoint 2010**.
3. If necessary, click the **Maximize** button in the upper-right corner of the PowerPoint window.

Introducing the PowerPoint Window

The PowerPoint window opens with a blank title slide where you can get started on your presentation right away. You can see similarities between the PowerPoint window and other program windows like Word and Excel. Notice the familiar File tab, the Ribbon, and the Quick Access toolbar.

Don't be concerned if your PowerPoint window looks slightly different from this example. The PowerPoint screen is customizable.

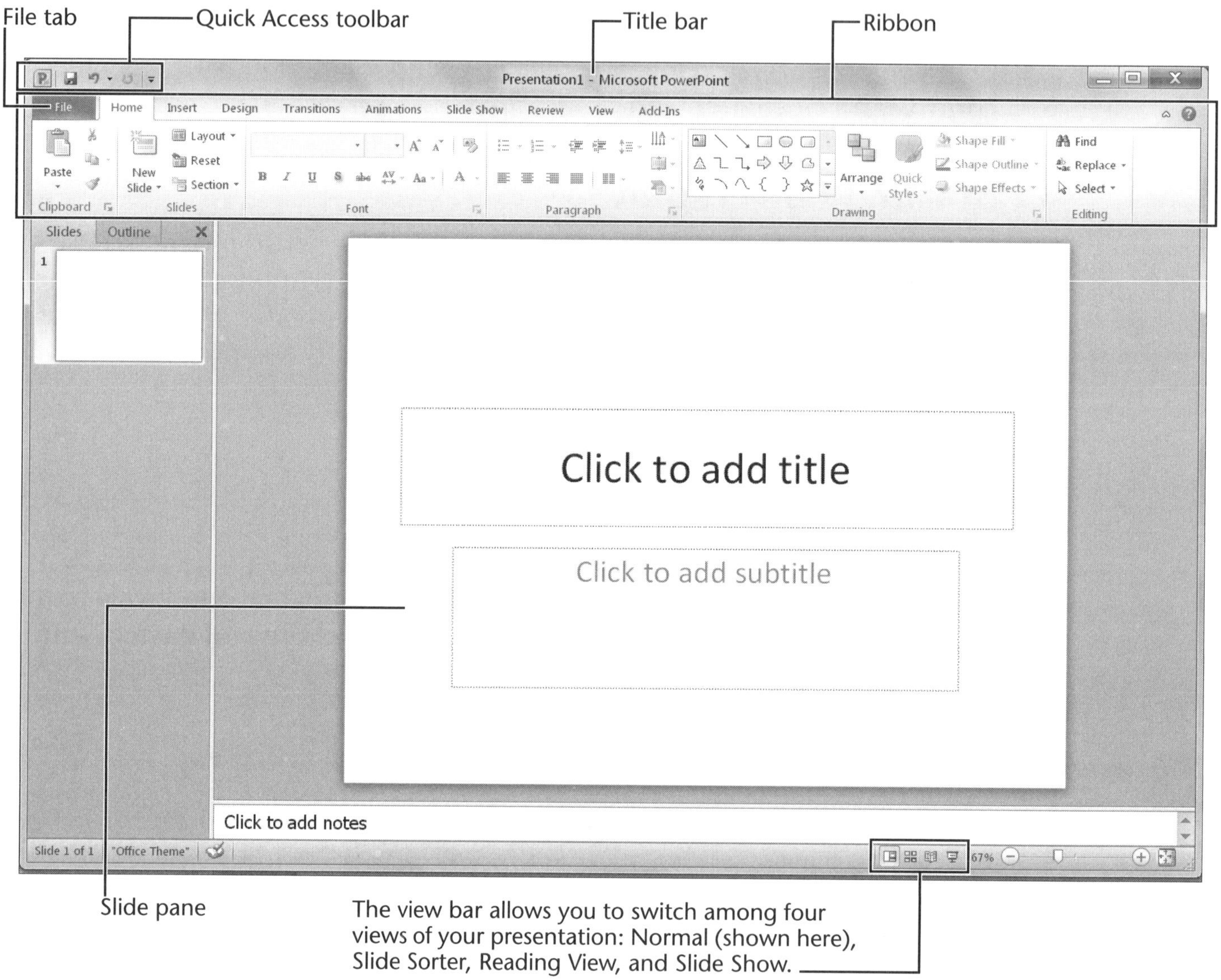

Navigating in a Presentation

PowerPoint has a number of features for navigating in a presentation. You can use both mouse techniques and keyboard techniques to move through a presentation. The technique you use is a matter of personal preference.

The Slides tab displays thumbnails of the slides in your presentation. Clicking a thumbnail icon switches to that slide in the Slide pane.

Dragging the scroll box moves through your slides while a ToolTip shows the slide number and the title of the slide to guide you as you scroll.

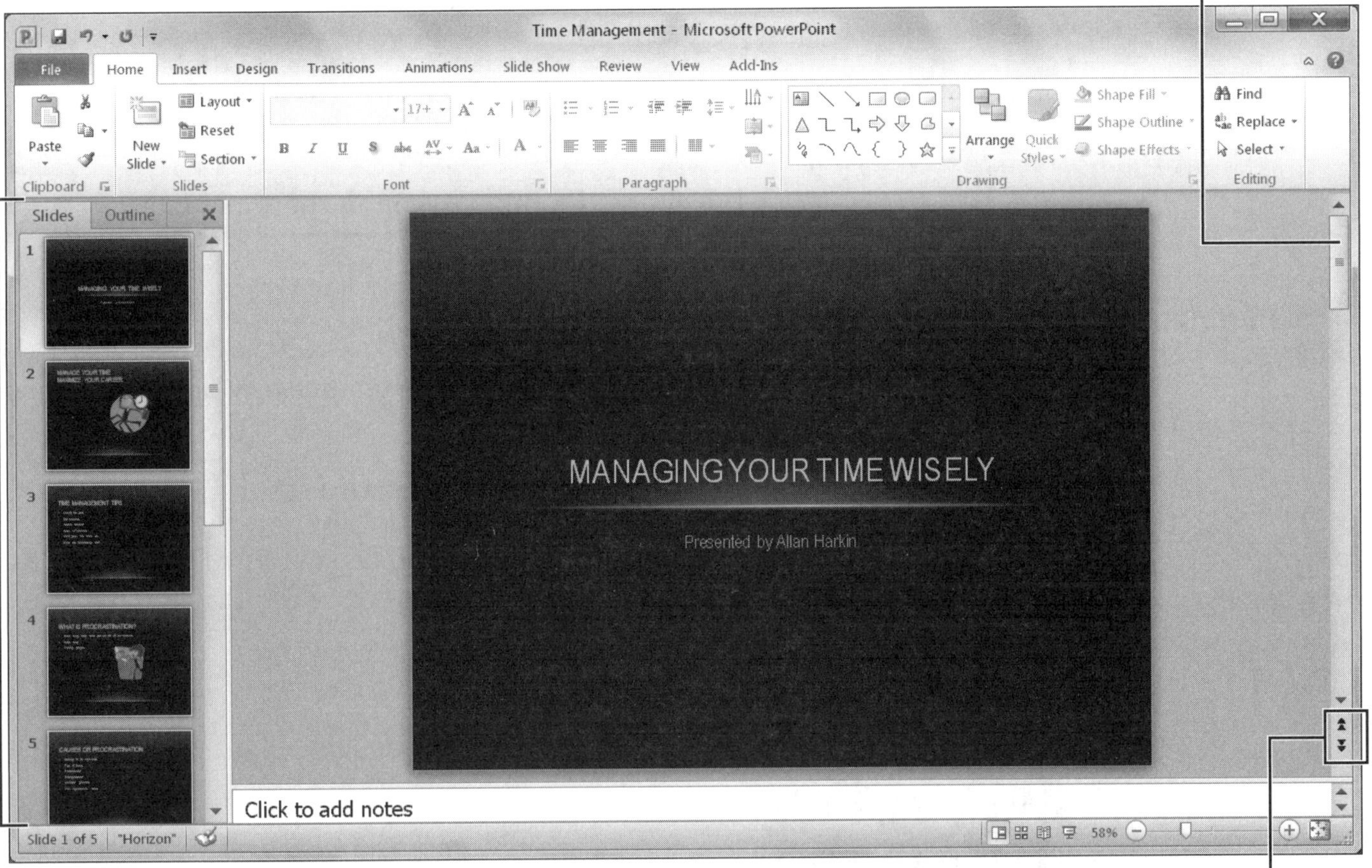

The Previous Slide and Next Slide buttons allow you to move through the presentation one slide at a time.

QUICK REFERENCE: Navigating in PowerPoint

Move To	Technique
The first slide in the presentation	Drag the scroll box to the top of the scroll bar. *or* Press Ctrl+Home.
The last slide in the presentation	Drag the scroll box to the bottom of the scroll bar. *or* Press Ctrl+End.

QUICK REFERENCE: Navigating in PowerPoint (Continued)

Move To	Technique
The next slide	Click the Next Slide button at the bottom of the scroll bar. *or* Press [Page Down].
The previous slide	Click the Previous Slide button at the bottom of the scroll bar. *or* Press [Page Up].
Jump to a slide	Drag the scroll box and observe the ToolTip which displays the slide number and title. *or* Click the desired thumbnail icon in the Slides tab.

HANDS-ON 7.2 Navigate in a Presentation

In this exercise, you will navigate through a presentation using several different methods, including both mouse and keyboard techniques.

1. Open the Time Management presentation from your Lesson 07 folder.
2. Click the **slide 2** thumbnail icon in the Slides tab to switch to that slide, as shown in the following figure.

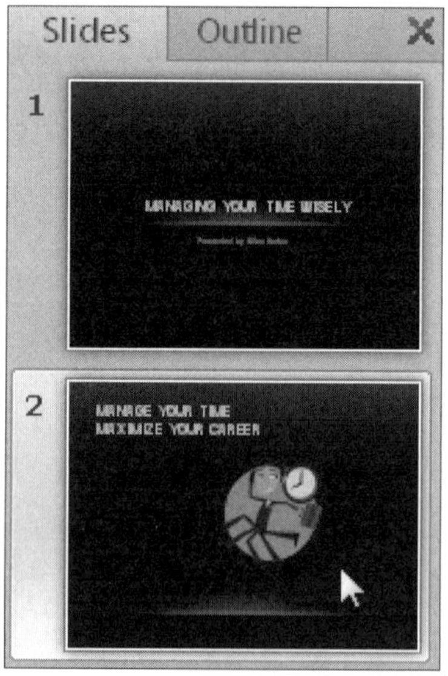

Slide 2 now appears in the Slide pane.

3. Follow these steps to use the tools in the scroll bar to navigate:

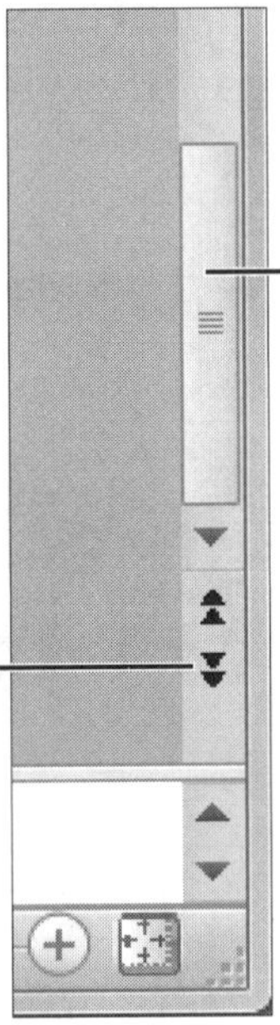

Ⓐ Click the **Next Slide** button at the bottom of the scroll bar to move to slide 3.

Ⓑ Drag the **scroll box** to the bottom of the scroll bar to display the last slide in the presentation.

4. **Press** [Ctrl]+[Home] to move to the beginning of the presentation.
5. **Tap** [Page Down] to move down one slide.
6. **Press** [Ctrl]+[End] to move to the last slide.
7. Drag the **scroll box** to the top of the scroll bar to return to slide 1.

   Leave the file open. You will use it in the next exercise.

Using PowerPoint Views

You can view a presentation several ways. The views you will use in this lesson are easily accessible in the view bar, which is located at the bottom-right side of the screen.

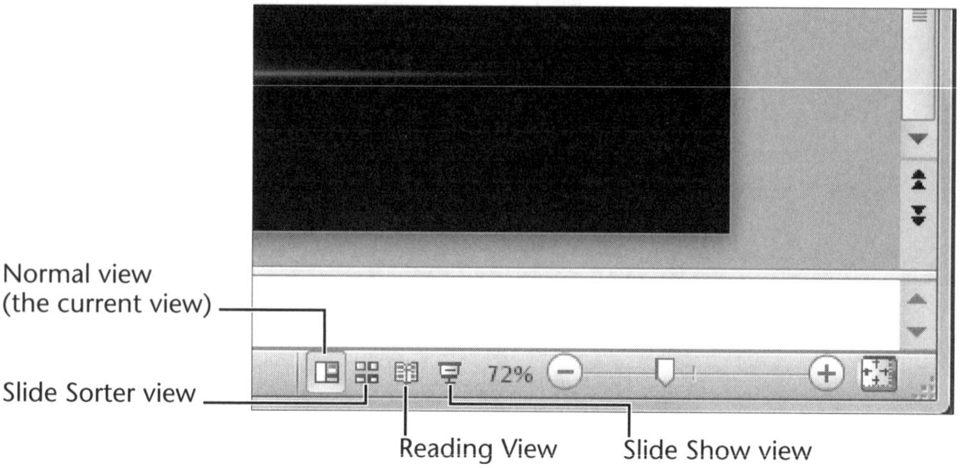

The four views on the view bar include Normal (the view you have been using), Slide Sorter, Reading View, and Slide Show. Each view is described here.

- **Normal:** Normal view is the primary view you use when creating a presentation. It consists of three areas: the Slides and Outline tabs on the left side of the screen, the Slide pane in the center of the screen, and the Notes pane at the bottom of the screen. This is where you can type speaker notes.
- **Slide Sorter:** Slide Sorter view displays all slides in a presentation in miniature. It is a good way to get a helicopter view of your presentation. You can drag and drop slides with your mouse to rearrange them in Slide Sorter view.
- **Reading View:** With this view, the slide takes over the full PowerPoint screen but not the full Windows screen. The taskbar is still visible, so if you are working with several programs at once, for example, you can switch among programs using the taskbar.
- **Slide Show:** This is the view you use when you are ready to deliver your presentation. All slides take over the full Windows screen.

HANDS-ON 7.3 Explore PowerPoint Views

In this exercise, you will use the view bar to explore other views of a presentation. You will also rearrange slides in Slide Sorter view.

Use Slide Sorter View

1. Click the **Slide Sorter** button on the view bar, as shown at right.

   Your slides now look like thumbnails similar to those in the Slides tab on the left side of the screen in Normal view. Notice the highlighted border around slide 1. This indicates that slide 1 is active.

2. Click **slide 2** one time to make it active.

   Notice that a highlighted border now surrounds slide 2.

Move Slides in Slide Sorter View

TIP! Slide Sorter view is one of the easiest views to use when you want to rearrange the order of your slides.

3. Follow these steps to move slide 4 to the left of slide 3:

A Place the mouse pointer over **slide 4** and then press and hold down the mouse button.

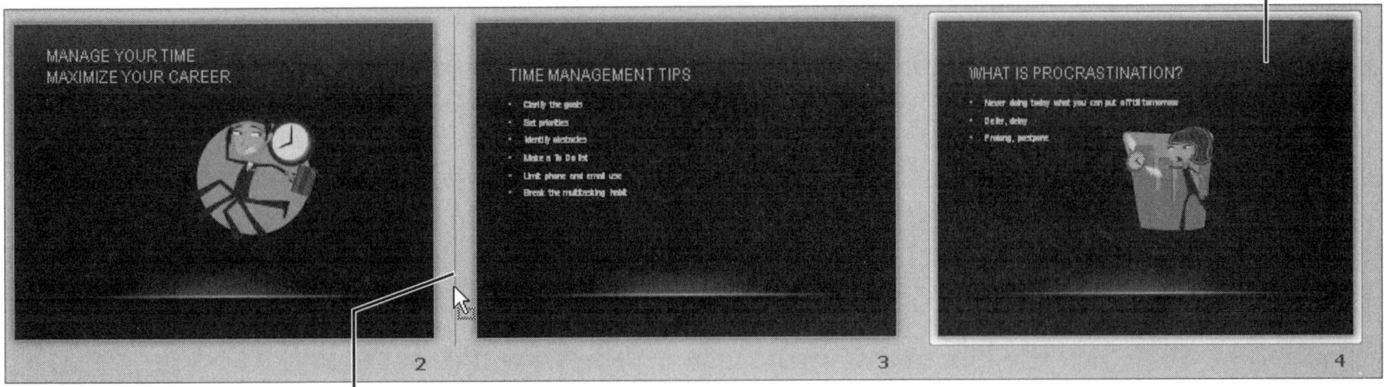

B Drag the mouse pointer between **slides 2 and 3**. A vertical line appears between the slides.

C Release the mouse button to reposition the slide.

4. Use the same technique to move **slide 5** between **slides 3 and 4**.

Use Slide Show View

5. Click **slide 1** to make it the active slide.

   The active slide is the first slide that will appear when you click the Slide Show button.

6. Click the **Slide Show** button on the view bar, as shown at right.

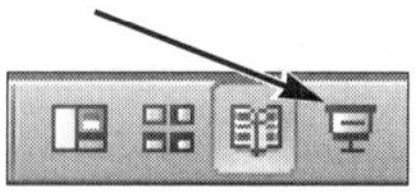

7. Click the **left mouse button** to advance to the next slide.
8. Click the **left mouse button** three more times to move to the last slide.
9. Click the **mouse button** again and notice the all black slide.

   How did that get there? PowerPoint put it there for you. It's not a slide that you can see in Normal or Slide Sorter view. The reason for this slide is to give the presenter an opportunity to wrap up the presentation without the audience looking at PowerPoint's Normal or Slide Sorter view. That would be distracting.

10. Click the **mouse button** again to return to Slide Sorter view.

    You can see that this view would be distracting for the audience to look at while the presenter is wrapping up.

Use Reading View

11. If necessary, click **slide 1** to make it active.
12. Click the **Reading View** button, as shown at right.

    You can see that this view covers the full PowerPoint window but that the Windows taskbar is still visible at the bottom of the screen. So, you can click a program icon on the taskbar to switch to another program, if necessary, while working in PowerPoint.

13. Click the **left mouse button** anywhere on the slide to advance to the next slide.
14. Continue clicking the **left mouse button** and notice the black slide at the end of the presentation—just as we saw in Slide Show view.
15. Click through the black slide to return to **Slide Sorter** view.
16. Click the **Normal view** button on the view bar, as shown at right.

17. **Save**  and then **close** the presentation.

Creating a Presentation

Now you will explore the exciting features that allow you to create powerful presentations effortlessly. You'll work with design themes, which add color and drama to your presentations, and with preformatted slide layouts, which make it easy to add text and graphics to your presentations.

As you add clip art to your presentation, you will find that working with clip art in PowerPoint is similar to working with clip art in Word. Once again, you are benefitting from the similarities among programs in a suite.

Using PowerPoint Themes

PowerPoint's built-in themes present professional-looking color schemes and background graphics at the click of a mouse. You can use Live Preview with themes to explore how various themes look before you apply them.

In addition, themes provide a consistent look throughout the presentation in terms of colors, fonts, and other design elements. Themes can also help set the mood for a presentation with their colors and graphic images. Easy to use themes allow you to concentrate your efforts on your message.

HANDS-ON 7.4 Use Themes in a Presentation

In this exercise, you will start a new blank presentation, use Live Preview to explore PowerPoint's themes, and apply a theme to your presentation.

1. Click File and then choose **New** from the menu.

   Blank Presentation is already selected in the center panel of the Backstage view, as shown in the following figure.

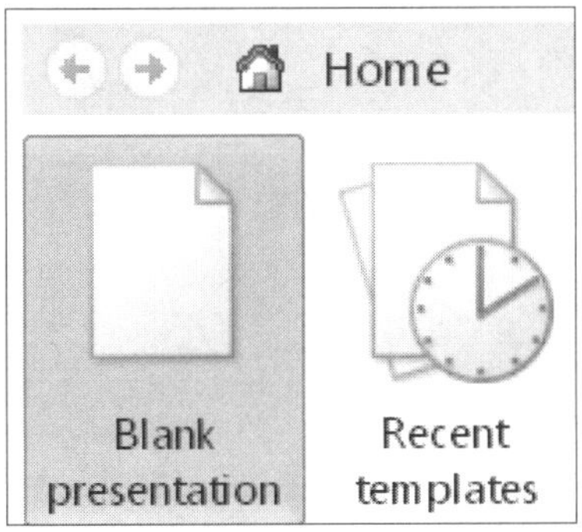

2. Click the **Create** button in the right-hand panel to start a new blank presentation.

   A blank slide appears on the screen so you can begin working with the presentation right away. The slide that appears when you start a new presentation uses the Title Slide layout. PowerPoint provides various slide layouts, which you'll learn more about shortly.

Apply a Design to the Presentation

3. Click the **Design** tab on the Ribbon and notice the Themes group.
4. Click the **More** button on the right side of the Themes gallery, as shown at right, to display the entire gallery.

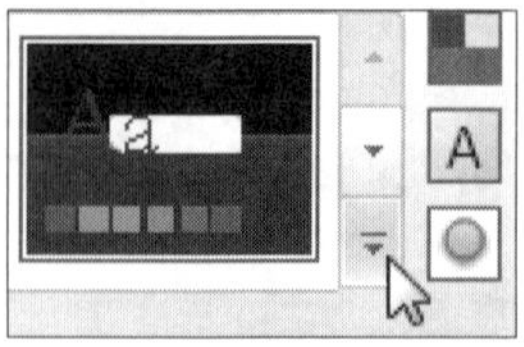

5. Hover the **mouse pointer** over several of the themes and watch as Live Preview displays samples of how the theme will look if you apply it to your slide.

   Notice that ToolTips displays the theme name when you hover the mouse pointer over a theme. Themes are listed in alphabetic order.

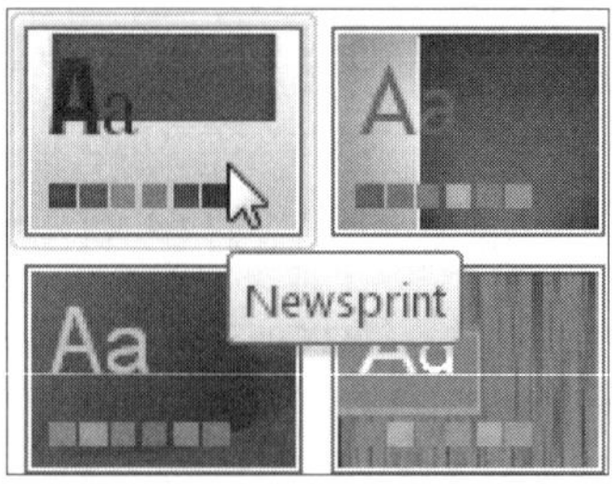

6. Use ToolTips to locate the **Angles** theme (white, orange, and blue) in the gallery.
7. Preview the theme for a moment, and then click to apply it to the slide.

Save the Presentation

8. Click 

and then choose **Save As** from the menu.
9. Navigate to the Lesson 07 folder in the Save As dialog box.
10. Type `Efficient Email` in the File Name box at the bottom of the dialog box, and then click the **Save** button.

    You are now ready to begin your presentation.

    Leave the file open. You will work with it throughout this lesson.

Typing Text in a Slide

Slides contain dotted boxes called *placeholders*. Placeholders can contain text or objects such as tables, graphs, clip art, and other elements. For now you will concentrate on adding text to the title and subtitle placeholders in your title slide.

HANDS-ON 7.5 Add Text to a Slide

In this exercise, you will add text to your title slide.

1. Click the text placeholder on the slide that reads, **Click to Add Title**.
   The placeholder is now selected and its handles (small circles) are visible. You can also see the flashing insertion point, indicating that you can begin to type.
2. Type **`Efficient Email`** in the text placeholder.
   The appearance of the font is part of the Angles theme.
3. Click in the placeholder that reads **Click to Add Subtitle**.
4. Type **`Presented by Alec Harkins`**.
5. **Save** the presentation.
   You are now ready to add a new slide to your presentation.

Working with Slide Layouts

Slide layouts vary based on the text and graphic placeholders that are embedded in the slide and based on the theme you are using. The Layout gallery offers a variety of different ways to organize your content on the slide.

The slide you just completed has the Title Slide layout, which contains title and subtitle placeholders. Next you will use a slide with the Title and Content layout, which contains a title placeholder and a content placeholder.

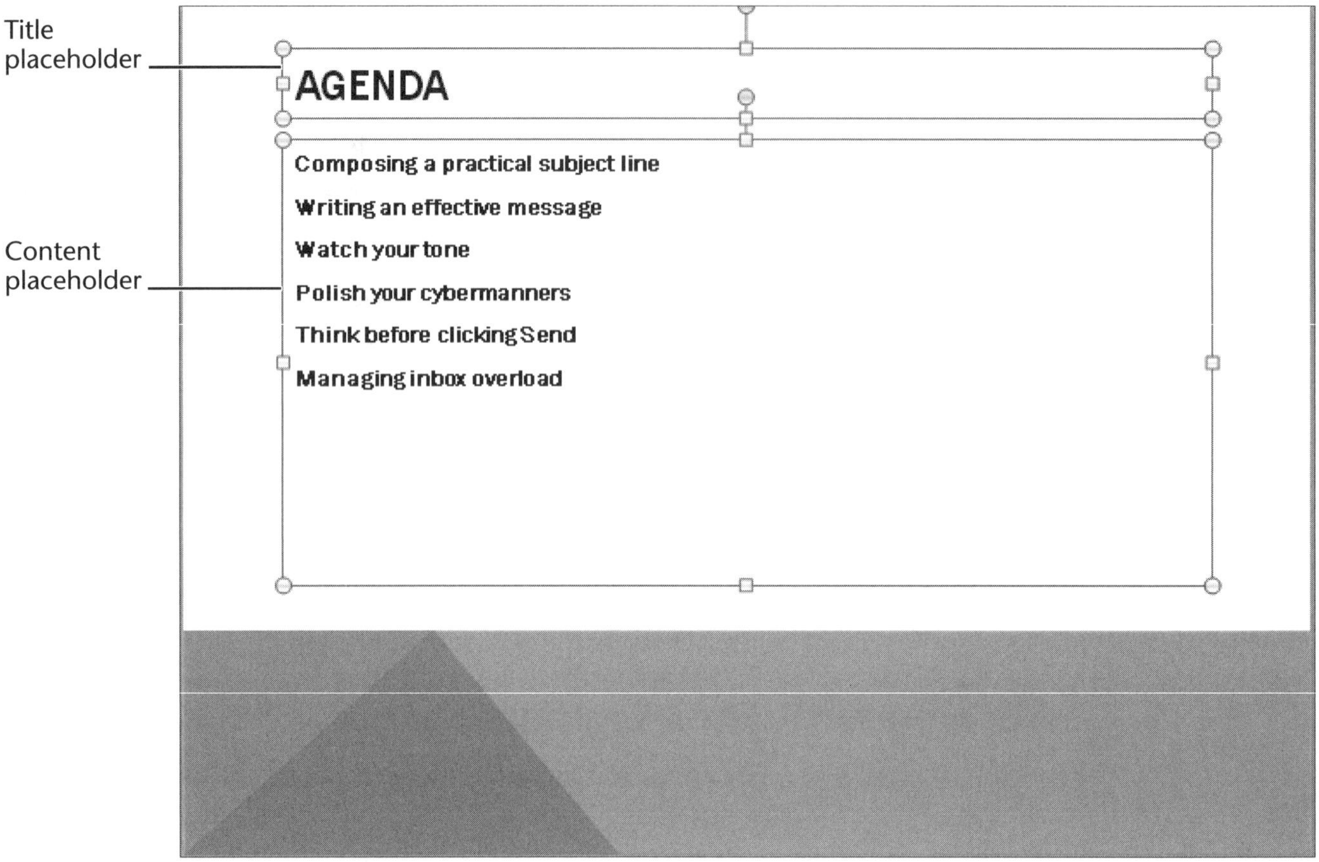

HANDS-ON 7.6 Add a Slide and Try Different Layouts

In this exercise, you will add a slide to your presentation and apply different layouts from the Layout gallery.

Add a Slide to the Presentation

1. Choose **Home→Slides→New Slide** from the Ribbon.

   A new slide is added to the presentation using the default Title and Content layout. Notice the icons that appear in the bottom placeholder. You can click these images to add elements such as tables, charts, and clip art to the slide.

Change the Slide Layout

The Layout gallery does not use Live Preview, so you have to apply a layout to your slide to see its effect.

2. Choose **Home→Slides→Layout** from the Ribbon.

3. Click to apply the **Section Header** layout, as shown in the following illustration.

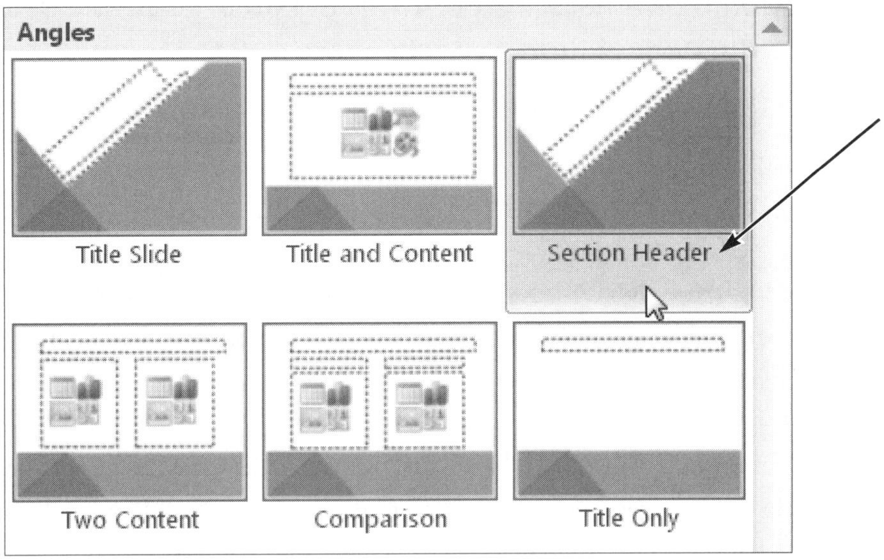

4. Choose **Home→Slides→Layout** from the Ribbon.
5. Click to apply the **Two Content** layout to the slide.
   Feel free to test other layouts if you wish.
6. Choose **Home→Slides→Layout** from the Ribbon.
7. Apply the **Title and Content** layout.
8. **Save** your presentation.

Presentation Design Tips

You are now ready to add more content to your presentation. Following are some tried and true recommendations from professional presenters. Keeping these guidelines in mind goes a long way in helping you design your presentation like a pro.

Don't Write an Essay People glaze over when they see dense text. Slide content should provide a roadmap of main points for the presenter.

- Use a maximum of eight lines per slide.
- If there is a lot of information, break up the lines over a few slides instead of crowding too much on one slide.
- Don't write in complete sentences; just hit the high points.

Font It's fun to play with different fonts, but keeping it simple is the recommendation for presentations.

- Size should be at least 18 points. If possible, go to the back of the room where the presentation will take place and see if you can read the slides.
- Limit the number of fonts to about three per presentation; that includes point size changes.
- Sticking with the fonts the theme provides is a good recommendation.

Design Theme Most people recommend a design theme with a dark background, but a dark background can look faded if the room is too light. If possible, check the room conditions first.

Special Effects Again, think simple. Special effects like clip art, animations, and slide transitions are fun, but they can detract from your message. Use special effects to emphasize a point, never to entertain.

HANDS-ON 7.7 Add Content to Your New Slide

In this exercise, you will add text to the title placeholder and the content placeholder.

1. Click the **title placeholder** and type **`Agenda`**.
2. Click the **bottom placeholder** and type the following items:

   `Compose a practical subject line`

   `Write an effective message`

   `Watch your tone`

   `Polish your cybermanners`

   `Think before clicking Send`

   `Learn to manage inbox overload`
3. **Save** your presentation.

Adding Clip Art to a Presentation

Using clip art is a great way to add zing to your presentations. Working with clip art in PowerPoint is similar to working with clip art in Word. Many of the techniques that you learned in Lesson 4, Word – Encouraging Recycling with Flyers, will apply in PowerPoint.

HANDS-ON 7.8 Add Clip Art to the Presentation

In this exercise, you will add a new slide containing a clip art icon embedded in it. You will use the icon to open the clip art task pane. Then you will search for a clip art image related to email and insert it in the slide.

1. Choose **Home→Slides→New Slide** menu ▾ from the Ribbon.

   This displays the Layout gallery where you can select the layout *before* inserting the slide.

2. Choose the **Title and Content** layout.

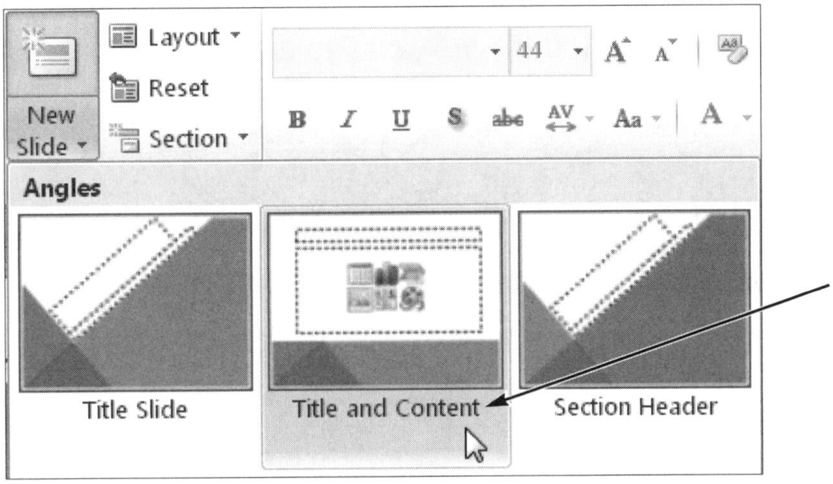

3. Click the **title placeholder** and type **`Over 100 Trillion Emails Last Year`**.

4. Click the **Clip Art** icon in the bottom placeholder, as shown in the following figure.

   The Clip Art task pane opens on the right side of the window. You may see a term from a previous exercise in the Search For box.

5. If necessary, delete any term that appears in the Search For box at the top of the task pane.

Search All Media Types

This time you will search for All Media File Types so you have more images to choose from.

6. Click the **arrow** ▾ on the right side of the Results Should Be field and, if necessary, check **All Media Types**.
7. Click the **arrow** ▾ again to close the menu.
8. Type **`email`** in the Search For box and then click the **Go** button.
9. Scroll down the list of thumbnails and click the image shown below to insert it in the presentation. If it is not available, choose an email image that blends with your presentation theme.

Move the Clip Art

10. Hover the **mouse pointer** over the image, and when the mouse pointer changes to a **four-headed arrow**, drag up and to the left a couple of inches; then, release the mouse button.

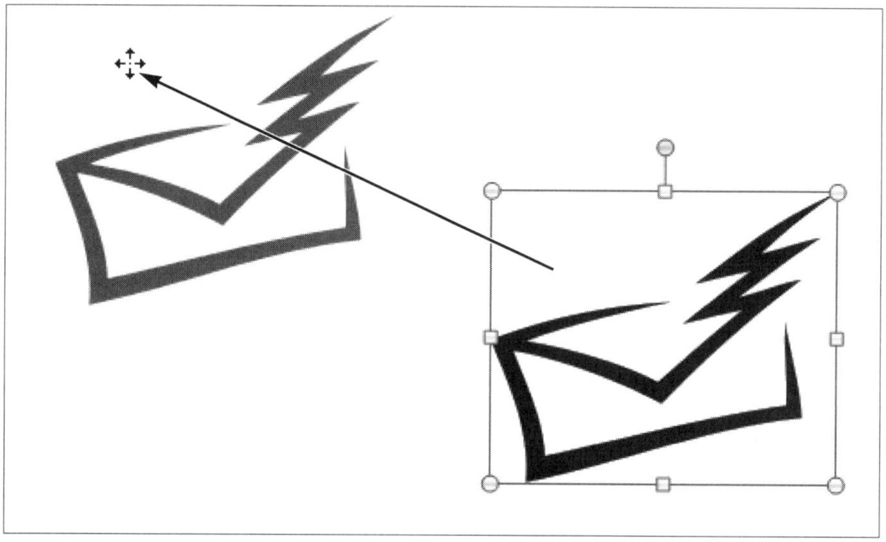

Resize the Clip Art

11. Place the mouse pointer over the **bottom-right corner handle**, and when the pointer changes to a **double-headed arrow**, drag down and to the right about three inches to enlarge the image.

12. Release the mouse button.

13. Adjust the **size and position** of the image as you deem necessary.

14. Click the **Close** button in the upper-right corner of the Clip Art task pane to close it.

15. **Save** your presentation.

Delivering the Slide Show

The slides are created and the presentation is complete. The first phase is over. The next phase, delivering the presentation, is just beginning. The successful communication of the presentation is dependent on the presenter.

The PowerPoint slide show is secondary to the message the presenter is delivering, and the manner in which you convey the message is critical to grabbing the audience's attention and keeping it. Before you stand in front of an audience, familiarize yourself with the following tips.

Delivery Tips

It is not only *what* you say, it is *how* you say it that makes the difference between an engaging and an unsuccessful presentation. Lead your audience. Help them focus on the message of your presentation. Use the following PEER guidelines to deliver effective presentations.

- **Pace:** Maintain a moderate pace. Speaking too fast will exhaust your audience and speaking too slowly may put them to sleep. Carry your audience with you as you talk.
- **Emphasis:** Pause for emphasis. As you present, use a brief pause to emphasize your points. Pausing gives your audience time to absorb your message.

- **Eye Contact:** Always face your audience while speaking. A common mistake is to speak while walking or facing the projection screen. Don't waste all of the work you have done in PowerPoint by losing your audience's interest now. If you are speaking from a lectern, resist the temptation to lean on it. Stand tall and look directly at your audience.
- **Relax:** You are enthusiastic and want to convey that tone to the audience. However, when you speak, avoid fast movements, pacing, and rushed talking. Your audience will be drawn to your movements and miss the point. Remember that the audience is listening to you to learn; this material may be old hat to you, but it's new to them. Speak clearly, maintain a steady pace, and stay calm.

Navigating in Slide Show View

You use different navigation techniques in a slide show than the ones you used in Normal view. There are several methods you can use to move through a slide show. They include using the mouse, the keyboard, and the Slide Show toolbar.

Navigate with the Mouse and the Keyboard The following Quick Reference table provides mouse and keyboard techniques for moving through a presentation in Slide Show view.

QUICK REFERENCE: Navigating in a Slide Show

Task	Procedure
Move to the next slide	Click the left mouse button. *or* Tap the [Page Down] button. *or* Tap the [↓] key or the [→] key. *or* Tap the [Spacebar].
Move to the previous slide	Tap the [Page Up] button. *or* Tap the [←] key or the [↑] key. *or* Tap the [Backspace] key.

Navigate with the Slide Show Toolbar When you launch a slide show and place the mouse pointer over the slide, the Slide Show toolbar appears faintly in the bottom-left corner of the slide. The buttons provide ways to navigate through the slide show. There's even a button that allows you to annotate or highlight your slides.

Button	Description
	Previous Slide
	Select a pen to annotate your slides during the presentation or select a highlighter to add emphasis
	The Navigation button displays a menu of navigation options
	Next Slide

HANDS-ON 7.9 Run the Slide Show

In this exercise, you will use various techniques to navigate in your slide show.

Start the Slide Show

1. Click **slide 1** in the Slides tab on the left side of the screen to move to the first slide in the presentation.

2. Click the **Slide Show** button on the view bar toward the bottom-right corner of the screen.

   PowerPoint displays your title slide in full-screen view.

Navigate in the Slide Show

3. Hover the mouse pointer over the **bottom-left corner** of the slide.

   The buttons on the toolbar in the bottom-left corner are dim, but these timid little buttons fade in when you place the mouse pointer directly over them.

4. Click the **Next Slide** button on the toolbar to move to slide 2.

5. Click the **Navigation** button on the toolbar and then choose **Go to Slide→Efficient Email** from the menu.

   This feature is useful if you want to jump a long distance in a presentation without having to move through a lot of slides.

6. **Tap** [Page Down] and then **tap** [Page Up].

   PowerPoint displays the next or previous slide each time you tap these keys.

7. Click the **left mouse button** to move to the next slide.

8. **Tap** [↑] on the keyboard to move to the previous slide.

End the Slide Show

9. Click the **Navigation** button on the toolbar and choose **End Show** from the menu.

   Next you will really jazz things up by adding animations and transitions.

Adding Animations and Transitions to the Show

Now that you have completed your slides and run a slide show, you decide to liven up the show using PowerPoint's animations and transitions features.

Animating Your Slide Show

Animation brings life to your presentation by affecting how text or objects, such as clip art, enter your slide. Following are a few buttons from the Animation group on the Ribbon to give you an idea of the possibilities.

If you have lines of text in the Content placeholder, you can have them fade, fly, or float into your slide when you click the mouse button. This keeps your audience focused on the point you are discussing.

HANDS-ON 7.10 Animate a Slide

In this exercise, you will add life to your slides by applying animations. You will test several different animation options.

1. If necessary, click **slide 2** in the Slides tab to place it in the Slide pane.

2. Click the **bottom placeholder** to make it active.

3. Choose **Animations→Animation→Fly In** from the Ribbon.

   Wow, pretty interesting! Notice the items are numbered 1 through 6. This is the order in which the items will appear in the slide show when you click the mouse button.

   Now you will check out how that works in Slide Show view.

4. Click the **Slide Show** button on the View Bar toward the bottom-right corner of the screen.
5. Click the **mouse button** to see the first point fly into the slide.
6. Click the **mouse button** to see the second point fly into the slide.

   Can you see how that keeps the audience focused on what the presenter is talking about?
7. Keep clicking the **mouse button** to see all of the items fly into the slide.
8. Click the **Navigation** button on the toolbar and choose **End Show** from the menu.

Try Out More Animations

9. Make sure the second slide is active, and then click in the **bottom placeholder**.
10. Choose **Animations→Animation→Float In** from the Ribbon.

    You can also hover the mouse pointer over a button in the Animation group and use Live Preview to get a feel for the animation.
11. Take a few moments to test other animations using **Live Preview**.
12. When you find an animation you like, apply it to the slide and then try it out in **Slide Show** view.
13. End the slide show and return to the **Slide** pane.
14. **Save** your presentation.

Adding Transitions to Your Slide Show

Transitions are like the six o'clock news effects. When the news commentator finishes one story and transitions to the next, there is typically some type of graphic effect that leads to the next story.

Following are a few of the buttons located in the Transition to This Slide group on the Ribbon. You can have a wipe, split, or reveal effect when moving from one slide to another in your presentation.

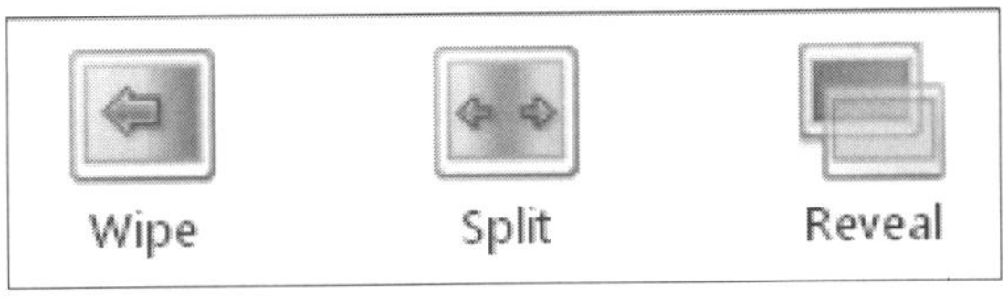

HANDS-ON 7.11 Add Transitions to Your Presentation

In this exercise, you will test out some transition effects. When you find a transition you like, you will check it out in Slide Show view.

1. If necessary, make **slide 1** the active slide.
2. Choose **Transitions→Transition to This Slide→Split** from the Ribbon.
3. Choose **Transitions→Transition to This Slide→Wipe** from the Ribbon.
4. Take a few moments to test some other transitions.
5. When you find the transition you like, switch to **slide 2** and apply the transition.
6. Switch to **slide 3** and apply the transition.

   Although you could apply a different transition to each slide, it would likely be distracting for the audience if you did. Some of PowerPoint's transitions are pretty lively and possibly distracting. Think "subtle" when selecting a transition.
7. Make **slide 1** active, then check out your presentation in **Slide Show** view.
8. **Save** and then **close** your presentation.

Concepts Review

To check your knowledge of the key concepts introduced in this lesson, complete the Concepts Review quiz on this and the next page. Or, you can take the quiz online by going to the URL **labyrinthelab.com/wtmo10**.

True/False Questions

			Page number
1. You can use Live Preview with themes to explore how various themes look before you apply them.	**true**	**false**	
2. Themes provide a consistent look throughout a presentation in terms of colors, fonts, and other design elements.	**true**	**false**	
3. The Slide Show toolbar provides the only methods for navigating in a slide show.	**true**	**false**	
4. Using clip art in PowerPoint is similar to using clip art in Word.	**true**	**false**	
5. Animation affects how text or objects enter your slide.	**true**	**false**	
6. You use Slide Sorter view when you are ready to deliver your presentation.	**true**	**false**	

Multiple Choice Questions

7. Which view displays the presentation in the full Windows screen?

   Page number: ______

   a. Normal

   b. Slide Show

   c. Reading View

   d. Slide Sorter

8. Which of the following is *not* a method of navigating through a presentation in Normal view?

   Page number: ______

   a. Dragging the scroll box

   b. Using the Slide Show toolbar

   c. Using the Slides tab

   d. Using the Next Side and Previous Slide buttons on the scroll bar

9. Which of the following is not a slide layout?

   Page number: ______

   a. Title and Content

   b. Title Slide

   c. Blank

   d. Clip Art

10. Which of the following views is *not* available on the view bar?

    Page number: ______

    a. Print Preview

    b. Slide Sorter

    c. Normal

    d. Slide Show

Skill Builders

SKILL BUILDER 7.1 Present the Giraffes

Your granddaughter, Leona, told her teacher about her trip to the zoo and how she made a graph of the giraffes' heights. Her teacher asked Leona to give a presentation about the giraffes during Show and Tell next week. Leona will use the picture icon embedded in a slide to insert a photograph she took of the giraffes. Then she will copy her giraffe graph into the presentation.

1. Click File and choose **New** from the menu.
2. Click the **Create** button in the right-hand Backstage view panel to start a new blank presentation.

Apply a Theme to the Presentation

3. Click the **Design** tab.
4. Click the **More** button on the right side of the Themes gallery, as shown at right, to display the entire gallery.

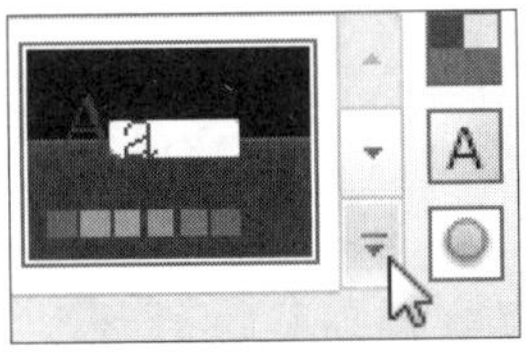

5. Apply the **Paper** theme to the slide.
   Remember, the themes are in alphabetic order.
6. Click the **title placeholder** and type **`My Trip to the Zoo`**.
7. Click the **subtitle placeholder** and type **`By Leona Goodspeed`**.

Add a New Slide and Insert a Photograph

Leona took her camera to the zoo and got a good picture of a couple of giraffes. She downloaded the picture to her PC and now she'll insert it in a slide.

8. Choose **Home→Slides→New Slide** from the Ribbon.
9. Click in the **title placeholder** and type **`The Giraffes`**.

10. Click the **Insert Picture from File** icon, as shown in the following illustration.

11. Navigate to your Lesson 07 folder and **double-click** the sb-Giraffe Picture file. Add a New Slide, Change the Layout

12. Choose **Home→Slides→New Slide** from the Ribbon.

13. Choose **Home→Slides→Layout** from the Ribbon.

14. Choose the **Title Only** layout.

15. Click the **title placeholder** and type **`Graph of Giraffe Heights`**.

16. **Save** the presentation as **`sb-My Trip to the Zoo`**.

    Next you will copy a graph from an Excel file. You haven't switched between software programs before, so saving at this point is just an extra precaution.

Start Excel and Copy a Graph into the Slide

17. Start **Excel**.

18. Click File and choose **Open** from the menu.

19. Navigate to your Lesson 07 folder and **double-click** the sb-Giraffe Graph file.

20. Click the **outside border** of the graph to select it.

21. Choose **Home→Clipboard→Copy** from the Ribbon.

22. Click the **PowerPoint** icon on the Windows taskbar to switch to PowerPoint.

23. Choose **Home→Clipboard→Paste** from the Ribbon.

    The graph appears in the slide, but it's a little too big. You'll resize the graph next.

Resize and Move the Graph

24. Position the mouse pointer in the **upper-left corner** of the graph frame and notice that the pointer changes to a double-headed arrow, as shown in the following figure.

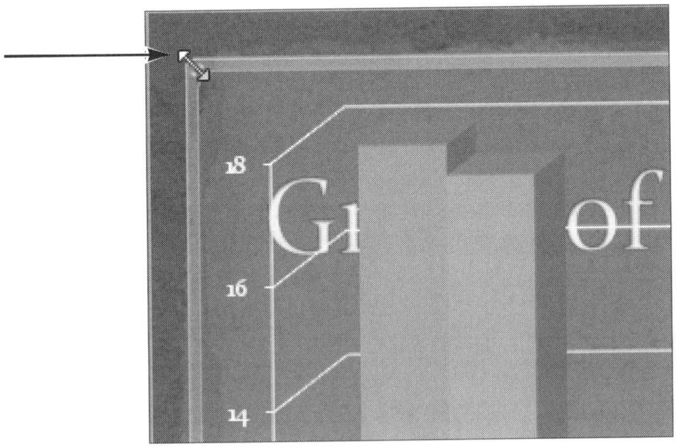

25. **Press and hold down** the **mouse button**, and **drag down** and to the **right** until the graph is below the title.
    The graph is not perfectly centered on the slide.
26. Place the mouse pointer on the **border** of the graph, but not on a dotted resizing handle.
    The mouse pointer changes to a four-headed arrow.
27. **Press and hold down** the **mouse button** and **drag** a little to the **left** until the graph is well centered on the slide; release the mouse button.
28. Make **slide 1** active; check out your presentation in Slide Show view.
29. **Save** and **close** the presentation.
30. Click the **Excel** icon on the taskbar to restore the Excel window.
31. Click File and choose **Exit** from the menu to close the Excel program.

SKILL BUILDER 7.2 Add Animation and Transitions to a Presentation

In this exercise, you will open a presentation and add some pizazz with animation and transitions.

1. Open sb-Tropical Getaways from your Lesson 07 folder.
2. Click the **slide 2** thumbnail icon in the Slides tab on the left side of the screen to make it active.

   Notice that slide 2 contains bullet points. That is part of the design for the Flow theme used in this presentation.

Add Animation to a Slide

3. Click in the **bottom-left placeholder** to select it.

   You now see a dotted-line box surrounding the placeholder.
4. Choose **Animations→Animation→Appear** from the Ribbon.

   Notice the items are numbered 1 through 4. That indicates the order in which the items will appear in the slide show when you click the mouse button.
5. Switch to **Slide Show** view and click the mouse button **four times** to display each of the first four destinations.

   Hmmm, that seems a little tedious. It might be better if the four destinations appeared at the same time.
6. **Right-click** a blank area of the slide and choose **End Slideshow** from the menu.

   TIP! If you select (highlight) all four of the items and then apply the animation, they will behave as one unit.
7. Place the **I-beam** mouse pointer to the left of the *T* in *Tahiti* and drag down to select all four destinations.
8. Choose **Animations→Animation→Appear** from the Ribbon.

   Notice that the numbering next to the destinations changed. Each item has a 1 next to it, indicating that they will all appear at the same time.
9. Switch to **Slide Show** view; click the **mouse button** once and all four items display at the same time.
10. End the slide show.
11. Drag to select **all four items** in the bottom-right placeholder and apply the **Appear** animation.

Apply Animation to Additional Slides

12. Switch to **slide 3**.

13. Click in the **bottom-left placeholder** to select it.

14. Choose **Animations→Animation→Fly In** from the Ribbon.

    Notice that all four items have a 1 next to them, meaning they will fly in together in Slide Show view. How did that happen when you didn't select all four items first? It's because the last three items are sub-bullets (indented) below the main bullet. That causes PowerPoint to assume that the items should act as one unit. (You create sub-bullets in a placeholder by pressing the [Tab] key.)

15. Click in the **bottom-right placeholder** to select it and apply the **Fly In** animation.

16. Go to **slide 4**, click the **bottom placeholder**, and apply the **Float In** animation.

    This time PowerPoint assumes that each of the main bullets and their associated sub-bullets are a unit. You have two main bullets, so each one floats in with its associated sub-bullets.

17. Go to **slide 5** and apply the animation of your choice.

18. **Tap** [Ctrl]+[Home] to return to the beginning of the presentation.

19. Switch to **Slide Show** view and enjoy the show.

    Remember, it's fun to play with different animations but you don't want to distract the audience. For actual business-related presentations, you might want to consider only one or two animation styles for the entire show.

Add Transitions to the Slide Show

Using a variety of transitions could be distracting, so in this example, you will apply the same transition to all slides. Using Slide Sorter view is an easy way to apply the same transition to all slides at the same time.

20. Click the **Slide Sorter** icon in the bottom-right corner of the window.
21. If necessary, click **slide 1** to make it active.
    It will have a highlighted border around it if it's active.

    TIP! If you select a slide, then hold the [Shift] key and click another slide, PowerPoint also selects all the slides in between.

22. **Hold down** [Shift] and click **slide 6**; release the [Shift] key.
    All six slides now have a highlighted border, meaning all six slides are selected.
23. Choose **Transitions→Transition to This Slide→Uncover** from the Ribbon.

View Your Final Presentation

24. Click **slide 1** to reselect slide 1 and deselect the other slides.
25. Switch to **Slide Show** view and run the slide show.
26. **Save** and then **close** the presentation.
27. Click File and choose **Exit** from the menu.

LESSON 8

Access – Accessing Raritan Clinic East

Have you ever wondered how service agents who take your order over the telephone know what questions to ask about the products you order...or how sportscasters come up with little-known facts about teams and players in a flash? In most cases, these service agents and sportscasters have access to a powerful database from which they obtain the information.

In this lesson, you will explore elements of the Microsoft Access 2010 application window, create a new database, and identify features of the database window. As you explore the tools available in Access 2010, you will begin building the new database.

LEARNING OBJECTIVES

After studying this lesson, you will be able to:

- Launch Access 2010 and identify elements of the application window
- Create a new blank database and database table
- Use the Navigation Pane and enter data into a table
- Save and close database objects
- Preview and print datasheets
- Close a database and exit Access 2010

Student resources ***labyrinthelab.com/wtmo10***

Case Study: Updating Raritan Clinic East

Raritan Clinic East is an incorporated medical practice staffed by the finest clinical diagnosticians in the Pediatric fields of General Medicine, Cardiology, Orthopedics, Pediatrics, Emergency Medicine, and Neonatology. The practice serves a patient community ranging in ages from newborn to eighteen years.

James Elliott has recently accepted a position in the human resources department with Raritan Clinic East. He has been tasked with reviewing the current records management system. From this review, he will be able to determine how best to organize data in new databases created using Access 2010. Then he will create a new database in which to store the data so that information can be located and retrieved more efficiently.

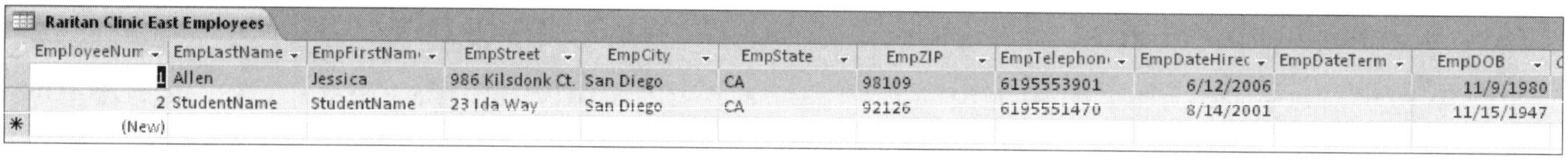
Raritan Clinic East Employees

EmployeeNum	EmpLastName	EmpFirstNam	EmpStreet	EmpCity	EmpState	EmpZIP	EmpTelephon	EmpDateHirec	EmpDateTerm	EmpDOB
1	Allen	Jessica	986 Kilsdonk Ct.	San Diego	CA	98109	6195553901	6/12/2006		11/9/1980
2	StudentName	StudentName	23 Ida Way	San Diego	CA	92126	6195551470	8/14/2001		11/15/1947
(New)										

The table created to hold employee data

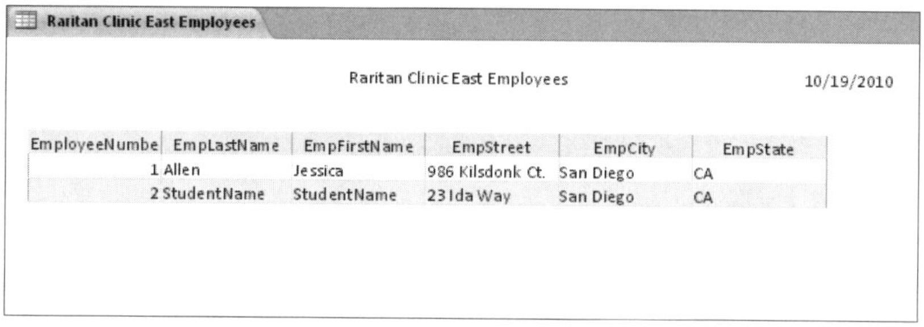
Raritan Clinic East Employees

Raritan Clinic East Employees 10/19/2010

EmployeeNumbe	EmpLastName	EmpFirstName	EmpStreet	EmpCity	EmpState
1	Allen	Jessica	986 Kilsdonk Ct.	San Diego	CA
2	StudentName	StudentName	23 Ida Way	San Diego	CA

A printout of data from the new database table

Defining Access Databases

If you have ever used a phone book or a catalog, retrieved a note card from a card file, or pulled a file from a file cabinet, you have used a database. If you have ever used an index or a table of contents in a book, you have also used a database—just a different type of database. Each of these items consists of individual pieces of *data* that, when combined, make up a *database*.

What Is a Database?

A *database* is a collection of related data stored together in one electronic file. Historically, individuals and businesses have used databases to store vast amounts of data in an organized fashion to facilitate quick and easy retrieval of facts, figures, and information. Prior to the computer age, database records were stored on index cards, on columnar tablets, and in file folders stored in file cabinets. While these data storage methods are still around today, computer-based databases have reduced the storage requirements of data and have improved the efficiency of data retrieval. As a result, reports from sportscasters, historians, politicians, stock sales, unemployment records, and many other details can be reported with amazing accuracy—and very quickly.

Exploring the Access Environment

When you launch Access 2010, one of the first things you will notice is that, unlike other Microsoft Office applications, Access displays the Backstage view rather than a new blank file. From the Backstage view, you can create a new database or open an existing one.

Starting Access

The basic procedures for launching Access 2010 are the same as those procedures used to launch other Microsoft Office applications. After you launch Access, you are prompted to take action to create or open a database. These procedures may vary somewhat, depending on the version of Windows installed on your computer as well as whether Access has been used on the computer or not.

HANDS-ON 8.1 Launch Access 2010

In this exercise, you will launch Access 2010 from the Start menu.

1. From the Desktop, click the **Start** button.
2. Choose **All Programs**.
3. Click the **Microsoft Office** folder.
4. Choose **Microsoft Access 2010**.

   After you launch Access for the first time, the program may appear on the Start menu. You can launch Access directly from the Start menu rather than displaying the menus from the All Programs list.

Identifying Elements of the Access Window

Access, unlike other Microsoft Office applications, displays the Backstage view each time you launch it. From this screen, you can choose to create a new database, open an existing database, open a sample database, or create a new database based on a template.

Using Database Templates

Access 2010 comes with a variety of built-in database templates that you can use as the basis for your new database. In Access, templates create fully designed databases so that all you have to do is enter data. Templates are available for creating the most common types of databases. Databases created using templates are often sufficient to meet the needs of most individuals and some small businesses and organizations. A database created with a template can also be used as a foundation from which a more sophisticated database can be developed.

Creating a Blank Database

An electronic database file serves as a shell that holds all the tools, data, and various database objects that help users enter and organize data and obtain meaningful information from that data. As a result, you must save the empty database shell and give it a name as you create it. After you create a new database, Access automatically creates a blank table named Table1. An Access database is composed of various objects including tables, queries, forms, and reports. Each object type can be created from scratch using a Design View for the particular type of object. Access also provides wizards to help you set up individual objects. You will use both of these techniques as you develop the databases throughout this unit.

Designing a Database

The first step in designing any database is to determine the type of information you will need to keep in your database. Examples of data include the names, addresses, telephone numbers, and email addresses of customers or contacts. Once the needed information has been determined, you can design the database to accommodate it. A database structure can be changed, but modifications to the structure should be kept at a minimum to prevent unwanted loss of data. Sometimes changing the structure can corrupt or delete data that has already been entered. This is why it is important to begin with a good design.

HANDS-ON 8.2 Create a Blank Database

In this exercise, you will create a new blank database named Raritan Clinic East.

1. Launch **Access 2010** and follow these steps to create and name the new database:

Ⓐ Click the **Blank Database** icon in the Available Templates section of the Access window.

Ⓑ Click the **File Name** text box and type **`Raritan Clinic East`**.

Ⓒ Click the **folder** button to open the File New Database dialog box.

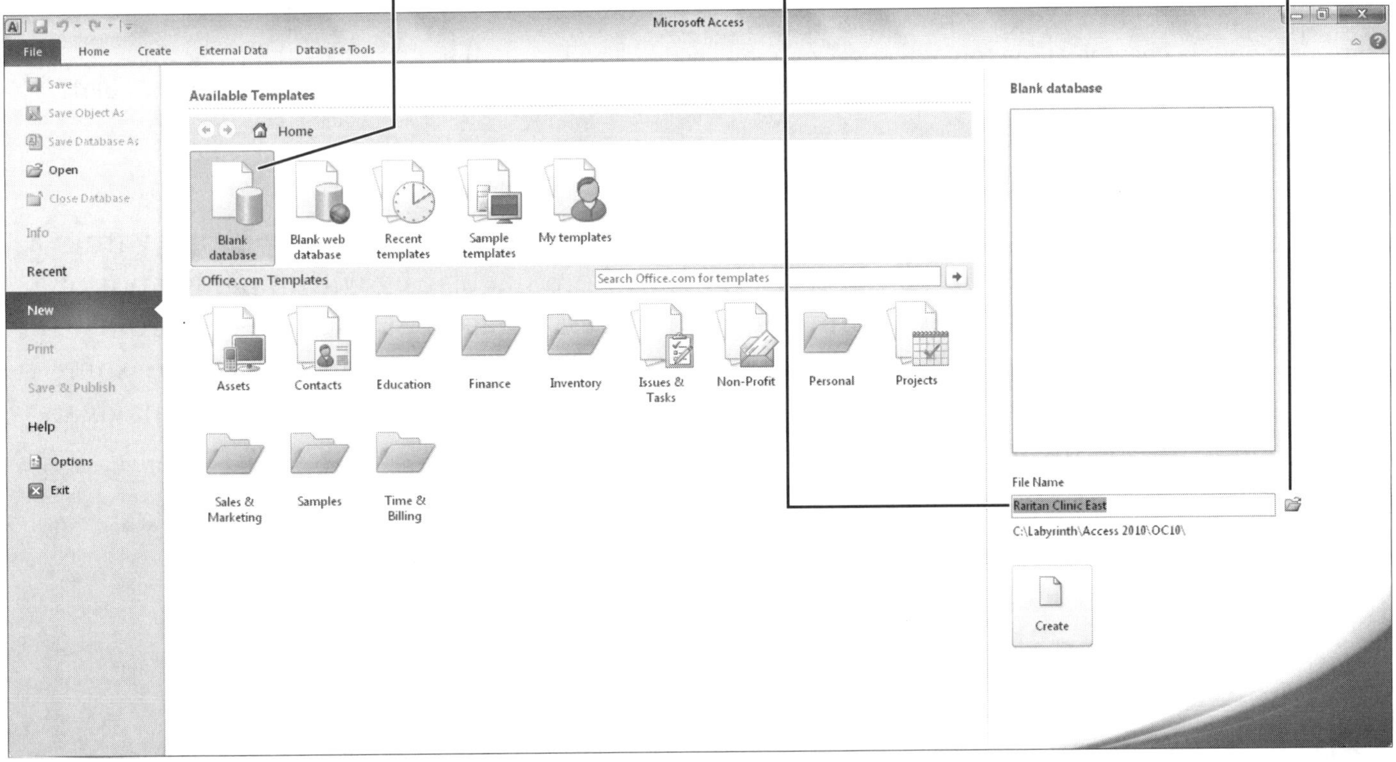

2. Navigate to the Lesson 08 folder or the folder in which you want to store your files and click **OK**.

3. Click the **Create** button.

   Access creates the new database, shows the database name in the application title bar, and displays a blank table named Table1 in the Access window.

Identifying Features of the Database Window

Now that you have created the database file, take a moment to study the layout of the window and compare the visual elements of the window with the features you have seen in other Microsoft Office applications.

The Navigation Pane appears on the left side of the window.

Tabs on the Ribbon display Access tools.

The title bar shows the database name and the file format for the version of Access you are using.

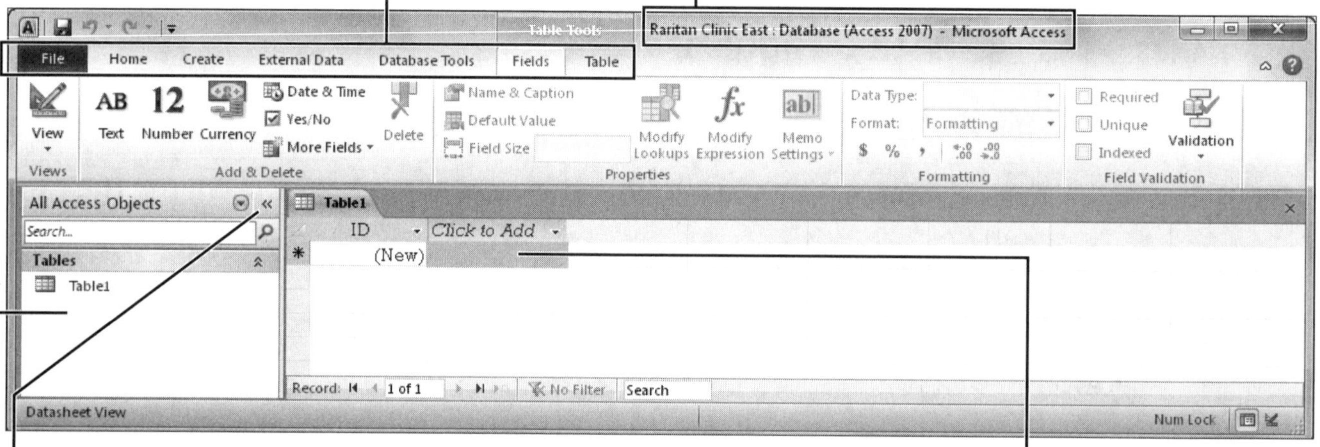

The double-chevron at the top of the Navigation Pane is called the Shutter Bar Open/Close button. It enables you to open and close the Navigation Pane.

The Work area shows a table named Table1.

Using the Navigation Pane

If you have used Microsoft Office Excel, you know that navigating within a worksheet or workbook is different from navigating within paragraphs of a document. Navigating within an Access database is also different from navigating in a document. As you begin working with the database, some basic procedures for using the Navigation Pane will enable you to navigate the file more efficiently.

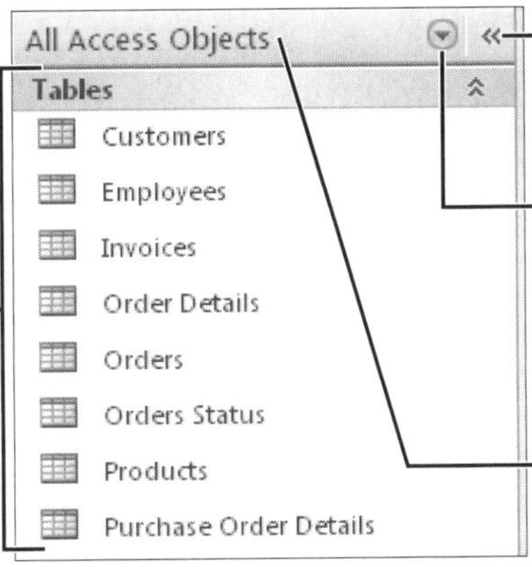

NOTE! For new databases, a Search bar also appears on the Navigation Pane, just below the Pane banner.

Creating Tables in Datasheet View

As you have already learned, all data stored in a database is stored in tables. As a result, Access creates a table for each new database you create, identifies the object using a generic table number (Table1), and creates one field named ID. Access also displays the Table Tools Fields and Table Ribbons so that the tools you need as you build the first table are available. When a database object is active, Access automatically places new Ribbon tabs at the right end of the Tab bar to make accessing appropriate tools more efficient.

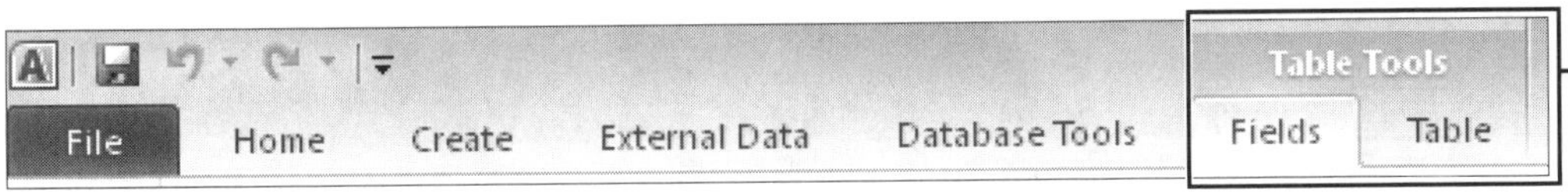

Before you begin building your first table, there are some terms and rules you need to know about tables.

Working with Tables

A database table is the basic object of any database because tables store all of the raw data placed into the database. All other objects in a database are based on data stored in tables. In most databases, you will find a number of tables, each of which holds data related in some way to data in other tables in the database.

Three key terms are used in relation to the data stored in Access databases:

- **Field:** The basic unit of database tables that holds one piece of data, such as first name, last name, street address, ZIP code, date of birth, and so forth. Each field is displayed by a table column.
- **Record:** A collection of all fields related to one item, such as all fields of data for each person or company, all items placed on an order, and personnel information for each employee. Each record appears on a table row.
- **File:** A collection of all related records stored together, such as all employee records found in a table, all customers, all suppliers, and so forth. Each field and record contained in a database table along with forms, reports, and queries used to input data and retrieve meaningful information make up a database file.

Tables are most commonly displayed in the Datasheet View that presents data from multiple records in the column/row layout shown in Table1. As you review the following sample table and work with tables, you will see how these elements fit together.

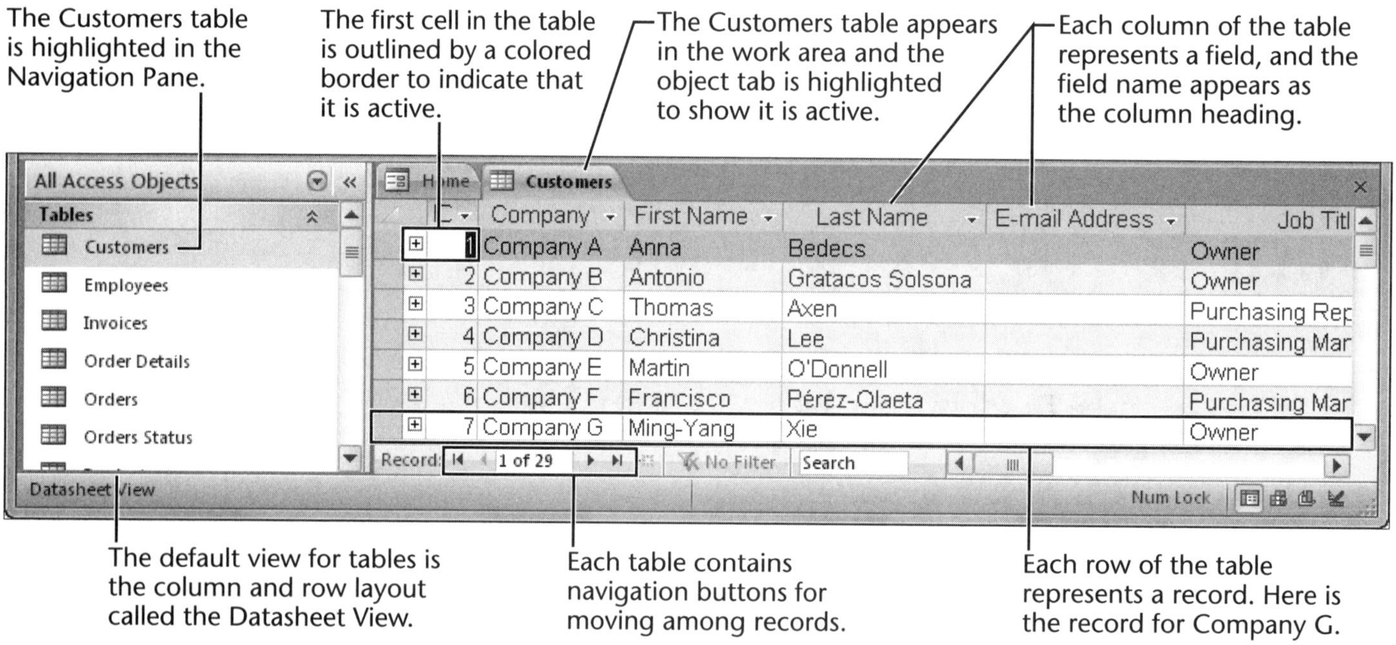

Identifying Table Guidelines

If you are acquainted with the Microsoft Word table feature or Microsoft Excel worksheets, you will find using the Access datasheet familiar. Because tables hold the field names and data used in other database objects, tables must be created first in Access databases.

Each table in the Raritan Clinic East database will contain fields that focus on specific data—patients, supplies, employees, etc. As you build the tables for the database, consider these guidelines:

- Each table should have a *primary key* field that contains unique data—data that will not be the same for any two database records. Social security numbers make a good example of unique data because no two people have the same number; however, most organizations have avoided using social security numbers for security reasons. As a result, most organizations use some type of coded ID such as employee number, patient number, or item number as primary keys.
- As you have discovered in the database you just created, Access creates the first field (ID) for you when you create a new database. It uses this field as a primary key field designed to hold unique data. To ensure that the data is unique, Access will assign sequential numeric values to each record you enter. You can leave the field as Access presents it or change the ID field to a different field name, depending on how your table is set up.
- The field identified as the primary key field must contain data—it cannot be empty. When Access creates the primary key field, it automatically sets the key field to automatically number the records. This ensures that each record has a unique number.
- Planning database tables to share data before you add them to the database reduces the amount of time spent editing and restructuring the tables.
- Tables have at least one field in common with another database table so that you can tie together information between any two tables to create reports and other database objects. These common fields are sometimes referred to as *foreign keys.* In an Employees table, the EmployeeNumber might tie it to the Customers table and serve as a foreign key.

Identifying Field Data Types

As you access each column in a new table datasheet, Access displays a drop-down list that enables you to identify the type of data you plan to place in the field. When you think about the data you plan to enter for a field, it's easy to see the different types of data—text, currency, dates, and so forth. By defining the type of data each field will contain, Access formats the data to some degree, and reduces the amount of formatting you must apply as you enter the data. A description of data types available for data in Access 2010 databases appears in the following table.

QUICK REFERENCE: Identifying Access Data Types

Data Type	Description
Text	The default data type that contains up to 255 characters consisting of any combination of alphabetic and numeric characters—such as names, addresses, and phone numbers—that will not be used to perform calculations.
Memo	Text entries that contain between 1 and 63,999 characters.
Number	Numeric data to be used in mathematical calculations.
Date & Time	Fields that hold date and time values.
Currency	Numeric values representing dollars and cents or fields in which you want to prevent rounding off during calculations.
AutoNumber	A field for which Access assigns a unique, sequential, or random number as records are added to a table. AutoNumber data cannot be modified or deleted.
Yes/No	Single-character entries in a Yes/No format that are used to enter data that can be only one of two possible values, such as true/false, yes/no, or on/off.
Hyperlink	Links to web pages or other documents that you access by clicking the link.
Attachment	A data type that identifies any type of file—such as a document, an image, and so forth—that will be included in the database as an attachment.
Lookup & Relationship	A field that displays values from another table or from a list of values on the basis of *criteria*—conditions you set so that you can select the value you want to enter.
Calculated Field	A field created by combining values in other fields within the table.

Saving Tables Each object you create in a database must be saved. As you save the database objects, you assign an appropriate name to the object. An appropriate name for each table, then, should help identify the data it holds. After you save the table, Access displays the name you give the table in the Navigation Pane.

HANDS-ON 8.3 Create and Save a Table Using a Datasheet

In this exercise, you will create a table to hold Raritan Clinic East employee data.

1. **Double-click** the ID field column heading to select the text and type **`EmployeeNumber`**.

2. **Press** Tab and then follow these steps to add a field name for column 2:

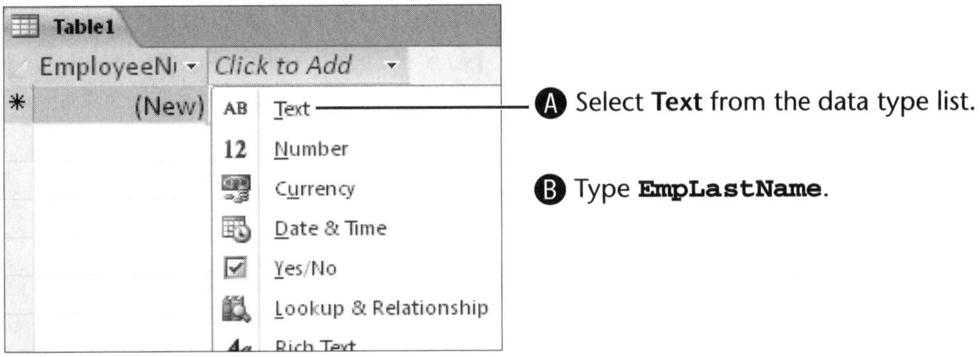

TIP! Notice the underlined mnemonic character identified for each data type. As you enter each column heading and prepare to set the data type, you can use the mnemonic character (such as T for Text) to select the data type and then type the field name.

Field names/column headings truncate because the columns are narrow.

3. **Press** Tab and repeat the procedures outlined in **step 2** to enter the following text fields in the order indicated by the letters:

   a. EmpFirstName
   b. EmpStreet
   c. EmpCity
   d. EmpState
   e. EmpZIP
   f. EmpTelephone

4. Repeat the procedures outlined in **step 2** to add the following three date fields to the datasheet, ensuring that Date & Time is the data type.

   a. EmpDateHired
   b. EmpTermDate
   c. EmpDOB

5. Follow these steps to save the table using a new table name:

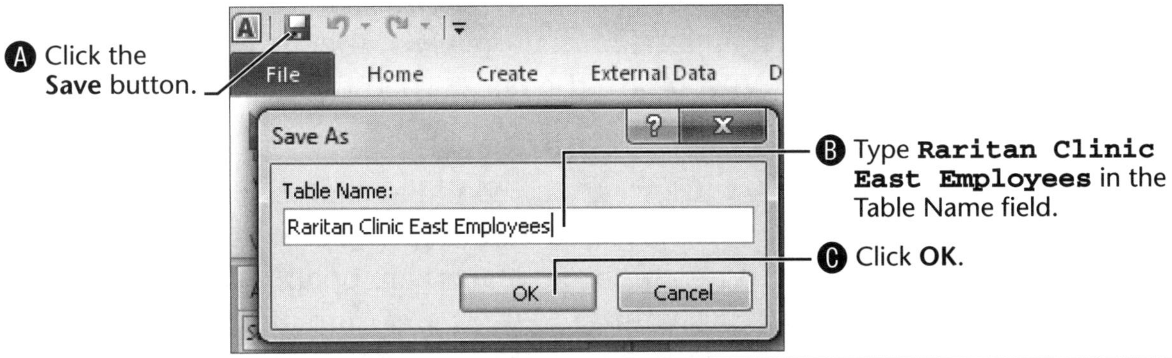

Navigating Tables and Entering Data

Now that the table is complete and saved as the first object in the database, you are ready to enter data into the table fields. Because of the column and row layout of the datasheet, moving from field to field within the datasheet is similar to moving among columns and rows of a Word table or cells in an Excel worksheet:

- Press Tab or Enter to move to the next field.
- Press Shift+Tab to move to the previous field.
- Click a field to make it active.

As you access each field, you simply type the data required for the record. When you complete the data in the last field, pressing Tab or Enter takes you to the first field in the next record. Access saves each record as you complete it, so each new record becomes part of the database table when you move to the next record.

Study the following figure to identify key features of the datasheet as you enter data.

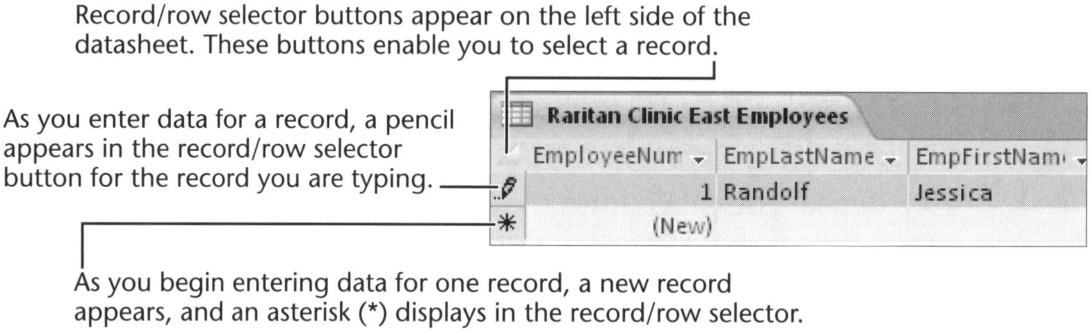

Working with Tabs and Closing Database Objects

As you have already learned, when you create a new database, Access creates a blank table and displays the table in the work area of the database screen. The tab that appears at the top left of the table displays the table name—Table1—until you save the table. Then the name you assign the table appears on the tab.

As you work with Access and build a database, the number of tables and other objects will grow, so you might have numerous objects open at the same time. When multiple objects are open, Access displays as much of each object as will fit within the work area, and all objects are layered, one on top of the other. The tabs make moving from one object to another more efficient.

At the far right side of the table datasheet window, you will notice the table Close button.

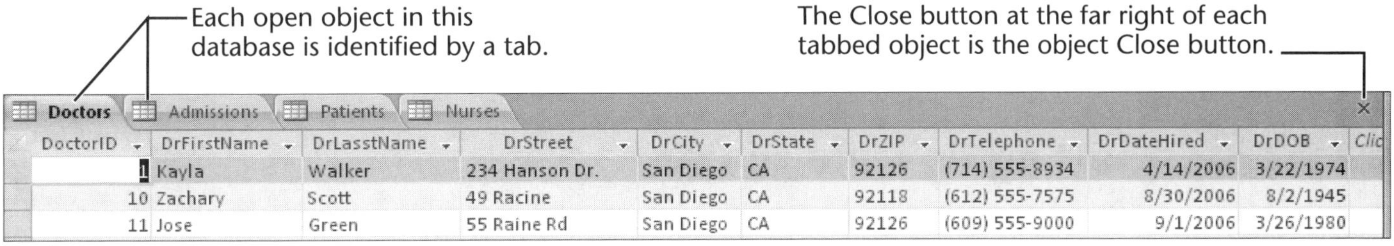

HANDS-ON 8.4 Enter Data into a Table Datasheet

In this exercise, you will enter data for two records into the Raritan Clinic East table of the Raritan Clinic East database.

1. Follow these steps to enter data into the first two fields of the first record in the table:

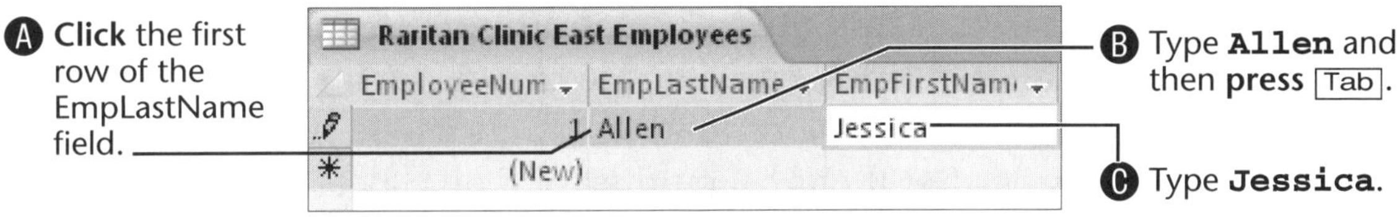

2. Continue **pressing** Tab to work through the record fields and enter the following values for the first record in the table:

EmpStreet	EmpCity	EmpState	EmpZIP	EmpTelephone	EmpDateHired	EmpDateTerm	EmpDOB
986 Kilsdonk Ct.	San Diego	CA	98109	6195553902	6/12/2006		11/09/ 1980

3. **Press** Tab to create a new record, add your name in the **EmpLastName** and **EmpFirstName** fields, and then complete the second record by entering the following data to complete the record:

EmpStreet	EmpCity	EmpState	EmpZIP	EmpTelephone	EmpDateHired	EmpDateTerm	EmpDOB
23 Ida Way	San Diego	CA	92126	6195551470	8/14/2001		11/15/ 1947

4. **Press** Tab or Enter after entering data into the last field to ensure that the record is complete.

Previewing and Printing Data

After entering data into a table datasheet, there may be times when you want to print raw data contained in a table datasheet. Access provides tools for printing all of these objects.

Setting Up Data to Print

When you print from a table datasheet, Access prints the data that actually appears in the datasheet when you issue the print command. You can hide columns to prevent them from printing, change the page layout settings to print the datasheet in landscape layout, and change the margins to fit a datasheet on a single sheet of paper, as you can when you print documents or spreadsheets.

Checking Data Accuracy

Ensuring the accuracy of data entered into databases is very important to obtaining meaningful information from the database. In addition, customers and other business contacts are troubled when they see their names misspelled and careless data entry errors. Be sure to check your data for accuracy after it has been entered. One way to check data accuracy is to print the contents of your tables. Proofreading a hard copy (paper printout) is often a good way to spot errors.

Examining the Preview Window

Previewing data before you print helps determine adjustments that need to be made to ensure that the datasheet prints on the page as you want it to. You can view multiple pages in print preview to see how columns line up, what columns appear on separate pages, and so forth, so that you can make the necessary adjustments to the datasheet.

Because the layout of database objects differs, options available in the Print dialog box vary depending on what you are printing. However, the basic procedures used to preview and print database objects are the same and are similar to the procedures used to print files in other applications. When you preview an object, the Print Preview tools appear on the Ribbon. These tools are used to change the layout of the page on which you print.

The Print Preview Ribbon contains tools for changing the layout of the printed document.

Preview settings enable you to change the number of pages displayed onscreen at one time.

Close Print Preview restores the access object window.

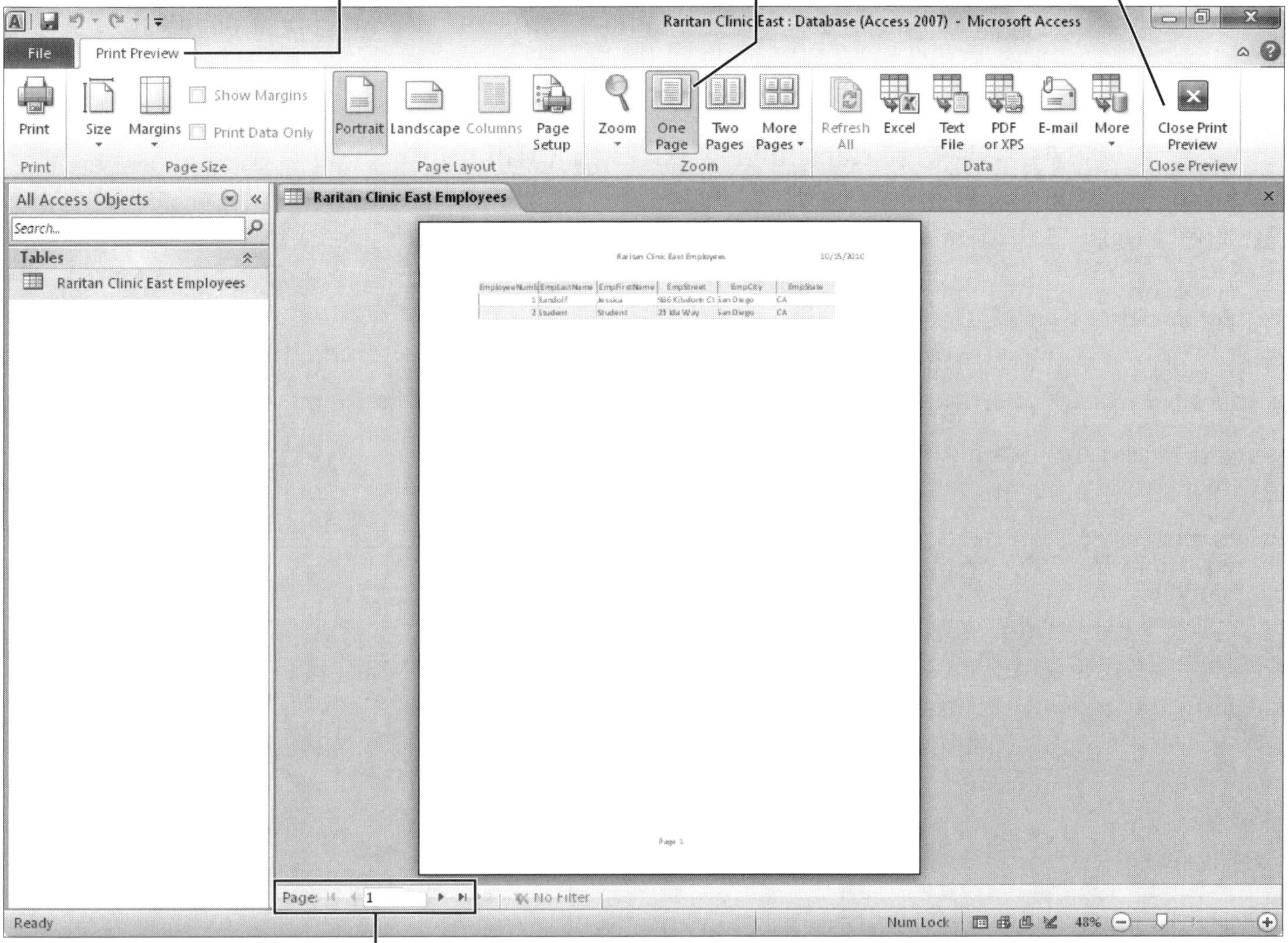

Navigation buttons enable you to review all pages as they will print.

HANDS-ON 8.5 Preview and Print Data

In this exercise, you will preview and print a database table. The Raritan Clinic East table should be open in Access.

1. Choose **File→Print→Print Preview**.
2. Follow these steps to view pages that will print:

Ⓐ Click the **Next Page** navigation button and review all pages of the document. As long as the Next Page button is active, another page is required to print the datasheet.

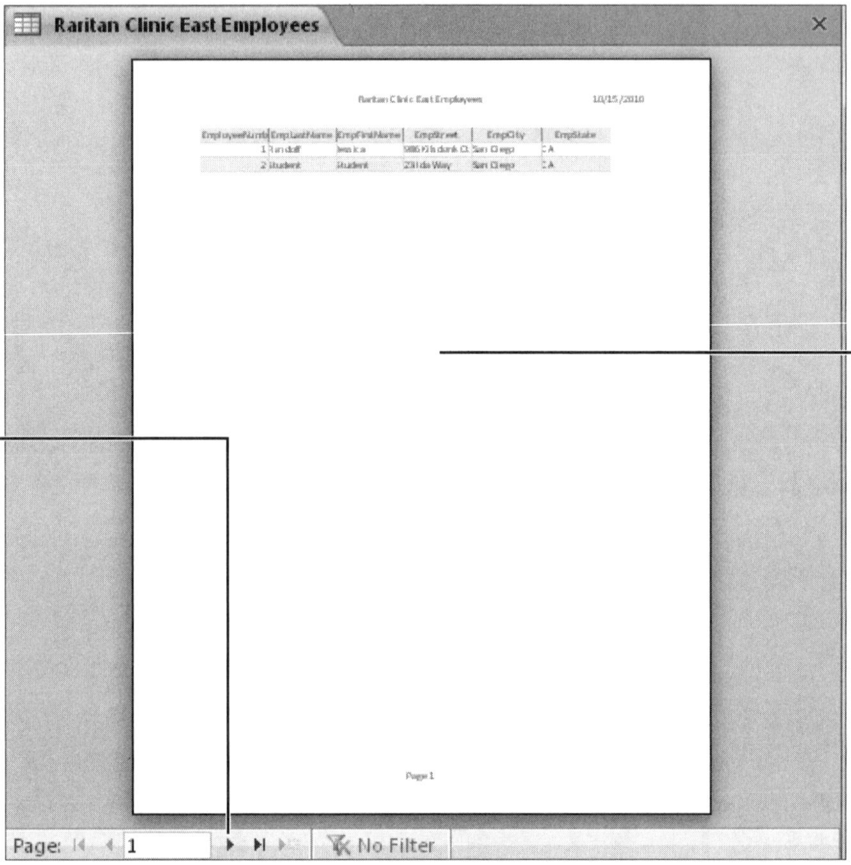

Ⓑ **Click** the middle of the document text to zoom in on the page.

Ⓒ Notice that some columns of the datasheet do not display.

3. Follow these steps to display multiple pages in the preview window:

A Click the **Two Pages** button to display two pages of the printout together onscreen.

B **Click** the text on page 2 of the document to zoom in on it.

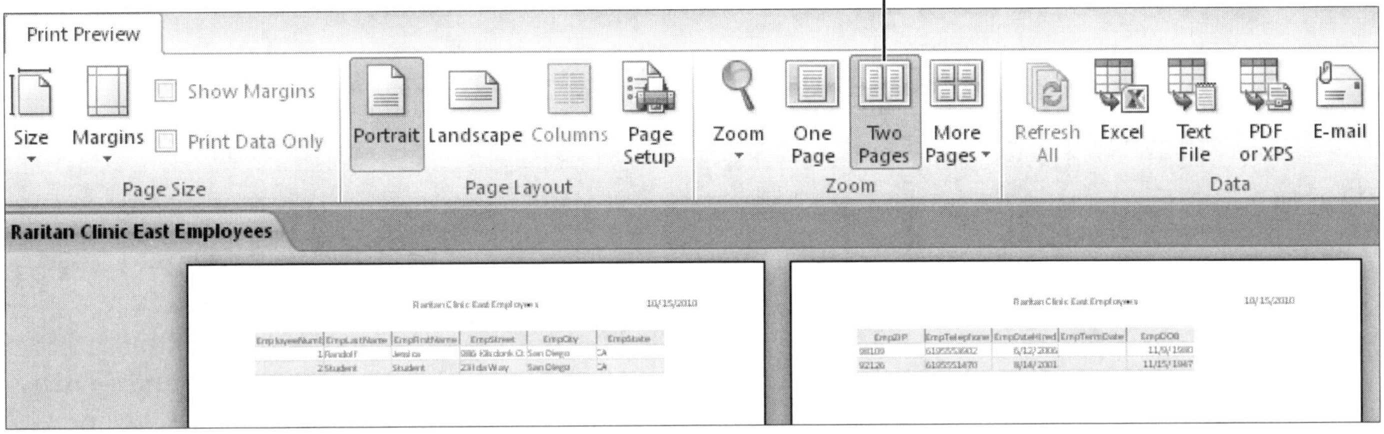

4. Choose **Print Preview→Page Layout→Landscape** on the Ribbon to display more of the datasheet on one page.

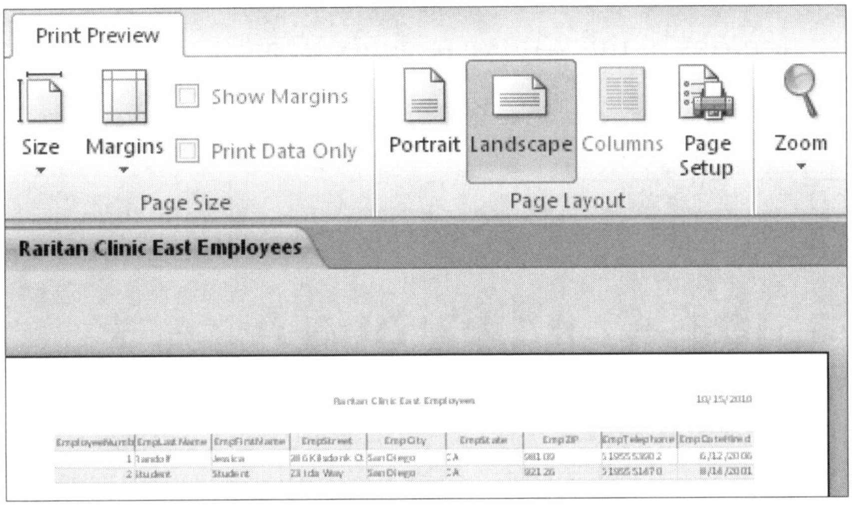

Landscape layout displays more columns together on a sheet.

5. Choose **Print Preview→Print→Print** on the Ribbon to open the Print dialog box.

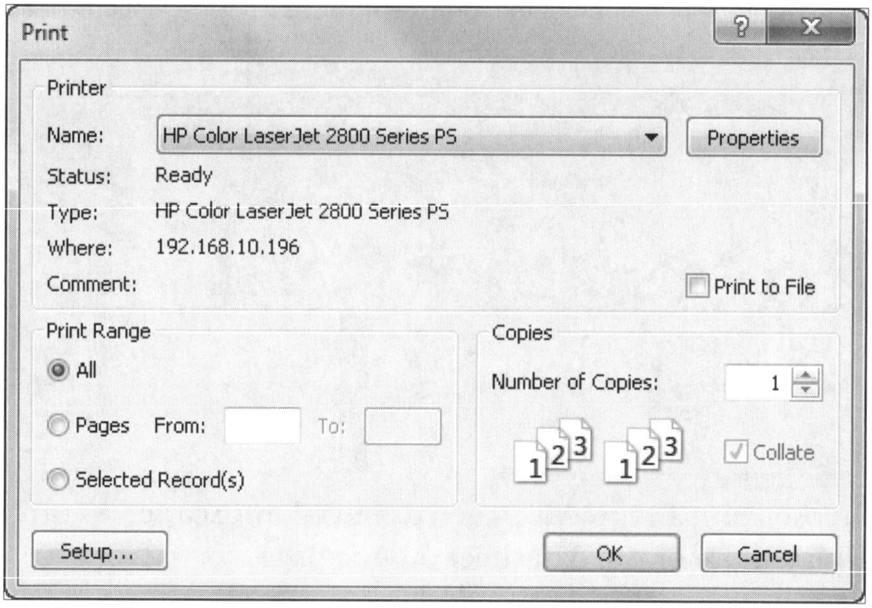

The Print dialog box you see may be different from the one shown here because of the difference in the printer that is active.

6. **Select** options in the Print dialog box to print only **page 1** of the datasheet.
7. **Close** the table. Choose **No** when prompted to save changes.
8. **Close** the Navigation Pane.

Closing a Database and Exiting Access

After all objects in a database are closed, you can close the database and exit Access. The procedures used to perform these tasks are the same as those used to close files and exit other Microsoft Office applications. Use these techniques to close a database and exit Access:

- Choose the File tab and select Close Database to close the database.
- Press [Alt]+[F4] from the keyboard to exit Access.
- Click the File tab and select Exit.
- Click the Access 2010 application window Close button.

Because Access databases contain numerous objects, it is always a good idea to close each database properly before exiting Access. This ensures that all objects in the database are put away carefully.

HANDS-ON 8.6 Close a Database and Exit Access

In this exercise, you will close the Raritan Clinic East database and exit Access.

1. Choose **File→Close** Database.
2. Click the Access 2010 application window **Close** ☒ button.

Concepts Review

To check your knowledge of the key concepts introduced in this lesson, complete the Concepts Review quiz on this page. Or, you can take the quiz online by going to the URL **labyrinthelab.com/wtmo10**.

True/False Questions

			Page number
1. Access databases contain multiple types of objects.	**true**	**false**	______
2. Access databases can hold only one of each object type.	**true**	**false**	______
3. The basic unit of data in a database is referred to as a field.	**true**	**false**	______
4. Every table must have a primary key field.	**true**	**false**	______
5. All data about one item is referred to as a file.	**true**	**false**	______
6. Access is the only Microsoft Office 2010 application that is always launched from the Desktop.	**true**	**false**	______

Multiple Choice Questions

7. Which Access database object holds the data in a database?

Page number: ______

a. Forms

b. Queries

c. Reports

d. Tables

8. Which of the following statements is true about the relationship between fields and records and databases?

Page number: ______

a. A record is made up of multiple fields.

b. A field is made up of multiple records.

c. A database is made up of multiple records.

d. All of the above

9. What purpose does a database file serve?

Page number: ______

a. As a holder for database objects

b. As a backup copy of database data

c. As a database window

d. None of the above

10. Which of the following organizations of data elements represents the structural relationship among the elements from smallest to largest?

Page number: ______

a. File, Field, Record

b. Record, File, Field

c. Field, Record, File

d. Record, Field, File

Skill Builders

SKILL BUILDER 8.1 Create a New Database with a Table

First Perk is a coffee shop that is getting ready to open in your town. Before opening, they would like to have a database in place that will enable them to track sales, supplies, menu items, etc. In this exercise, you will create the First Perk database and the first table.

1. Launch **Access** and click the **Blank Database** icon.
2. Type **`rs-First Perk`** in the File Name text box and click the **Browse** folder to select a folder in which to save the database.
3. Choose **Create** to create the database.
4. Change the ID field name to **`ItemNumber`**, and then **enter** the following field names into the **Table1** column headings, selecting the data type shown for each field:

Field Name	Data Type
`ItemName`	**`Text`**
`Price`	**`Currency`**

5. **Save** the table using the table name **`Menu Items`**.
6. Add the following records to the **Menu Items** table:

Item Name	Price
`Cappuccino`	**`2`**
`Latte`	**`3`**

7. **Print** a copy of the datasheet and then **close** the database.

SKILL BUILDER 8.2 Create a Database Using a Template

In this exercise, you will create a new database using the Tasks template.

1. Launch **Access**, if it is closed, and choose **File→New→Sample Templates.**
   Access displays a list of sample databases in the Backstage view.
2. Follow these steps to select the database type and save the new database:

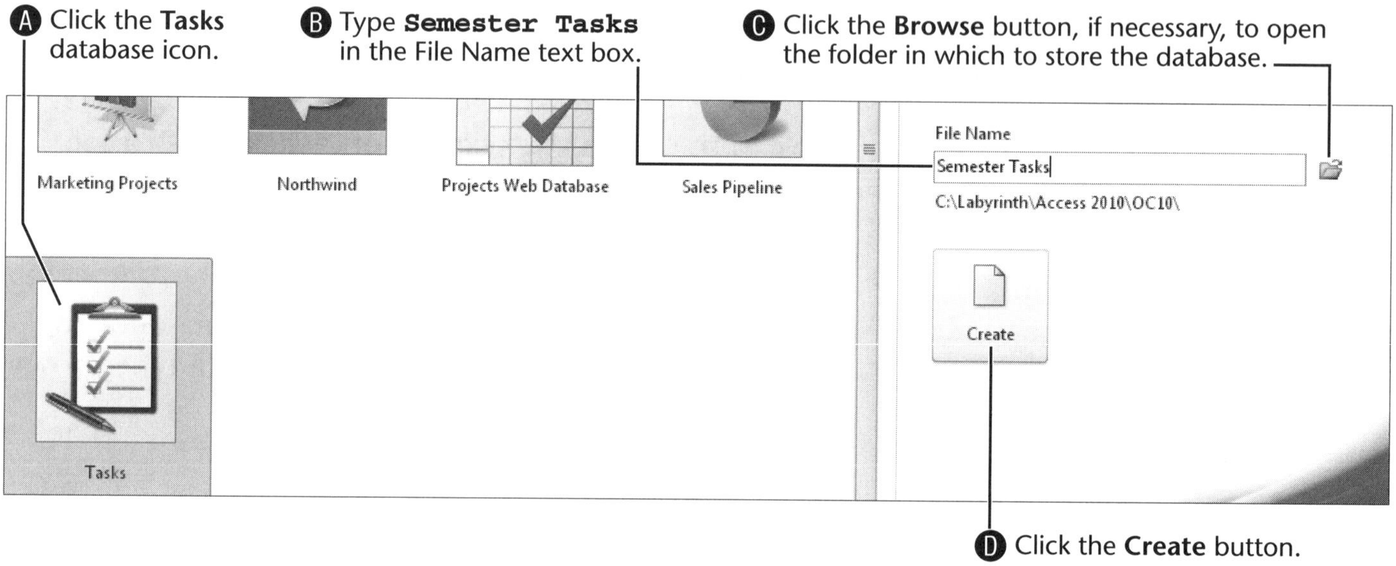

Access downloads the template, saves it using the filename you assigned, and then opens the database.

Review Database Objects

3. **Enable content**, if necessary, **open** the Navigation Pane, and then change the display in the Navigation Pane to display objects by **Object Type.**
4. **Open** each table, form, query, and report and review the arrangement of data in each object.
5. **Close** the database.

Glossary

AutoComplete Feature that recognizes certain kinds of entries, such as dates, and offers to complete them for you as you type

AutoCorrect Feature that automatically corrects commonly misspelled words as you type, based on a built-in dictionary

Backstage View Feature that contains commands to manage your files, such as Open, Save, and Print; available from the File tab

Cell Small rectangle that appears wherever a column and row intersect in a table or spreadsheet

Character Formatting How text or numerical characters look; includes font type, font style, font size, and special effects

Clip Art Collection of photos, images, and pictures you can use in your documents

Clipboard Area in your computer's memory where data that you cut or copy is temporarily stored before pasting it in another location

Compatibility Mode Documents created in earlier versions of Microsoft Office open in Compatibility Mode; this limits the application to using only features available in earlier versions

Contextual Tabs Tabs on the Ribbon that appear only when certain objects are selected; for example, the Table Tools→Layout contextual tab appears only when a table is selected in Word or PowerPoint

Crop Feature used to hide any unwanted portions of a graphic image

Data Type Category of data that determines the type of data a field can contain, such as numeric, alphanumeric, date, or currency

Database Collection of related information (e.g., name and address list); typically stored in an electronic format that allows users to select and sort records of information

Field Column of information in a database

File Collection of data saved on your hard drive or other storage media; saved documents are called files

File Format Consistent pattern for storing information in a computer file; application programs normally have a special file format that they use by default; examples are docx (Word), xlsx (Excel), pptx (PowerPoint), and accdb (Access)

Find and Replace Feature that finds a word, phrase, or format that you specify and, optionally, replaces it with another word, phrase, or format

Folder Area in a computer filing system in which you store files (documents); can be made on USB drives, hard drives, or network drives

Formula Equation that performs calculations on values in a spreadsheet

Freeze Panes Excel feature that allows you to freeze column or row headings so they remain visible on the screen when you scroll through a spreadsheet

Function Formula built into Excel that performs calculations on cells in a table or spreadsheet

Handles Small squares or circles that surround an object when it is selected; you can drag a handle with the mouse pointer to resize an object

I-beam Shape of the mouse pointer when in the typing area of a document; resembles a capital "I"

Icon Small GUI (graphical user interface) that represents an object, such as a folder in which you store your files

Insertion Point Blinking indicator where text will appear on the screen; when typing you must position the insertion point at the desired location before typing; also referred to as the cursor

Live Preview When pointing at formatting commands on the Ribbon, Live Preview displays how the format would appear on selected text and objects without actually applying the format

Mathematical Operators Signs used for addition, subtraction, multiplication, and division

Mini Toolbar Contains frequently used formatting commands; appears when you select cells or text or when you right-click on cells or text

Non-printing Characters Symbols that represent typing elements, such as spaces and tabs; you can display the symbols on the screen, but they will not appear on the printed page

Presentation Program Software application (such as PowerPoint) that allows you to create dynamic multimedia presentations that can be displayed on your computer or projected on a screen

Primary Key Unique identifier in a database field (e.g., a social security number); helps ensure that a database does not contain duplicate records

Quick Access Toolbar Toolbar that contains buttons for frequently used commands; can be customized by adding command buttons

Range Group of adjacent cells in a spreadsheet, such as A1:A100

Record Row of information in a database

Redo Feature that allows you to successively repeat your last action(s), starting with the most recent

Relative Reference Excel automatically changes cell addresses in copied formulas and functions relative to where they are copied

Ribbon Band running across the top of the screen that contains software commands for Office 2010 applications; organized in tabs that relate to a particular type of activity and groups that contain related commands

Scroll Bar Means of moving to different areas of a document

Select To choose an object or to highlight text in order to manipulate it in some way

Selection Bar In Word, the white space at the left margin from which you can select text

Slide Layout Preset layout of placeholder boxes on a PowerPoint slide

Slide Show View used in PowerPoint when delivering a presentation

Sort Arranges data in alphabetic, numeric, or date order

Spell Check Feature that monitors your spelling as you type; underlines suspected misspellings with wavy red lines; right-clicking displays a pop-up menu of possible correct spellings

Spreadsheet Document that allow you to organize data in columns and rows, analyze data, and perform calculations on data; also known as worksheet

Suite Collection of software applications sold as one package; less expensive than buying the individual applications; applications typically contain features that work in a similar fashion

Task Pane Screen element that contains links and icons you click to issue commands to the computer

Theme Set of formatting selections you can apply to a document; includes colors, graphic elements, and fonts all designed to work well together

Toolbar GUI (graphical user interface) containing buttons that represent commands

ToolTips Small balloons that appear when you hover the mouse pointer over a Ribbon or toolbar command; contain a description of the command

Typing Area In Word, the area between the margins of a page; where you type

Undo Feature that successively undoes changes you make in a document, starting with the last one

USB Flash Drive Stores your data on a flash memory chip; plug it into a USB port on any computer and Windows recognizes it as an additional disk drive

Views Varying ways you can look at a document, spreadsheet, or presentation; optimized for specific types of work

Word Processor Software application that allows you to electronically create and edit text

Word Wrap Feature that wraps to the next line a long string of text that extends beyond the right margin

Worksheet *See* Spreadsheet

WordArt Gallery of stylized, decorative text

Index

A

Access, Microsoft
- (*see also* databases)
- exiting, 248–249
- introduction, 233
- launching, 233–234
- navigating in, 236–237, 242
- object types, 234
- overview, 3
- window elements, 234–236

alignment
- cell data, 140–141
- paragraphs, 99–100
- table data in Word, 45–48

animations
- transitions between slides, 221–222
- within slides, 220–221

argument in formula, 167
arithmetic operators, 163, 164
Attachment data type, 240
AutoComplete, 33, 35
AutoCorrect, 69–70
AutoFill, 129
AutoNumber data type, 240
AutoSum, 167–170
AVERAGE function, 167, 171

B

backgrounds, slide, 209–210
Backstage view, 233, 234
borders, 52–53
bulleted lists, 37–38, 51

C

Calculated Field data type, 240
calculations (*see* formulas)

cells
- addresses for, 129, 165
- alignment, 140–141
- borders, 52–53
- copying and moving, 144–146
- defined, 45, 129
- deleting, 150–153
- editing data, 139
- entering data, 136–138
- formatting, 45–46, 47–48
- in-cell editing, 139, 140
- inserting, 150–153
- merging/splitting, 45–46, 47–48
- ranges of, 141–144
- references for, 129, 165, 172
- replacing data, 139
- selecting, 141–144, 174–175

characters, text, formatting, 91–96, 214

charts
- chart sheet, 176–177, 178
- column, 174–175, 177
- creating, 177
- designing, 182–188
- embedded, 176–177
- layout, 184, 186–187
- legend, 175
- moving, 180–182
- pie, 174, 175–176, 178–179
- printing, 177
- selecting cells for, 174–176
- selecting chart, 178
- sizing, 180–182
- styles, 185, 187–188

Chart Tools command group, 177, 182
clip art, 105–114
colors, text characters, 96
column charts, 174–175, 177

columns and rows
- deleting, 151, 153
- freezing, 133–136
- inserting, 48, 51, 150–152
- resizing, 48–49, 149–150
- sorting, 147
- spreadsheet organization, 128–129
- switching in chart, 183, 185

commands, Ribbon, 8
Compatibility Mode, 12–13

contextual tabs, 9
Convert command, 13
copying and moving objects
    cell contents, 144–146
    clip art, 216
    formulas, 172–173
    text, 74–76
cropping images, 112, 113
Currency data type, 240
cut/copy and paste functions, 74, 75, 144–146

D
data, defined, 233
data accuracy, 244
databases
    closing database, 248–249
    closing objects, 242–243
    creating from blank, 234–236
    Datasheet View, 237–243
    defined, 233
    designing, 234–235
    entering data, 243
    navigating in, 236–237, 242
    previewing data, 244–248
    printing data, 244–248
    saving, 234, 240, 241
    tables in, 237–248
    template-based, 234
Datasheet view, 237–243
data types, database fields, 239–240
Date & Time data type, 240
Design tab, Excel chart, 182–188
Design view in Access, 234–235
documents
    (*see also* text)
    bulleted lists, 37–38, 51
    closing, 19, 20
    creating new, 19–20
    navigating in, 14–18
    opening, 12–14, 19
    printing, 43–44
    saving, 39–42, 97–98
    selecting entire, 66
    tables in, 45–53
    versions of Word, 12–13
DOCX and DOC file formats, 39

E
embedded charts, 176–177
Enter button in Excel, 137
Enter key in Word, 36
envelopes, 54–55
Excel, Microsoft
    (*see also* charts; formulas; spreadsheets)
    Auto features, 129, 167–170
    entering data, 136–138
    introduction, 127
    navigating in, 130–136
    overview, 3
    starting, 127
    window elements, 128
exercise file storage, 12

F
fields, 238, 239–240
file formats, 39
files
    compatibility and converting, 39
    database definition, 238
    renaming, 97–98
    storage of, 12
File tab, 7
Find and Replace feature, 77–81
finding clip art, 105–107, 216
Float In animation, 221
Fly In animation, 220–221
folders, 97–98
fonts, 91–92, 95–96, 214
foreign key fields, 239
formatting
    alignment of cell data, 140–141
    borders, 52–53
    cells, 45–46, 47–48
    charts, 184–188
    field data, 239–240
    fonts, 91–92, 95–96, 214
    nonprinting characters, 32–33, 34
    paragraphs, 31–33, 66, 99–100
    presentation slides, 209–210, 213–214
    tables, 46
    text characters, 91–96, 214
    WordArt, 100–105
formula bar, 139, 140
formulas
    (*see also* functions)
    copying, 172–173
    defined, 163
    editing, 166
    entering, 164–166
    introduction, 163
    mathematical operators, 163, 164
    references to cells, 165, 172

freezing panes in Excel, 133–136
functions
  AVERAGE, 167, 171
  copying, 172–173
  defined, 167
  MAX, 167, 171
  MIN, 167, 171
  SUM, 167–170

G
grammar checking, 72
graphics (*see* images)
groups, Ribbon, 8

H
Help feature, 21–22
highlighting (*see* selection methods)
Hyperlink data type, 240

I
I-beam symbol, 15, 16
images
  clip art, 105–114
  WordArt, 100–105
in-cell editing, 139, 140
insertion point, 8, 14, 16, 31
Insert tab, 11

K
keyboard
  creating formulas, 163–164
  document navigation with, 17–18
  Enter key in Word, 36
  nonprinting characters and, 32
  selecting text with, 66, 68
  Slide Show navigation, 218
  spreadsheet navigation with, 132–133
keyboard shortcuts
  copying/moving objects, 75, 76
  line spacing, 32
  ToolTips, 9
keys, primary field, 239

L
layouts
  charts, 184, 186
  slides, 211–213
  table, 46
Layout tab, 46
legend, chart, 175
line spacing, 31–32, 34–35
lists, 37–38, 51
Live Preview, 93, 95
Lookup & Relationship data type, 240

M
mathematical operators, 163, 164
MAX function, 167, 171
Memo data type, 240
memory, computer, 39
merging/splitting cells, 45–46, 47–48
MIN function, 167, 171
Mini toolbar, 11, 92
mouse pointer shapes
  Excel, 129–130
  Word, 15, 16
moving and copying objects (*see* copying and moving objects)

N
naming files and folders, 97, 98
Navigation Pane, 77, 236–237
Next Page button, 14, 17
nonprinting characters, 32–33, 34
Normal view in PowerPoint, 206
Number data type, 240
numbers, sorting in Excel, 147, 148
numeric keypad, 163–164

O
Office 2010 suite, overview, 3
Open dialog box, 12, 13
operators, mathematical, 163, 164

P
paragraphs, 31–33, 66, 99–100
PEER guidelines for presentation delivery, 217–218
pictures (*see* images)
pie charts, 174, 175–176, 178–179
placeholders in presentations, 210–211
PowerPoint, Microsoft
  (*see also* presentations)
  introduction, 201
  navigating in, 203–205
  overview, 3
  starting, 201
  themes, 209–210, 214
  viewing options, 206–208
  window elements, 202

presentations
adding slides, 211–213
animation, 220–221
clip art, 214–217
creating, 209–217
delivering, 217–220
design tips, 213–214
formatting, 209–210, 213–214
inserting text, 210–211
layout of slides, 211–213
sorting slides, 206–207
themes, 209–210, 214
transitions, 221–222
previewing printouts, 244–248
Previous Page button, 14, 17
primary key fields, 239
printing
charts, 177
data from databases, 244–248
documents, 43–44
Print Preview feature, 244–248
program icons, 4, 127
proofreading tools, 72, 73

Q
Quick Access toolbar, 7, 10

R
ranges of cells, 141–144
Reading View in PowerPoint, 206, 208
records, database, 238, 239
Redo and Undo buttons, 72–74
references, cell, 129, 165, 172
relative cell references, 172
Ribbon
Access defaults, 237
introduction, 8–10
Word, 7, 8–10
rotating objects
clip art, 108, 109
WordArt, 102
rows and columns (*see* columns and rows)

S
Save As command, 39–40, 97
scroll box, 17
scrolling
documents, 14–15, 16–17
worksheets, 130–132
searching
clip art, 105–107, 216
text, 77–81
selection bar in Word, 65, 67–68
selection methods
cells, 141–144, 174–176
charts, 178, 180
records in database, 242
text, 65–68
WordArt, 102
shortcuts (*see* keyboard shortcuts)
Show/Hide button, 32–33, 34
sizing objects
charts, 180–182
clip art, 108, 110, 217
columns and rows, 48–49, 149–150
text, 92, 95
WordArt, 102, 104, 105
slides (*see* presentations)
Slide Show, 206, 207–208, 217–220
Slide Sorter view, 206–207
sorting
data, 147–148
slides, 206–207
special effects in presentations, 214
spelling checking, 72, 73
splitting/merging cells, 45–46, 47–48
spreadsheets
(*see also* cells)
copying/moving data, 144–146
defined, 128–129
deleting data, 139
editing entries, 139–141
entering data, 136–138
formulas, 163–173
functions, 167–173
navigating in, 130–136
replacing data, 139
sorting data, 147–148
spreadsheet tabs, 128
Start button, Windows, 4–6
status bar, 8
storing exercise files, 12
styles, charts, 185, 187
(*see also* formatting)
SUM function, 167–170

T

tables
- (*see also* columns and rows)
- borders, 52–53
- creating in Access, 237–241
- creating in Word, 45–52
- Design view, 234–235
- entering data in, 49–52, 242, 243
- formatting, 46, 47–48
- merging/splitting cells, 45–46, 47–48
- navigating in, 48, 50, 242
- printing, 244–248
- saving, 240
- selecting records, 242

template-based databases, 234

text
- adding, 69
- copying and moving, 74–76
- deleting, 69, 71
- editing, 69–74
- finding/replacing, 77–81
- fonts, 91–92, 95–96, 214
- formatting, 91–96, 214
- inserting in presentations, 210–211
- replacing, 69, 71
- selecting, 65–68
- sizing, 92, 95
- sorting options in Excel, 147, 148
- wrapping option, 36, 37, 111, 112–113

Text data type, 239

themes, PowerPoint, 209–210, 214

Title bar, 8

title slide, 211–212

toolbars, 10–11

ToolTips, 9

transition animation, 221–222

typing area in Word, 65, 68

U

Undo and Redo buttons, 72–74

V

view bar in PowerPoint, 206

W

Word, Microsoft
- (*see also* documents)
- Compatibility Mode, 12–13
- exiting from, 22
- Help feature, 21–22
- navigating in, 14–18
- overview, 3–4
- proofreading tools, 72, 73
- Ribbon overview, 7, 8–10
- selection bar, 65, 67–68
- starting, 4–6
- tables in, 45–52
- typing area, 65, 68
- window elements, 7–8

WordArt, 100–105

Word Wrap, 36, 37

workbooks/worksheets, 128–129
- (*see also* spreadsheets)

wrapping text option, 36, 37, 111, 112–113

Y

Yes/No data type, 240

Z

zoom control, 8